A True Fantasy | A Fantastical Memoir

An Unsuitable Princess

Jane Rosenberg LaForge

An Unsuitable Princess

A True Fantasy | A Fantastical Memoir

Jane Rosenberg LaForge

DISCARD

Jaded Ibis Press
sustainable literature by digital means™
an imprint of Jaded Ibis Productions

© 2014 copyright by Jane Rosenberg LaForge

First edition. All rights reserved.

ISBN: 978-1-937543-56-3
Library of Congress Control Number: 2014902192

Published by Jaded Ibis Press, *sustainable literature by digital means*™ An imprint of Jaded Ibis Productions, LLC, Seattle, WA USA

Cover and interior art by Mary Ann Strandell

This book is available in multiple editions and formats. Visit our website for more information. jadedibisproductions.com

60918257

For Norma and Adam; and mostly for Noah, so he might know.

how to read this book

An Unsuitable Princess is both a coming-of-age memoir and a meditation on how people construct their daydreams when their realities inevitably disappoint.

The first half ❀ is a true fantasy that takes place in Renaissance England, where a mute stable girl finds herself punished for saving the life of the boy she loves. It looks like this, and the **flowers** ❀ will direct you to the modern-day explanations like the one below.

> ❀ **The second half** is a fanstastical memoir that takes place in the late 20th Century and explains the inspirations for the first half. It looks like this.

> ❀ And the **flowers** show you the connections.

chapter one

Sir Robert Drake's ❀ horse appeared normal enough that morning, but to anyone who had the humanity to look into the eyes of that animal, it was clear that the mount had been roughened by pain. The whites of a horse's eyes are not always apparent, as though its vision flooded its entire given eyeball. But in this case it was observed that the horse's pupil shifted within its white backdrop, from forward to back, as though it was looking for the source of its grief, but could not find it.

❀ **Robert Drake** is the name of a boy in my sixth-grade class. We had a fine time with his name the day we learned about Sir Francis Drake, but his real import to this story comes from his proximity to celebrity. His mother, Sylvie Drake, was a theater critic for the *Los Angeles Times*, and she even appeared at my high school on career day one year, to discuss the life and times of becoming a writer. She was one of the many celebrities populating my universe as delineated by the boundaries of the Los Angeles Unified School District. For I am a graduate of Wonderland Avenue School, in Hollywood's storied Laurel Canyon, which was in my time host to any number of celebrities and their offspring: kids who were brighter, shinier, and so much smarter than the rest of us cretins. It has long since been documented that Laurel Canyon was home in those days to a particular type of celebrity, whose flavors and fixations seemed to drive the counterculture, and inevitably the mainstream, of our nation.

Laurel Canyon is where Robert Mitchum got busted for smoking dope and to where actors and screenwriters blacklisted during the McCarthy era supposedly retreated. It was where people did not so much live in houses as in cabins, carriage houses, rabbit hutches, and *pieds-à-terre* on stilts. Raymond Chandler's Marlowe, for a time, rented a house in Laurel Canyon, and this little artistic and intellectual hinterland was very happy to be left to its own devices. In the days of Flower Power and Ah Fong's—the Chinese restaurant at the bottom of the hill—Joni Mitchell and Graham Nash also lived there, in a very very very fine house, immortalized in song.

Circa 1960, however, the philistines embarked on an invasion, and that includes my parents, who, if they hadn't moved in as early as they did, probably would never have been able to afford the neighborhood. These people did not build their houses in the canyon proper, but in the neighboring subdivision of Laurel Hills, an arrangement of stucco-and-palm trees that backed up against Mulholland Drive and the shopping districts of the San Fernando Valley. Laurel Hills attracted a distinguished, if not predictable, stream of clientele: clothing salesmen, also known, among the Jews in the neighborhood, as rag, or *shmata* men; psychiatrists, plastic surgeons and G.P.s; lawyers of every stripe and even a few stars from television.

The entrance to Laurel Canyon, on Laurel Canyon Boulevard and Lookout Mountain Drive, was seemingly guarded by two sentinels: Houdini's castle on the east and a large, mysterious cabin on the west. This cabin was said to be inhabited by either the Beach Boys (or perhaps just a single Boy at any one moment); or by Charles Manson and a smattering of his followers. We neighborhood kids, particularly the ones from the new subdivision, who had not been taught not to stare at such sights, gawked at the fences and trees that obscured the house's façade with a mixture of fear and wonderment.

Laurel Canyon was free love, free drugs, and full of speculation and landmarks. It was where peyote grew wild on the vacant hillsides, and where we could point to the house on Rothdell Trail where Jim Morrison had lived. In fourth grade I knew all the words to Carole King's *Tapestry* album, because her daughters were either the prettiest or the most talented girls in the school; I don't remember which. Laurel Hills was sedate, uptight, conventional and exhaustingly boring. Laurel Canyon was where it was at, and its children were wise and with-it, seemingly emancipated from our side of the generation gap so that they might participate in all forms of the era's new freedoms. The parents, meanwhile, experimented with their minds, bodies, and marital arrangements. Laurel Canyon was where people went because they hadn't turned to asses on Pleasure Island.

Among the canyon celebrity children, there were the daughters of Tommy Chong (the Canadian half of the Cheech & Chong stoner comedy duo); one in mine, and one in my sister's class. Rae Dawn Chong (who became a star-actress in her own right, in the 1980s) did not know me from a speck of dust, but her sister, Robbie, was friendly with my sister. Oh! To be noticed by the few, the chosen, the famous! One year, Rae Dawn invited all her friends to a Halloween party—at the Roxy nightclub on the Sunset Strip. Cheech & Chong were performing *Big Bambú*, and provocative things were supposed to happen at midnight. The next day, all of Rae Dawn's friends came to school wearing T-shirts with the *Big Bambú* logo (designed to look like a pack of rolling papers) on the back, and a picture of an illicit cigarette on the front. "Do A Number," it said, and although I had no idea what it meant, I was insanely jealous.

We were not completely bereft of celebrities on my side of the neighborhood. I used to play with Gigi Perreau's daughter, Gina: Gigi Perreau as in *The Rifleman* TV show, which was then in syndication. Country music star Glen Campbell, his second wife, and three of his children lived on our street, and the Iron Butterfly was supposedly headquartered at the top of our block, although I was too young at the time to have noticed or remembered. But they offered little competition to the Laurel Canyon residents, such as Sylvie Drake, pop installation artist Edward Kienholz, the film editor Frank Mazzola and many other players to be named later: these were the people with the real canyon credibility, and I spent a good portion of my childhood yearning to be like them.

(You don't know who Frank Mazzola is? From kindergarten through twelfth grade I went to the same school as his daughter, Dina, and probably exchanged five words with her during all that time. Except for one day in elementary school, when she consented to play with me on the schoolyard: It was grand to be associated with her ilk, even if her interest in, or attraction to me was short-lived. Her father is perhaps best known to the world as Francisco Mazzola, who worked with director Donald Cammell on *Demon Seed*. He's plain old Frank Mazzola when he appears in documentaries about Cammell and his half of the masterpiece that was the cult film, *Performance*. Nicolas Roeg was the other half of the directing team of that film; Mazzola's editing work on *Performance* is not credited. More importantly, though, he was a one-time member of the Athenians, which was the coolest, hippest, tightest gang at Hollywood High School, and its members were recruited to play the coolest, hippest, and cruelest teenagers in *Rebel Without a Cause*. Now if that's not fame, I don't know what is.)

I instead enjoyed a different kind of fame: I was the scion of a crazy family. At least my mother was crazy, certifiable and hauled off in straitjacket one evening during my fourth-grade year. I don't think there actually was a straitjacket, even though my father went around the neighborhood lamenting as much; my mother told me later that she went voluntarily. The expensive hospital in West Los Angeles where her brother, the doctor, arranged for her to be taken   only accepted patients who could walk in on their own power, she once assured me. Although her official diagnosis was never revealed to me, not even when I was adult, she was later said to have had a "nervous breakdown." In today's language it might be called a manic episode that was followed by its partner in the bipolar universe: depression.

I didn't know I was crazy, or that my mother was crazy, until several weeks into my mother's hospitalization. I had said or done something during the course of my fourth-grade school day that prompted the teacher to tell me to calm down, because my mother would be released soon. How he knew my mother was sick, in a hospital or in an institution—I only knew that one night, my sister and I were taken into her bedroom to say goodbye, and the weeks that followed were a combination of chaos and the doldrums—I still haven't figured out. I knew that my mother was sick, and that it wasn't with some run-of-the-mill gall bladder problem. But when the teacher (whose name is being withheld here because, as I was to learn in adulthood, he was having affairs with a number of the PTA moms) said those words in front of the class, I immediately understood something intangible, yet hard and fast about myself. I was not a celebrity, but I was on my way to becoming infamous.

Once my mother returned home from her mysterious sojourn, she had to keep herself busy, and if not with her own children, then with the children of others. She began collecting canned food and old clothes as the chairwoman of child welfare for the Wonderland PTA, which turned out to be a den of vipers if there ever was one. It too was infested with celebrities, real and imagined. Having eventually matriculated from the PTA, my mother liked to tell the story of how Mark Volman, first of the Turtles and then of Flo and Eddie (he was Flo) helped build booths for her for the annual school Halloween Festival. Sadly for her, though, those celebrities also included Martin Bernheimer, the classical music critic of the *Los Angeles Times*, who did not spare my mother his critical faculties when reviewing the PTA circulars she wrote. They were in rhyme, extolling the virtues of an upcoming PTA bake sale or a family sing-a-long. Bernheimer was known not only to tangle with my mother on policy issues, but also complain he could not understand the point of the circulars long after they had been published and distributed.

Sir Robert, Lord of **Berwinshire** ❀ had yet to insert himself into the saddle when **Samuel Bright**, ❀ escorting his younger twin sisters on **Market Day**, ❀ noticed this about the horse, although what Samuel paid his foremost interest to was the horse's attendant. This stable slave was a girl, unusual enough for any day, but of particular interest to Samuel, but not for the expected reasons associated with a young boy. She was holding the horse on a short rein, nearly up to its chin, and she might have been whispering to the horse, although she was not known to speak, or perhaps, it was sometimes thought, that while she refused to speak to people, she spoke to animals, horses, primarily. From where he stood, with a sister on each hand, Samuel watched as the girl stroked the horse on its face and neck. His sisters recognized her too, and pointed the girl out to each other, as if she were one of them, inconsequential and small. The girl had to stand on a box to reach the horse, to rub her cheek against its own and breathe, if not whisper, into the horse's ears. She was not particularly beautiful, even in Samuel's eyes, and the color of her hair, indeed, was not much distinguishable from the horse's Chestnut coat. Yet at moments the girl's hair and the horse's mane blended into a picture of the remains of a sunset, the sun's last gasps smeared and sinking behind it.

❀ **Berwinshire** is the name of the house that overlooked one portion of my neighborhood, lording over Mulholland

Drive as if it were the mansion from television's *Dark Shadows*. It was built sometime after the rising middle class of Laurel Hills settled into their ramblers and ranch houses, so that the daughter of the Berwinshire household, who was old enough to be one of my babysitters, could have a horse in her backyard. Berwinshire turned out to be the neighborhood's first visible mansion—when Glen Campbell moved away from our street and up the hill to bigger digs he had designed and built for himself, we were never told his exact address—and soon after its completion, the horse moved in. It was with foal, and for the twelve months it took for that foal to be born, I watched both horse and house carefully, scheming and dreaming how I might be taken in by that family. Each time the Bancroft Junior High-Hollywood High school bus drove past that house I rose in my seat to get a better look, and in the whinnies and nickers the horse threw out, the jerks of her head and her trotting about, I knew she was calling out for me. At least I hoped as much. For I was going through my equestrian phase at that age, and the only beings that could threaten celebrities and rock stars off their perch were Ruffian or Secretariat, or the two horses my friends owned, Mesa and Pebbles. Whether my family owned land zoned for horses was a big debate my father and I carried on, and it would turn out that I discovered Mesa and Pebbles lived on land my father owned, but that is just one of many grievances my father and I were to wrack up against one another, in my adolescence.

❧ **Samuel** was the formal name of my most significant boyfriend in high school: Samuel Brian Waynert, Ulysses S. Grant High School, Class of 1980.

❧ **This Market scene** is essentially based on the Renaissance Pleasure Faire, a recreation of Elizabethan England born in Laurel Canyon and mother to all such other fairs across our liberated nation. Phyllis Patterson, a leading lady of Laurel Canyon and an elementary school teacher, staged the first fair in her backyard for her students. Since I was neither old enough nor cool enough to be present at the creation, I can only guess as to how it grew into the behemoth I eventually became acquainted with. I can only be thankful that it did.

The conceit of the Faire is a celebration day for a visiting Queen Elizabeth I. Merchants and craftsman bring out their best wares; guilds assemble; nobles display their finery in pomp and parade, and entertainers pay tribute. It's essentially a carnival, and the prizes, literal and figurative, are hippie lust objects: candles, blown glass, hand-bound books with parchment pages and velvet covers; pottery and leather goods; airy dresses and musical instruments: drums, harps, mandolins, penny whistles and dulcimers.

Over the years the Faire grew into the Living History Centre, which did all kinds of good works. The Faire later mutated into two separate productions, a Southern Faire at the mouth of the Malibu canyons; and a Northern Faire, across the Golden Gate Bridge, through the psychedelic tunnel depicting the Founding Fathers, and down into the flat lands of Marin County. In terms of both audience and participants, The Faire attracted a heady combination of families, drunkards, drug addicts, geeks, nerds, actors, artisans, and punks. A motley but profitable atmosphere that would eventually spawn the singing, dancing, and comedic jugglers of The Flying Karamazov Brothers; the countercultural improvisational actors of the Firesign Theater (one founder, David Ossman, was the father of two of my contemporaries at Wonderland); and the Reduced Shakespeare Company, whose name should be explanation enough as to the source of its notoriety and profit.

For a time the Faire functioned as a fundraiser for the Los Angeles Pacifica radio station, KPFK. Its survival became a cause célèbre of the *Los Angeles Free Press* (before that newspaper turned pornographic), as the Faire's fidelity to bawdy old England offended the gentlemen and ladies in whose metaphorical backyard the Faire was staged. There were some adults from our neighborhood who were regular participants, including one reputable father who dressed in tights to play his bagpipe. His wife volunteered along with my mother at the elementary school, but this was not enough to ease the scourge my parents perceived as the Faire, and I was to be kept away from the place.

The horse was trying to throw its head free of the bridle as Sir Robert approached. He was, as far as Samuel's knowledge extended, not knighted for any great act of bravery or chivalry. But he was wealthy, tall, and important, and was very possibly related to the Queen, through some method. He was not armed, and yet he moved brusquely through the stable and onto the courtyard facing the Market, as though he were on some extraordinarily charged errand. The stable girl, in her way, may have tried to tell him to slow his pace, but he took the reins from her hands without so much notice to her, and he swung himself into the saddle even as the girl kept her hands on the horse's nose. When the horse kicked forward just before raising itself on its hind legs, the girl pitched forward, as if forced into the horse's hooves and the riling and weight they threatened with.

Samuel wanted to shake his hands free of his little sisters'. He wanted to run, toward the rearing horse, the prone girl. He might rescue her; steal her away from the danger. He lunged forward, as if preparing for flight. But in unison his sisters clasped onto his hands with a new ferocity. They set him back off his toes and onto his heels. Suddenly there was motion all around them. "Stand back," "Clear away," "Down, down, down," people shouted. Market-goers, stall owners, fish and laundry swirled and plunged in front and behind Samuel. There was loose poultry at his feet: ducks, chickens and geese; dogs bayed in his ears. People retreated and surged about the center of attention: the stable courtyard, the rearing and now bucking horse, the felled noble man and his stable girl. On his toes Samuel could see only the horse's movements. With its voice it was screaming, but with its head it was braying, as if a stubborn donkey, although with a violence that was unfamiliar.

Like a belt snapping out its length, the crowd bounced, backwards, sideways. People breathed together: there was an audible intake of surprise. Samuel saw hands; the girl had righted herself. In the face of the hooves, the force of shoulders, she did not cower. She stood before the horse with her arms stretched as wide as she could deign, with her palms open, empty to the horse's vision. She had once explained to Samuel, through her signals and signs, how a horse sees best on the periphery, and what it sees most is threats. Samuel knew what the girl was telling the horse, based on the girl's posture, but the sound of the horse's protests was diligent and exhausting. Samuel caught a glimpse of the horse rearing, as if the weight of its tack and body were too much for it.

"Watch," Samuel heard; he might have said as much to his sisters. They were hardly tall enough to see past the hips and waists of the tightening crowd, let alone above the heads and shoulders. Samuel looked down on them, as if to check on their welfare after all the jostling. They may not have seen much but each wore a contented expression, as though they were listening to a story they well knew to be suspenseful if not dangerous, but peacefully resolved at its end. By the time Samuel returned his attention to the fighting horse, the stable girl, and the noble, he could see only the horse. It had ceased bucking and rearing, but was clearly still disturbed. It alternated between walking and trotting around the perimeter of its fit. If anyone from the crowd, or another stable hand or steward dare to approach it, the horse prepared to charge, its ears swinging between bewilderment and anger. Samuel had to rise on his toes to see what became of the stable girl and Sir Robert; she was kneeling by his side as the murmurs of the crowd thickened and lifted around him.

To the sound of people sighing, more in shock than in respect, he thought he saw the girl whisk her fingers across the nobleman's forehead. It was a gesture he found stunningly familiar, although Samuel refused at that instant to place it. The girl next took something from a pouch on her belt, ran a finger over Sir Robert's lips, and gently placed what appeared to be a leaf into his mouth. The taut interest of the crowd threatened to choke what remained of Samuel's view.

"Is she poisoning him, then?" someone asked into his chest. "Potions," someone else suggested. "Treachery," another spat out. "Why doesn't someone send for a surgeon?" a woman cried out. "Hush," a number of people advised, although not in unison. With each attempt to discern the going's on, the crowd became more confused although it could not shake its curiosity. The horse slowed to a degree, but refused to relinquish all its agitation. It swayed during the intermittent seconds when its gait inexplicably halted. The blacksmith's apprentice ran into the courtyard, his gloved hands gripping the handle of a cast-iron pot. By the reaction of the gathering chorus circling around Sir Robert, Samuel judged that the apprentice was carrying boiling oil for the noble's wounds. Kitchen hands, stable waifs, the blacksmith's children and individual stewards had summonsed themselves if not to help, then at least to dread, and observe.

The girl was shaking her head at the blacksmith, his apprentice, and their pot of boiling oil. The horse stopped at Sir Robert's feet, but took no conciliatory sniff. When the apprentice made a go for its reins, the horse bolted. The girl was begging, but for what, she could not make clear to the men. As the horse finished its renewed round about the courtyard, the girl seized the reins as they dangled past her. Before he could protest, she had pushed the reins into the blacksmith's hands. Having occupied the blacksmith for the moment, she ran to the well closest to the stable entrance. Her hands were busy at what once was the hem of her skirt. She had ripped it into shreds, to douse them into the water, and was just as quickly back at the side of Sir Robert.

Samuel recognized the girl's methods, as far as they applied to horses, but he had never seen her work on a man. He did not know how to feel, as he watched her apply a cool strip of her skirt to Sir Robert's forehead; and as she demanded, with her arms and hands, that Sir Robert be kept absolutely still. In Samuel's chest, his heart coiled and unfurled in spurts, and the girl squeezed another strip of her skirt hard against the back of Sir Robert's head. She was applying pressure to the wound, he knew, for he had seen her do as much to horses that fell under her care. She breathed without speaking into Sir Robert's ear as one hand cupped his lower lip, to wipe away the spittle chewing the herb might force from his mouth. Samuel's little sisters did not need to see this at present; they, too, had witnessed it plenty of times earlier.

The girl was **a healer**, ❀ although many had other names for the gift she had reserved for animals until Samuel's own recent illness; a gift that had come to seem like a curse when she was ordered to leave her home upon Samuel's cure. Still Samuel did not hesitate to recount for his sisters what they could not see from their height in the crowd, although he did not mention the whisk of the girl's fingers across Sir Robert's forehead.

❀ My uncle, who lived around the corner from our family as I was growing up, was **a doctor**. Not only that, but at one point he was chief of staff at Cedars of Lebanon Hospital, which made him, in our neighborhood, practically famous. A sizeable portion of the children of Jewish, West Side, or Jewish- and West Side-minded families in the Los Angeles of a certain era were born at Cedars of Lebanon (including one college roommate and one college boyfriend), which was eventually abandoned for the newer, shinier, and bigger Cedars Sinai that we know today. (The old hospital was later to become a Scientology building.) Cedars also was a place of employment for a few other dads in our neighborhood, including one stepfather who was the administrator of the entire operation; and another doctor who was said to be so brilliant, and so consumed by his brilliance, that his rather pedestrian wife and children were unable to communicate with him. That was one of the many marriages in the neighborhood that ended mercifully, via divorce; although my parents didn't pooh-pooh that particular divorce, given the circumstances.

My uncle lived around the corner from us because, as my sister and I liked to believe, he could not take care of himself and had to live with his parents. His parents were of course our grandparents, and our grandfather, whom we called Poddy because I apparently believed at some point that this was a diminutive, was a retired colonel in the United States Army. This was not quite the same thing as celebrity, although he was known as The Colonel in the neighborhood and most of the kids liked him because he had a swimming pool (the pool and house were in fact my uncle's, I was to learn later). But we did have entrée to some of the most exclusive establishments in all of Southern California, the cafeteria and commissary, or PX, at the U.S. Army base at Terminal Island, where we cruised through the meat crisis of the early 1970s as though nothing had happened at all.

"She has done it again," Samuel told his sisters, for whom their brother's voice no longer sufficed. "Pull me up, Samuel," the one on his right, Grace, begged. "Me first," the other, Lucy, implored with a yank on Samuel's shirt. "I want to wave to her," Grace argued. "We want to see her again," Lucy said. Samuel squatted to address his sisters at their level; there was surprisingly more room now to mill about. Perhaps it was obvious at this point that no one was going to die. "Not right now," Samuel told them, as he noticed clumps of the faces in the crowd directing their attention away from what must have proved to be a disappointment to them, and now toward a new source of awe: his sisters and him. "We will ask our parents," he promised. "We will, when we get home. They know best. Now, do we have tasks ahead of us?" The girls nodded a bit dejectedly. Struggling to conceal his own measure of resignation, Samuel rose, reclaimed the hands of his sisters and laced his way out of what felt like a gawking crowd.

"But what will she be doing now?" Lucy was asking. "Yes, Samuel," Grace came out in support of her sister. "What will she do next?" "Darlings, darlings," Samuel said between breaths. "Not now." He led them away. The Market was returning to normal. At the fruitier he traded a few coins for berries, which mercifully engaged his sisters for the moment. As they gathered the groceries their mother had set out for them—milk, butter, bread and fowl, Samuel felt anxious, unsettled, although the precise source of his feelings eluded him. He did not know if it was because he was so eager to relay all that he had seen to his parents, or sensed he lacked the discipline he would need to rightly keep them to himself.

Samuel delivered the girls home with a determination that nothing be said about the morning's incident. It was nowhere near as difficult as he had anticipated, for he quickly fell into the routines of the household, and he loved the household, as much as he loved the house itself. The main room, kitchen, and his parents bedroom had been built by his father, Thomas, before Samuel was born, but he had worked with his father to add the one other bedroom, once Jenny had come, and the twins were said to be on arrival. He loved the wood his father had used, the wood he and his father had milled and stained, red as the wine they drank for their celebrations: the twins' birthdays, his parents' anniversaries, the feast his mother had made when Samuel recovered from the illness no one thought he would recover from; still no one knew what it was, or what had gotten him through it. Samuel only recorded that his parents and Jenny had nursed him through most of it; Jenny, actually, had never left him, in his memory, while his parents seemed to come and go according to what time of day it was and whether a priest, or a surgeon, or an apothecary could be fetched. In his mind he could see Jenny constantly, on her knees while he lay beside the stove atop a layer of blankets; sometimes he thought he could recall the way her fingertips whisked across his brow in the morning, letting him know that despite his coughing and sweating, he had made it through another night; that soon enough another night would pass.

But mostly he loved the house because it contained everything he knew, from its scent of wood smoke, wax, and charcoal, to all of the events of his life: his father and mother teaching him and Jenny their letters and the Bible by the stove; his mother teaching him how to sort wheat, and fruit, and meat from the skin of the animal, in the shambles out back. In his parents' bedroom he slept once he was recovered and Jenny slept on the floor beneath him; in the twins' room, where he had slept on a bunk with Jenny above him—until the twins were too big for their crib, and they had to be moved into his bed. Then Samuel returned to the main room. There were two old oaks outside the front of the house where Samuel hid from his father when Thomas first insisted that Samuel work in the shop, and Samuel thought himself too young and frail to assist him. Soon enough he would be teaching the twins how to scale those trees in their time of need, and he would teach them to read and write there beside the same stove where their mother was cooking. As dinner approached, the twins were left with their mother to observe her mastery. This was the world, he delighted in knowing, that was to be his inheritance, and it was more than enough in riches to satisfy him.

Dinner was always a feast, it seemed to Samuel, with its meats and cheeses, fruits and bread. There was ale for the twins, wine for his mother, and mead for Thomas. Samuel drank a kind of mull tea, warm and savory with chamomile, golden seal and marshmallow. A recipe of Jenny's, it was said to strengthen his lungs in the wake of his **illness**. ❄ Samuel's mother insisted on serving it to him each evening, as though she believed the sickness still lived within him, and was merely waiting for the proper moment to make itself known again.

❄ My father has suffered from **asthma** all of his life. I believe, given the current medical chatter in the popular press, that had he not been a poor Depression child, he might have been nothing more than just another snot-nosed kid with allergies. But he was the son of struggling immigrants, always one step ahead of the landlord or the bill collector, and he missed so much school because of his wheezing and fevers that he was held back for a year. He spent the rest of his life catching up.

He claimed he "grew out" of his condition after working as a junior high school teacher for two years in the California desert. Yet many a family trip out of the Los Angeles smog—to the mountains, or the beach in Santa Barbara—would be marred by one of his asthma attacks, and we would have to come scurrying home. My father's childhood, to her my grandmother recall it, was devoted to experimental asthma treatments, allergy shots, and expeditions to the Children's Hospital on Vernon Boulevard.

As an adult my father kept an inhaler (next to the bottle of Maalox) by his bed and tooted up constantly as we watched television together. Psychedelics were all the rage in Laurel Canyon, or so the gossip at my elementary school led me to believe. But my father, who couldn't drink because of his ulcer, was instead hooked on the inhalers' contents: adrenalin and other inert ingredients.

Until my mother's nervous breakdown, my father's various sufferings (he was also partially deaf owing to an explosion he set off as a teenager; and he suffered through rashes and hives that arose without explanation) were the primary focus of my family's hypochondriac tendencies. His asthma also had one peculiar effect, one that might arouse a Freudian's interest: My first crush, in second grade, was an asthmatic. I carried a torch for this boy long before I knew about his illness. To me he was blond-haired and had wide, brown eyes, and was the best handball player on campus. But once the fifth-grade teacher made this public (it was during our health unit, and I suppose the teacher thought outing this kid as an asthmatic was the closest thing he could provide to a hands-on experience), I was hooked for life. A real Florence Nightingale I resolved to become, until I learned the woman was celibate, preferring her career to love's consummation.

When Jenny was ordered to remove herself from their home, Samuel slowed his disappointment by taking the breaths Jenny had taught him during his illness, when his heart raced and a chill gripped at his shoulders. These breaths, however, were the deepest he could ever imagine. Thomas sent himself into his workshop for more work, as though to forge his way beyond Jenny's departure. Grace and Lucy, mercifully, were not entirely aware of what had been decreed. Samuel's mother, meanwhile, was inconsolable. She plunged into tears at every meal, which were just as sumptuous as they had ever been, although Samuel's mull was missing. Not even the affections of the twins could make up for Jenny's silence, until Thomas somehow obtained the missing ingredients. It seemed to all that with the herbs in hand, their mother's sadness lessened considerably. Whether she was relieved to again be treating her eldest son with Jenny's magic, or whether she had resigned herself to the girl's absence, no one made mention.

The mull was the first thing his mother placed before him at every sitting, and Samuel nursed it this evening with special attention. He told himself he was studying its taste, the plainness matched against the sweet and bitter; he was gauging the effects of the drink, as though he could feel it accomplish its aims, its embrace of his lungs. All this concentration, however, apparently allowed his sisters special access to the grapes at the center of the table. Their mother rapped on her plate to shake Samuel out of his focus.

"Your sisters, Samuel," his mother said.

"Yes?" he asked.

"Are you watching?"

Grace and Lucy stretched their faces, as if to hide the grapes they had stored in their cheeks. "Darlings," Samuel chided them, but he could not conceal his own smile at their cleverness.

"Watch them," his mother reminded.

"We'll need **the fire** early tomorrow," ❦ his father announced at supper, between the passing of bowls.

> ❦ It was not my boyfriend Sam's profoundest wish that he become **a blacksmith**; I think he would have liked to have been an actor, or an agent for MI5 or MI6, or a poet, or something else my parents would deem unreasonable, if not romantic. But when pressed on a career choice, he'd opt for blacksmithing, which, while not paving a traditionally middle class Jewish route from academic glory to financial security, was sufficiently exotic enough to shut down people's curiosity.

"Yes, sir," Samuel complied.

"Bellingham has got a brood to bring by."

"Yes, sir," Samuel said.

"And we'll need to see to that hoof file."

"Yesterday, didn't you see, I tried my hand at fixing it."

"You should give it another good blast," his father said. "If you want any of those fine shoes you've made to fit any of Bellingham's."

"Yes, sir," Samuel relented. The twins giggled.

"Women always find work amusing," Thomas observed. To the twins, he asked: "And what, on Market Day, did you fine young beauties accomplish?"

"We saw her," Grace offered. "We saw J—,"

"Grace!" Samuel admonished, before she could finish.

"We didn't see her really, Father," Grace explained. "There was a crowd, and a wild horse, Samuel told us, but he wouldn't lift us up to see—"

"That is enough, Grace," Samuel said.

"Yes, your brother is right," Thomas said.

"He said she was magnificent," Lucy said.

Now it was Mother who spoke. "Lucy," she said in her voice, slow and swaying with disappointment.

"Father said nothing about my speaking," Lucy said plainly.

Samuel and his father instantly read Mother's expression. She took pride in the nimbleness of her girls, and more so, Samuel thought, than she did in her boy. Together he sometimes thought the women in his family were a conspiracy—not necessarily against him, but in a tide of snickers and smiles.

"Now that is enough," Thomas proclaimed. "Enough for now."

It would not be until the twins were sent off to bed that Samuel would revisit the issue with his father. For as the meal continued, and Grace and Lucy took turns relating the purchase of every grocery that afternoon, Samuel could not dismiss the feeling between his parents that neither had finished with the topic. They did not display the curiosity the twins delighted in yet they could not help but be aware of the absence of the girl from their lives. She once sat beside his mother, on the same side of the table as the twins, to feed them and wipe their faces; in his father's shop she juggled the tongs and the hammers and the chores relating most directly to the animals. Tomorrow, with hooves to be trimmed and flanks to be cooled, she would be missed even further. As he ate, Samuel watched the faces of his parents, and he could see the empirical effect of her exile. She was not their own but perhaps they had imagined her as much; so much so that now whatever expression befell their eyes and lips, they were thinner, less resolute, without her presence.

After the meal, Samuel approached his father while Thomas whittled in his chair. He was relieved, to a degree, that his father was so absorbed by this task, unaware of the layers of soft wood his sisters played at sweeping at his feet. His father must have been in a pliant mood, and Samuel's first instinct was to make his request immediately. But Thomas would not appreciate Grace and Lucy having to play witness to whatever agreement might follow. His father was tolerant on many issues, although not when it came to protecting his children from arbitrary or foul temperaments.

So Samuel sat at the foot of Thomas, watching the abstract slab of wood melt into a more agile shape—a pipe, or a weaving needle, or something for simple household use. To Samuel his father's hands were a miracle, of sorts. They were more than large, with an enviable reach; they were able to take the most intransigent of materials and coax them into necessities. It was as though his father was able to see something, in the most silent and stubborn gifts Mother Nature had provided. It was what Samuel hoped to inherit from his father, the one coveted nature of his birthright.

"I should like to see her," Samuel asked, certain enough time had passed for the twins to fall to sleeping.

"See who?" Thomas asked, shoving off another layer of wood.

"Father." Samuel felt the words he had practiced rising too quickly in his mouth to tame them. "You weren't there, you have no idea what happened today at the Market—"

"I do, son. The news preceded you."

"How—?"

"Bellingham," Thomas said. "He wanted insurance that she would not be here tomorrow, meddling. As he put it."

"She could have been—"

"But she wasn't, so you needn't speak of it. She can take care of herself quite nicely."

On that score, Samuel could not broach an argument. He appealed to Thomas: "Please, Father. I should take Lucy and Grace along."

"You think that would be wise?" Thomas asked. Now he took his eyes away from his work to look directly into Samuel's. Whatever Thomas meant to say next, he meant to bore it into his son, into his soul through the very panes of its windows. "I wouldn't think so, two little girls in that atmosphere. It could be rough for them."

"Yes, sir." Samuel relented, but he did not steal a glance away from Thomas.

"What I mean to say, Samuel: It is rough for all of us. Your mother and I—well, especially the girls. It's as if they lost a mother." Samuel watched his father's grip on the wood, the hold his other hand practiced on the knife: whether the subject of their conversation would enforce itself upon his project. It did not, as far as Samuel could gauge it.

Samuel nodded, and set his attention on the growing pile of wood curls. It seemed at that moment he could keep time, all the rest of the days of his life, by the number of layers his father was adding to it.

"Forgot the fire you'll need to start tomorrow?" Thomas asked after a moment, as if to strike Samuel out of his wondering.

"No sir," Samuel said.

"Then you should be at rest," Thomas said, "or at least tucking in those you love." Thomas paused, as though he was taking the measure of how much of the day's work he had accomplished. "No matter how far they be from your hearth."

Samuel jumped to his feet, but found he could not venture further.

"Take care not to be noticed, Samuel," his father said.

"Thank you, sir."

"And send her our love."

"Yes, sir."

✄<✄<❀

"**Jenny**," ❀ Samuel said softly. There was nothing wrong with her hearing. And if he should spook the Chestnut as it had been frightened that morning, Jenny would likely send him away, and was not likely to welcome him back any time soon.

> ❀ **Jenny** is the name shared by two of the mothers in my neighborhood, one of whom was our next-door neighbor. It should be noted that for the Jenny next door, it was not her true name, but one she took on once she converted to Judaism so she could marry her husband. Her given name was somewhat of a secret, but her daughter told me it was Jeanette; and her daughter had a wooden lapel pin with Jeanette written in script.

Her mother had given it to her as a token of her pre-married life. The way the daughter wore that pin drove me nuts, as though she had an extra "Jeannette" persona she could retreat into while she wore it: sophisticated and mysterious, something altogether inaccessible to someone like me, a girl whose mother's name was Nancy and would always be Nancy; there was no possibility of change or even improvement. (In all fairness, it should be recorded that during her marriage, my mother signed her checks "Mrs. Leonard Rosenberg," as if Nancy Rosenberg had no standing on her own, but that changed after she divorced my father, and Nancy Rosenberg came to mean quite a bit, thank you very much, but that is her story, not my own.)

The other mother named Jenny was a Scottish immigrant, whose English husband was a great source of admiration for my father, but we'll get to him soon enough. Jenny also is a Scottish form of another, more traditionally English name, which should become self-evident through the course of this narrative.

She was already accustomed to hay for a pillow and a mattress, and he could see, as he was entering the stall, ❀ that she had already made for the night such arrangements.

❀ No doubt this setting is reminiscent of the **Pickwick Stables**, an old if not venerable institution on Riverside Drive in Burbank. You knew it was a cheap stable by the likely hollow, but life-sized plastic stallion placed above its identifying sign and the horses were said to be several rungs closer to the glue factory than the horses at the neighboring Sunset Stables. The Sunset Stables catered to the expert equestrians, who included a fair number of Laurel Canyonites, but Pickwick is where they had riding lessons. And so onto Pickwick I was taken and put under the tutelage of a man named Harold. To us kids he didn't have a last name. He was a hard case with a heart of gold who called out when we were supposed to post on a trot and when, for brief intervals, we could canter in the ring. His stomach shook with each instruction that he gave, as if it were posting and cantering on its own. Another one of Harold's protégés explained Harold did this because he was probably drunk and his entire body was in a welter of cirrhosis and associated deterioration.

From behind the side of the horse she appeared, as if she had been hiding behind the animal. The hair that had been loosened by the day's events still ran over her face and shoulders, although one of her green eyes was visible. The hem of her skirt was still missing. Samuel thought she looked mischievous, this unkempt, and but also possibly pleased to receive his call. Samuel had always found himself deciding on her attitudes, since she could not describe them herself.

"Jenny," he repeated, feeling as though he were heaving off a great weight. "How are you?" She shrugged and set her eyes on her boots, as if embarrassed. "Grace and Lucy—we saw it all," Samuel went on, and under the glance of Jenny's one green eye he realized this was the first he could remember, speaking to her without any one else present. "Mother and Father— they were worried," he said, and it seemed to him that he was diving after the words he needed, or wanted. Nothing he wanted to say would stay in his mind long enough. "They send their love," he said, almost as an afterthought.

Jenny put out both hands and lowered them toward the floor until they reached a point in the air that approximated the size of the twins.

"The girls, they were not worried," Samuel promised. "They knew it would turn out well."

Jenny smiled, as if she could take credit for the girls' courage. But she was just as soon discomfited again, her glance returning to the tips of her toes.

"They wanted to be here, to see you," Samuel said. "But we did not think it safe." Samuel himself had never been here at this hour, when the snorts and panting of horses combined with the sounds of human restlessness. The roars and voices, some drunk, some scared, made the stable sleeping quarters feel as though they were in motion, the people and animals no longer tethered as he was in his world. But this is where Jenny had to live now. This was her sentence. "I am sorry," Samuel said.

Jenny moved her head; whether to shake it, as if to say his apology was not necessary, or to direct his attention back to the Chestnut, Samuel could not be sure. She put her arms around the horse's neck and embraced what she could of the mount, and then pointed with a finger toward the horse's back. There was something she wanted Samuel to see; he tried taking a step toward the horse but it swung his head nastily, and stamped and shifted in the stall. Jenny put her cheek to the horse's own, and then her finger to the horse's mouth.

"I don't suppose he fancies any more attention," Samuel said, and Jenny pointed again to the horse's back. She then withdrew her finger, now put to her lips, as if to reinforce the need for stillness. Samuel looked more closely, from where a saddle blanket and saddle would fall over the horse's shoulders to just above the horse's hindquarters. Midway on the back he saw the hide roughened, reddened, as if it had been chewed upon. The exposed skin was hideous, but shining, Samuel guessed, from the dressing Jenny most likely had made for it.

Jenny had moved away from the horse, toward a haystack outside of the horse's vision. When she walked around horses her steps were light, and fleet, almost unfathomable. On the haystack were the saddle and saddle blanket Samuel recognized from the morning. Jenny lifted the saddle and pointed to a hole in its underside, and the corresponding tears in the saddle blanket's fabric.

Then she opened her palm to Samuel's eyes and displayed an unfamiliarly shaped piece of metal. It could have been a coin or a badge, or the head of a dagger, but it had a prohibitive edge of a razor framing it. Still Jenny was able to easily slide the object into the hole in the saddle and saddle blanket. She made a fist with one hand and shoved it into the other, twisting her fist into her palm several times for emphasis. She pointed in the direction of the wound on the horse's back.

Samuel made a second hesitant move toward the Chestnut; it was as though he understood now what had happened to the horse that morning, with Jenny's explanation. He put out one hand himself, now, and although it contained no offering, he aimed it toward the horse's mouth, his nostrils. The

Chestnut observed Samuel with a new confidence before smelling and licking his palm.

"There, there you go," Samuel said to the horse, and he thought, if only for an instance he wanted to keep to himself, that Jenny was smiling at him with approval. "I won't hurt you, ask Jenny, she knows," he said. "No one wants to hurt you."

Jenny was most definitely shaking her head, as if to disagree with his statement. She tossed her glance quickly outside of the stall, as if in the direction of the castle, beyond the sounds of the servants and their harangues.

"Sir Robert," Samuel said. He felt the horse withdraw from his attentions. "Someone wanted to hurt Sir Robert?" he found himself asking the girl.

She returned her stare to her boots, again, as though the truth was also a threat to her.

"Does he know?" Samuel continued, and the feelings he had experienced that morning in the square, once Jenny had been felled by what was now understood to be an obvious attack on the horse, returned with a new significance. "You must tell him, Jenny," Samuel concluded.

Jenny nodded, although not as much in agreement as in resignation.

"I will tell him for you, if you desire," Samuel volunteered.

She might have leaped at him, as if to insist, "No," with her entire body making the plea for quiet. Instead she pointed at herself, her chest, and nodded more assertively. She was making a promise. Not to Sir Robert, it seemed, but to Samuel, because she then put a finger to Samuel's lips. But he wanted to ask more questions at this gesture; he wanted to know who might plot against Sir Robert, and why? What would the Queen make of it? Did the conspirator or conspirators know what had become of their game? Was Jenny herself jeopardized as well? Samuel Bright felt the roughened edge of Jenny's finger against his lips; her touch was not unfamiliar. Yet now he detected a pressure, an urgency he could not account for. For her, clearly, the subject was finished.

Jenny withdrew and resumed her place by the horse's side, preventing Samuel from studying the wound further, as he had intended. She smiled faintly and patted the mount on his neck, reassurance to both the animal and the young man whom she had so efficiently taught to commune with it.

"I will say goodnight, then," Samuel said. He wanted to give her a kiss, as he had done when he thought of her as a sister, but the sounds and movement of the stable seemed to forbid it. "You will take care," was his statement, although his voice implied more of a request.

Jenny closed her eyes in reply.

"I, we, we all miss you, Jenny," Samuel said. "Mother and Father and the twins. We all love you as well." As he walked out and away, he wondered if it were possible, her smelling the mixture of regret and reluctance in the air he expelled; then he wondered whether that mixture was in fact in the air he inhaled.

chapter two

In public, Sir Robert Drake was rarely outfitted in anything less than the most complex finery. His underclothes were as meticulously prepared as his ruffs and doublets, his shoes and his hose, and the white-powdered feathers in his hat. He was not thought to be a vain man, although those in court knew he had reason to be so careful about his appearance. He was a knight but one who had long since dropped all calculations as to his place in line to inherit anything. His rivals thought him complacent and made no secret of their assessment. Sir Robert thought himself realistic.

True, the Queen favored his looks and his occasional deeds but he was a disposable noble, easily inconvenient should alliances and circumstances take any particular turn. He had married into the court; a cousin-in-law to some other cousin-in-law and these auspicious links to the most royal of all personages had technically been severed. She was **a young bride who had died rather quickly;** ❀ Sir Robert rarely thought her death was of a deliberate design, but there were times, in confrontations with the Queen's closer advisers, he thought otherwise. There were times, more often in recent days, that he indulged in such speculations, even though he knew them to be ridiculous.

❀ **Widowhood** was permitted in our neighborhood, although the widows I can remember were alternately talked about, marveled at, or suffered through some kind of *de facto* segregation. Of those I remember, one went on to make a very good marriage, in everyone's opinion, with a prominent executive. One moved away because of the financial difficulties that followed (her husband dropped dead during a Brownie-Girl Scout Jamboree, and my mother was so upset upon hearing the news that she left me behind at said Jamboree to come home and mourn); and a third became a lady hermit. Her driveway was a popular gathering spot, and while we loitered and watched her property fill up with motor scooters, bicycles and dune buggies, we knew she was inside, roaming through bedrooms, into the kitchen and back again, in a pair of slippers and housecoat. We also had a couple of widowers in the neighborhood; one was a lawyer successful enough to hire a live-in nanny for his daughter, and some were very impressed. But widowers did not inspire the tongue-wagging that widows did. No one found fault in them but there was shame, oh the shame, in how they persisted without their husbands.

There was something worse than widowhood, however, and to my parents, it ran rampant in the canyon: divorce. This final solution to bad marriages was inexcusable, particularly where my father was concerned, and no matter the cause, alcoholism, social diseases, and juvenile delinquency could be its only results. It did not matter that alcoholism caused at least two of these divorces (I was witness to several messy episodes of drunken motherhood during my youth and they nearly branded me a teetotaler for life. I mean: People thought my mother was nuts, but she was a font of reason compared to the women who drank like lunatics.). The children involved were sweet little girls in my ballet class. On my street, we were swaddled in the knowledge that no divorces could happen there, until one couple at the top of the block broke up (a psychologist and his wife; it was blamed on his profession); and then another (a psychiatrist and his wife, who subsequently enrolled in law school, an action which offered its own explanation); and then another, until divorce veritably swarmed around our house, and my father was compelled to do something about it. More about that later.

My mother did not publicly berate divorcees and divorcers, but my father certainly did, even though his father's family would not have been possible without it. My great-grandfather had obtained a "get," the Jewish form of divorce, in the Old Country so that he could leave a barren woman and find another one more suitable to his purposes. The one he found had already been married herself (we were never told whether she was divorced or widowed), and had a son. This was talked about only as often as it took for me to understand it, for we have a bevy of cousins in Canada we visited every year, even though they were technically stepcousins, the product of my great-grandmother's first marriage.

Yet in his costume, with his width of his chest expanded, his legs wrapped and strapping, and his arms twin bulks of menace and pressure, he was grand and authoritative. Certainly there was no deceiving the Queen herself, but he believed that the two shared a particular understanding. As long as he made himself presentable, and did not share his opinions too loudly with the wrong persons, he was welcome to kiss her ring and bow at her brow, and live within her grace.

In his bedclothes, however, Sir Robert reverted in his manifestation to what he had been born to: a pale ordinariness; a man so engaged with the pedestrian and the pastoral that he gave no thought to where his next enemy might be nurtured; a man caught unaware. The linens and blankets had overtaken him, or perhaps he had allowed himself to drown in this atmosphere, or he had been poisoned.

"We had to see for ourselves," Sir Robert heard her saying from his bedside, or that was as much Sir Robert could hear, upon being awakened. "How a man appears after such a battle." The woman did not smile as she spoke, and her voice had a distinct tenor of disappointment. "Between himself/ and his horse, was it? Or some phantom challenger?" Her expression in that moment was one reserved for her lovers or perhaps her ministers. But in the haze of the potion that the girl must have given him, the Queen was feigning something close to satisfaction, the rise and the red in her cheeks matching the velvet in her costume.

"Would his injuries also be invisible?" the Queen went on. "So as to appear perfectly unharmed?" Her tone, he was beginning to register, connoted that there were others in the room, but from where he lay, Sir Robert could not see anyone other than **Queen Marion**. ❀ "Or perhaps his injuries would be so much more real, as if to emphasize a very real danger that only he can see."

❀ The universe that was Laurel Hills and Laurel Canyon had its closest approximation to a queen in the form of **Eleanor Marion**. This woman derived her great power from Mann Realty, the firm that packaged the area as a suburban development. I don't know whether she owned or simply managed the place but she was most definitely in charge, and she had lived in the canyon long before the squares like my father even knew where it was.

Eleanor Marion was a large woman, and she wore sandals and maxi-length dresses. Her regular uniform hid "a multitude of sins," as my mother would say, and she was a regular sight at the elementary school. With a school district-issued bullhorn she patrolled the playground for those who could not play well with the others; and she sold candy canes and lemon slices on Tuesday Treat Day. And in this way she generally strutted about her authority, so that she was invincible at the ramparts of the school's PTA.

Eleanor Marion bred early and often, and her sons were great-looking redheads who lived in the houses she collected. One of these houses was across from the school, and was notable for its garage, with a mural of a long-haired hippie painted on it along with the words "Peace/Pax." It was more than a landmark, but also the neighborhood's sentinel, advising all those who glanced upon it that yes, this was it, the famous Laurel Canyon and here was the mural to prove it. I don't know what the presumed head of the Marion family did—Mr. Marion—although I was led to believe he was a blacklisted actor, only owing more credence to my father's suspicions about canyon denizens. My sister was regularly invited to one of the son's birthday parties and I knew the same boy from the playground, but where Eleanor Marion came into our lives with such force was at the Parent-Teacher Association meetings, where she and my mother regularly tangled.

I can remember my mother dutifully studying Robert's Rules of Order as part of her anti-Marion strategizing; they were fighting over some kind of PTA arcana, according to my father. My mother's backers were scandalized that Eleanor Marion sometimes breastfed her younger sons in public. But Eleanor Marion's forces were evidently stronger, and when my mother challenged her in a run for PTA president, Mrs. Leonard Rosenberg was absolutely, completely, devastatingly slaughtered. To this day, my father credits the blips in my mother's recovery to that Marion woman.

Sometime when I was in college, which is where the crux of this memoir will end, I promise, I had a very strange conversation with Eleanor Marion. It occurred as I was working at the Renaissance Pleasure Faire, which I thought made me a real Canyonite, since participating in the Faire offered simultaneous opportunities for self-expression and self-inebriation. Here I was, inserting myself into the same milieu as the kids and adults I'd idolized and feared, and lo and behold, there was Eleanor Marion, waving at me as I was literally covered in mud.

I was working at a dunking booth at the Faire and to meet her I had to climb down from the terrace where I flung water and yelled Elizabethan-flavored obscenities to a drunken but dehydrated crowd. Eleanor Marion asked after my mother. She apologized for upsetting her in those olden days, and then Eleanor Marion was gone. I never saw her again. I was on the outs with my mom at the time over my parents' divorce, and so only reported this encounter to my father, who laughed at the irony and unimportance of it.

The Queen put her palm to his forehead, as if to test her thesis. Sir Robert wanted to speak, but the Queen's smile lessened to the point of vanishing when he tried, and Sir Robert dared not test her. He closed his eyes, as if to say he could not stand the confusion, and felt the Queen's hand gently slide over his eyes and nose and onto his cheek, where it was cool and comforting, almost loving.

"And how strange, for an enemy to attack, but without any discernible signature," Queen Marion explained. But the reach of her voice had suddenly lessened. "I cannot imagine any enemy of my own that would make such an effort with no hope of credit."

"Perhaps it was not an enemy with which Her Majesty is familiar," Sir Robert answered in a whisper.

"Perhaps not," she said as Sir Robert opened his eyes, and confirmed that the two were fully alone in the room, his own chambermaids and the Queen's escorts having departed. "Yet any enemy of your own would certainly be an enemy of the Queen." She paused, as if to renew her seriousness. "Who did this?" she demanded.

"I haven't a clue."

"Whom do you suspect?"

"I suspect sabotage," he responded.

"By whom?"

"Any number of Her Majesty's nobles," Sir Robert began. "Sir William and Sir Thomas of Glencord, that Beechum fellow sneering around court these days, Sir Gaines, or Sir Matthew—which one—**Payne**? 🏵 Shall I continue?"

🏵 As far as I can remember, the boy named **Matt Payne** in my elementary school had absolutely nothing against Robert Drake; I don't even remember their being together in the same class. By the time I was in sixth grade with Robert Drake, Matt had long since disappeared, either for greener pastures or into that mystery land of post-divorce arrangements. But one of my friends supposedly had a crush on Matt Payne, whose name set him up for his share of teasing. So we teased my friend about her attraction, but one day, I learned that her crush was not without reason.

I was reading the second- or third-grade reports we had written about Africa or Asia or some other continent whose inferior culture and technologies we were being made to memorize, and Matt's report had been typed. Typing a report, rather than handwriting it, was a major innovation. Reports that were typed required either some kind of parental intervention or a mound of hunt-and-peck patience, of which I had none, so my reports had to be presented in pencil and dull attempts at mature, cursive strip. Reading Matt Payne's report that day, I began to think that Matt was incredibly articulate, much more so than I could ever to be. At first I attributed his newfound intelligence to just the typewriter. The machine had made him this way, I told myself; it was even possible that his parents had in fact written this report for him, and he had nothing to do with it. But as I continued to read, I realized that these dreary facts and figures about hunger, poor sanitary practices, illness and ill-fated attempts at democracy had been arranged by Matt himself, not his parents, and that this boy was a good deal more mature and erudite than I could ever hope to be.

"No," she ordered, but the smile had resumed its key position upon her countenance. If they had not come to an understanding about what had happened the day before, they had at least reached an agreeable stale mate.

"We can't have our nobles fighting among themselves as if this were some sort of—" The Queen hesitated. "...Some sort of monastery, with its intrigues."

"As you can see, I am not fighting with anyone—"

"At the moment."

"Isn't there some other business Her Majesty might want to sort through at this moment?" Sir Robert asked. Although he could not fathom who might want to do him harm, the prospect that someone harbored such a desire was a rational possibility. He did not suffer his opponents lightly, and their force and number had been growing, owing to the war they insisted on pursuing. There was nothing wrong with war, Sir Robert reasoned, but **this war** ❀ had no aims, no end game. It dawdled on with its death and deformities, and for no land, no booty, no articulated prize the Queen could one day count on displaying.

❀ **The Vietnam War** was not a real war for my cohort; no war could be real, I suppose, for children as insulated as we were, in an upper middle class neighborhood in the hills above Los Angeles. But there were lines of demarcation over Vietnam in our little piece of heaven, and they were easy to sight. Kids from the canyon side tended to be anti-war, as were their parents, and they wore precious silver Prisoner of War bracelets to prove their loyalty. Kids from the hills were not necessarily pro-war (although my father was), but, like their parents, they lacked the resources to articulate any position beyond tacitly backing the establishment.

The closest our neighborhood took to any form of confrontation over the war came in the form of a riot at UCLA (the center of all that is true, holy, and righteous) that swept up one of the neighborhood dads into its maelstrom. UCLA (my parents' alma mater) was no Berkeley in terms of political upheaval. It never had a Free Speech Movement or a People's Park, no Mario Savio and no Jack Weinberger. But UCLA did screw up Angela Davis' tenure pretty good, and once it hosted a shootout between rival branches of the Black Panthers. So when UCLA (also the alma mater of my parents' best friends, Jack and Bobbie) exploded in protest over the shooting of anti-war students at Kent State, the LAPD of *Adam-12* and *Dragnet* was at the ready, and surged into the campus and shut the place down for a week. And one of the neighborhood fathers, a linguistics professor named Peter Ladefoged, wound up being hauled away with all the draft dodgers, outside agitators and other social debris for rioting against the police.

Ladefoged and his wife, Jenny, and their children lived on the canyon side of the neighborhood. The family was famous for many reasons, chief among them being their British accents. Ladefoged was a Cambridge don and his wife was a Scottish lady whom my father insisted smoked an incredible number of cigarettes, even though my mother was also a notorious chain smoker, although not when my father was watching. Ladefoged had other claims to celebrity as well; he was a consultant on the film of *My Fair Lady* and helped the police identify, or rule out, whether Howard Hughes was speaking on a particularly significant moment of reel-to-reel tape that turned up during his hibernation in Las Vegas. Ladefoged's youngest daughter was in my class and I took ballet lessons with her, when she wasn't trotting around Africa with her father on some sabbatical.

Mrs. Ladefoged once made a special appearance at our school to lecture about life on the "Dark Continent." She recalled that during one visit, she was pregnant, and the women in the African villages where her husband documented dying languages treated her with a special deference. During some kind of disturbance, they immediately circled around her and carted her off, separating her from her husband to make sure she was not injured. She was trying to explain to us something about infant mortality in Third World nations when most of us kids could only giggle when confronted with Africa, thanks to the pictures on the covers of *National Geographic* magazines.

All the Ladefogeds' proximity to celebrity was to become painfully close to me one year, perhaps in third grade. All ex-pat Brits apparently know each other, so the Ladefogeds knew the chief ex-pat Brit in the U.S.A., Alistair Cooke. When Cooke was filming his iconic *Alistair Cooke's America* series, Ladefoged's daughter and three or four of her best friends were chosen to appear in it. They were required to run up and down a set of stairs at the Baskin-Robbins ice cream parlor and then were filmed eating banana splits. It was a long, rough evening of working under hot lights and a presumably anxious director, but it was worth it. How do I know? Because they told me about it, over and over again, much to my bewilderment.

The Ladefogeds also were the family that held a Boxing Day party every Dec. 26—these I was invited too, and often— and Ladefoged himself was to become a durable source of fascination for my father, who considered him his only intellectual equal in the vicinity. Whether this is accurate, you'll have to decide for yourself. My father attended Los Angeles City College after graduating from high school; transferred to UCLA after two years and received his bachelor's degree in political science; was turned down for a fellowship at Washington State University; taught English and social studies at a junior high in the desert town of Barstow, but failed to get tenure because the school board thought he was a Communist; and dropped out of a master's of education program at UCLA.

To my father's mind, only he and Peter Ladefoged spoke the same language, as my father's favorite story of Ladefoged is intended to communicate: During one of our Girl Scout ceremonies, my father and Peter Ladefoged stood side by side, and watched the Girl Scouts in their uniforms lining up and saluting and performing other ceremonial tasks. We raised flags and said the pledge of allegiance and recited the Girl Scout promise, as the professor muttered, "I really can't stand these paramilitary organizations."

So my father was quite beside himself when the vaunted Prof. Ladefoged was arrested during the UCLA riots over the Vietnam War; how could one of his types wind up in such questionable circumstances? Prof. Ladefoged said he was not rioting, but trying to break up a fight, and then he had the audacity to sue the LAPD for false arrest. He won that lawsuit, a feat that was documented on the nightly radio broadcast we listened to at dinner, as well as by the television news we watched and the newspaper we read. At the Ladefoged house, there hung a banner celebrating Ladefoged's release from jail—it proclaimed him to be a "yardbird" or some other British slang for convict—and it had been autographed by all his supporters. Here was proof that you could fight the power, my father had to concede, but only if you were truly and breathtakingly innocent and prestigious. Only if you were Peter Ladefoged.

As divorced as we were from the course of the war, the professor's court victory and Walter Cronkite's nightly casualty and death counts were among the more consistent notes in the background noise of my childhood. This noise was particularly prevalent at dinnertime, when my father, who called himself "hard of hearing" but was in fact "deaf as a doorknob," struggled to listen to the KNXT/CBS radio broadcasts at full volume. Afterwards my parents snuggled together in their king-sized bed where they watched Eric Sevareid looking down on everyone, themselves included. But he was so eloquent in his criticisms of the middlebrow patriots (and in a pitch and rhythm that my father could latch onto), they did not seem to mind. What my grandfather, The Colonel, thought of the war was a mystery to me, but had it been up to my father, we would have planted a victory garden and sent its products to Lyndon Johnson. For my father the war in Vietnam was nothing less than the defense of his way of life, his own neighborhood, a cluster of Jews and a few tolerable goyim under siege from a great tide of unwashed, undisciplined, and quite possibly unemployed hippies.

It was not until I was in college, the Reagan administration's covert war in Nicaragua was well under way and my parents were in the midst of their divorce that my father personally apologized to me for his role in the Vietnam War. Yet such an apology would not be enough for some of our fellow neighborhood residents.

Classified as 4-F for the Korean War and thrilled he

was unfit for service, my father was riddled with all sorts of impediments: besides the asthma, ulcer, and deafness, he also suffered from poor eyesight, *and* flat feet. This of course meant nothing to one kid in my school, whose father was a M*A*S*H* surgeon who had fallen into the hands of the North Vietnamese. On top of this travail, this poor, besotted boy was forced to sit at the same table in sixth grade as a girl whose dad was a certified wimp. There was no way he was going to let me forget that my fat and happy father was at home living the good life of canned vegetables and Dutch Master cigars only because his father was sacrificing his sanity, income, and relationship with his kids to preserve the dignity of American democracy. He reminded me of it every day in his mortifying remarks and teasing. Nowadays we would say this boy, hurt and confused, was simply acting out. Still, I find it hard to conjure even a wedge of sympathy for him. He was pretty prolific with his fists and fingernails, when he was not suffering seizures from his epilepsy on the schoolyard.

My elementary school was riveted, then, by these subtle "divisions," but if only for a moment, we students were united in spirit and purpose. In fourth grade, we as a class committed some sort of horrible offense, and marching during our recess was said to be the only adequate punishment. It must have been hard for us to take this punishment seriously, because of the teacher who ordered it. He was no hippie—I remember once his hesitation on letting someone play a Beatles record in class, because it might have "swear words"— but was given to wearing the stars and stripes on his shirts and ties, and he sported a Van Dyke beard. He also used the words "cool" and "far out," which were strictly prohibited in my household. So when he had ordered us to march, someone decided we would assuage the penalty with song. "We are marching to Pretoria," we sang, but one of the long-haired canyon boys changed the words soon enough. "We are marching to Cambodia," he sang, and I was honored to sing along with him.

"I am at your disposal today," the Queen answered, and after taking a quick glimpse about the room, she placed herself on the edge of the bed beside Sir Robert.

"Then I must dispose wisely," he said, and found himself wondering if he could sink even more deeply into the bed, and tempt Her Majesty to dive in after him. At some point in their careers, all knights fall in love with their Queen, and he knew his position depended, to a degree, on continuing for her this tradition. But the physicality of his situation, the throbbing weakness he still sensed in his head, the fatigue that had him feeling he was strapped to the bed, was more overpowering.

"Who is she?" he asked.

"Who?" the Queen asked, all too innocently.

"The stable slave, the servant. The nurse maid."

"That is a mystery, tripled," the Queen observed.

"There was one girl in all those roles," Sir Robert said, and as the Queen shifted both her posture and glance, he realized how she had always known this was the case. It was possible, Sir Robert realized possibly too late, that this was not an area open to inquiry.

"That girl," the Queen said firmly, "is an outcast."

"Cast out from what?"

"Haven't you summoned enough trouble for the moment?" the Queen asked.

"I only wish to thank her," he said, because it was the explanation most readily available to him. He well knew, however, that there was no way to pay tribute to an outcast. As an outcast, the girl could hold onto nothing, not even to gratitude; she was as good as a ghost, a figment of his imagination.

The Queen's face lost all expression. Her age did not show, and neither did her frustration, but she was hesitating, obviously, still formulating the final word, the decree that could not even be affectionately answered. Yet even with her make-up, the bearing she still maintained in her back and neck, the cool touch of her palms against his, she had no strategy to disguise what she was doing. Sir Robert could not be certain whether he had happened upon a secret of the Queen's; for knights bound to delve into the Queen's heart, there were said to be many. He tried to disguise his own moves in response, how he watched her eyes, his own reflection in them, his reaction to this horrible pause.

"I should not be questioned as to why man behaves so inhumanely, casting out one of his own, accepting another," she said. "But this girl: she does not speak. She has cast herself out. She perhaps favors it that way."

"She does not speak," Sir Robert repeated. "Perhaps she has nothing to say."

"They also say she is a witch," the Queen warned.

"Perhaps she is merely bewitched," Sir Robert offered back, but the Queen remained unmoved by his play.

"Robert," the Queen addressed him at her most intimate.

"Maggers," Sir Robert offered; the endearment was all he had at the moment. She was beautiful, Sir Robert believed; she was dark and bright and mesmerizing and frightening all at once.

"If you wish to see this girl, no one will vouch for the consequences," the Queen said.

"Does she have a name?" Sir Robert asked.

"No family name," the Queen insisted. "But they call her Jenny."

❀ ❀ ❀ ❀ ❀

Sir Robert felt the girl's return before he could witness it; the dry, papery wisp of her hand ministering to his head. The touch was older, more hesitant, than he had anticipated of an outcast; he expected someone careless, in the sense that she had long since bothered to take heed of other's opinions. But this girl's hand, at its first press against his forehead, and then in the gentle sweep across his brow, immediately communicated an altogether different message. It contained both need and sensitivity, as if it called out for healing more than its patient could. This did not provide an unpleasant sensation as it traveled from his hairline to his eyes, and to his cheeks, and Sir Robert allowed himself to languish in it as if it were the cautious, modest stroke of a kitten auditioning for a benefactor.

When he opened his eyes, the girl quickly withdrew. She could have curtsied in apology, or averted her glance, but apparently she was too frightened to.

"Good morrow to you," Sir Robert said, as deeply as he could muster. But in neither her expression nor her manner was the girl affected. His voice, Sir Robert thought, may very well have also been injured.

"I was asking after you earlier," he said. "Were you informed?"

She shook her head.

"Then I must be failing in some new way," he guessed.

The girl again shook her head, but this time her gesture was punctuated by the curtsy due to a noble. In the next moment she left the room. Before Sir Robert could decipher her actions, she returned, with a large tray that she placed on the room's table. It contained a pitcher and towels, a glass bottle, and some sort of instrument made from wood and metal; Sir Robert readily detected its gleam in the remaining sunlight. The girl raised her index finger to her lips and moved toward him, more confidently now, with a purpose.

"I was told you have a name," Sir Robert said.

The girl took his face between her palms, and guided his chin into his chest.

"Jenny, is it?" Sir Robert went on. In response, he heard the stopper removed from the glass bottle. "No parents, no guardians? That must mean no enemies, but no allies." From what he could see of her working, she had brought over one of the towels and placed it on his pillow; another, he sensed, was placed around his neck as if it were a collar. "That is an enviable position in these times," Sir Robert continued, although he was no longer certain of what he was saying. The girl raised his face again to show him what was in her hand: something like a fork with only two prongs and a wooden handle. Sir Robert knew asking after its purpose would be useless, so he took the moment to discern what it might be on his own.

What he saw, though, was nothing of the instrument. Its bearer, meanwhile, was not wholly unattractive, although in size and weight she was dreadful. The bones of her neck and shoulders showed through the rags she had somehow maneuvered into a bodice and blouse. Her black hair was braided down her back but at the right angle could appear unaccountably sleek, like a fur. But it was her eyes that made her what she was in this world, **an orphan** ❀ if not also an outcast, silent and impenetrable. Neither crystalline nor dull, they were a rushed, wild green, untraceable in origin and motive.

❀ Given the conventions of children's literature, there's little doubt that at some time or the other, most children fantasize about being **an orphan**. I know I did. But just as war was unreal, so were orphans in my cloistered neighborhood. But in junior high I would actually meet one—along with all the various other undesirables whom my parents feared.

We'll call this girl Wendy. She wasn't undesirable in any way, although her living arrangements originally befuddled my parents, strict believers in two-parent families with mothers chained to the hearth and all-powerful patriarchs at the head of every dinner table. Wendy lived with her grandmother; her mother was a mystery; and her father and stepmother were somewhere in a far better neighborhood than Wendy could ever aspire to. Perhaps because Wendy was so prodigiously gifted, or perhaps because she was Jewish, my parents did not immediately disapprove of her, as they did with most of my other friends. Or perhaps because of her story, as it unfolded before us, they were particularly sympathetic.

Wendy's mother died when she was a few months old. She might even have died in childbirth, or as a result of it, but this much was never clear. When her father remarried, he chose the prototypical stepmother to replace her. This woman beat the girl and made her eat her cereal after she had vomited into it. Once, she plunged the girl's hands into boiling hot water. Wendy couldn't tell me about being taken to the doctor or a hospital afterward, but she did remember the day the bandages came off. Her father decided it was time to remove them, for no discernible reason, other than she was watching "Hobo Kelly" on television. It was far too soon and she had the scars on her forearms to show for it, as though her skin was a topographical map of what must have been happening to her internally.

Because of her stepmother's venality or perhaps because her father was at a loss to protect her against it, this girl was sent to live with her paternal grandmother, which is how I came to know her. Together they lived in a small house in what was considered a downscale part of town, in the downscale attendance area where Bancroft Junior High was centered. Her father, a lawyer, presumably sent money, although Wendy and her grandmother did not live as if this were the case. She suffered through all the indignities of having to rent a horse, rather than own one; and of having to sit in the nosebleed seats during the best rock concerts, as the rest of us did.

How I dropped from the heights of Wonderland to the down market of Bancroft is a tale of *de jure* segregation, and my father's battle against white flight if not racism; and it's not entirely relevant to the matters at hand. But what is relevant is that Wendy was one of the first people I befriended in the big bad city of Hollywood, where not only terrible things transpired in families, but they unfolded in front of everyone, all over the place.

I don't know how to describe Wendy's sense of identity other than to say it was absolutely foreign to me. There was a time I was at her house and members of her mother's family, whom she had never met, came to pay a call on her grandmother. She was completely oblivious to these people, who looked as though they might be her grandparents. I adored both sets of my grandparents and loved meeting new second, third, and fourth cousins, but these were just more old people to her, uninterested in the things that she cared about, apparently.

And what she cared about was boys, and horses, and rock 'n' roll stars. She was incredibly talented in all three departments, in terms of copying them: she could draw like nobody's business. From the small, yearbook-ready mug shots of our classmates she produced amazing, life-like portraits.

She was particularly adept at animating pictures of the boys we stalked. I suppose she was so assiduous at copying reality because she had no expectations for it: for her there were no happy endings, no house that was a sanctuary at the end of the road, no balance between the public and private sphere that would allow the imagination, with a necessary set of moorings, to flourish. So she stuck to what she could grasp, and the results were meticulous.

Our interests, as you might imagine, came to be finely meshed, and I spent hours on the telephone with her. In school we were perceived as ugly, awkward (and I was intolerably loud), but in fact she was beautiful, with a face so clear and deftly formed that it did not seem human. She was what my mother and grandmothers would have called a real Dresden doll. By high school she had grown into a truly fantastic specimen, and the boys were lining up in front of her door, fumbling in their pockets.

By his shoulders Sir Robert next felt himself being pulled forward; the girl's hands were fastened onto his shoulders. She was obviously much stronger than she appeared, or he had sensed at the beginning of this encounter; one of her forearms held him down as the other guided his head forward. His chin was in his chest, his scalp in her lap. She smelled as he expected her to—sharp, unwashed, but alluring in a way he could not make words capture. There was pressure at the back of his head, her fingers teasing through his hair, and then a tug.

"What's this?" he asked, but now it was his turn to be silent, for there was also something of the familiar in all this: the scent of her, or perhaps it was the scent from the glass bottle. The pattern of pressure, teasing, and tugging against the back of his head. She must have treated his wound in a similar fashion yesterday, with the same effect, a sudden dreariness in all his limbs that demanded attention.

He began to speak again, or perhaps he only thought he did; and then he thought he was being lifted, re-arranged, rolled onto his side or onto his stomach, into some new position. Her scent or the scent from the bottle increased in his nostrils as it ferried itself up somewhere behind his eyes, and then it dug into his eyelids. He needed to close them, to close his breath, to see and hear and feel nothing. All he could sense was her presence.

❀ ❀ ❀ ❀ ❀

Because he had slept so completely, he assumed he was due for some sort of revelation, or at least a transformation, upon waking. There was none, but he did not feel himself wanting. The girl was still there. Immediately Sir Robert knew that she had been there throughout his dreaming, calculating the number of breaths he had been taking, cooling his brow with cold cloths, brushing her hands against his own. He did not see any evidence of this; she sat apart from the bed now, on a stool, her eyes and hands engaged with some sort of book, as if he were not there at all. Yet he knew she had not left throughout the hours he had been sleeping; he felt it in the calmness of his own breathing, in the lightness of his skin across the forehead. There had been no alteration in his circumstances and yet he was altogether stronger now, his thinking no longer preoccupied with the sensations of his injury.

Sir Robert watched as the girl studied the book, her eyes presumably following the course of lines on the page, and her hands massaging the paper as if its texture were meant to give up meaning too. The sunlight had either diminished a great deal, or he had re-gained the ability to truly assess this girl's appearance; for her hair no longer contained the sleekness he had seen earlier. It was plain, offering none of its earlier reflections. Her eyes had changed as well. Their meaning was no longer muddied, but bright, as if inspired by what they were seeing. If this outcast had a human heart, it was beating at that moment, through her leaf green irises and infinitely black pupils. If this girl was an outcast, she had to have been cast out after her schooling. She was a literate creature, who knew more than just medicine. She must have known, after a sort, a religion.

"What does it say?" Sir Robert asked casually, because he did not want to frighten her off, as he had done upon their initial meeting.

She shut the book quickly and placed it on the table beside the bed, and shook her head. But she smiled this time, like a child relieved to acknowledge its foolishness.

"What do the pictures say, then?" Sir Robert tried.

She shook her head again with the same smile.

"Can you not show me?"

To this the girl rose from her stool and retreated to the large table at the room's center, where she had placed the tools of her trade, whatever it might precisely be, at the beginning of the afternoon's episode. Silently she went through what must have been an inventory of her materials, and then returned to the side of the bed with a cup of liquid and something else, squirreled into the fist of one of her hands.

Sir Robert let himself be raised up higher onto his pillow and then his head and mouth guided toward the liquid the girl was offering. It was warm, and vaguely sour. She did not force him to drink the entire contents, and he found himself breathing deeply, as if exhausted, when she returned his head and upper back to the pillow; it was as if she knew he suddenly required the additional rest.

Before his eyes her palm opened, revealing a blackened, bloodied curl of something. It was too thin to be a worm or a maggot, such as those that sometimes prey upon injuries; it was no wider than a strand of sewing thread. With her other hand, she reached for his forehead, and then traced a line to the back of his scalp, the site of his wound from yesterday. It was not clear to him whether this was something she had removed from him, or whether it was meant to soothe and heal him.

He was not permitted to ask after her methods either, because she was offering him the warm drink again. This time he was able to handle the cup himself and drink on his own. She smiled approvingly now as she re-took her seat on the stool, and waited for him to finish it.

"You cannot read, and yet you know more than the Queen's own alchemist," Sir Robert said into the cup.

She nodded, but it could have been for encouragement, he knew, to keep on with the draught.

"I don't suppose you could learn, could you?" he asked. "To read and to write."

No, she shook her head, but again it wasn't necessarily a straight answer. Her hand went to the bottom of the cup, as if to remind him on what he should be concentrating on. She must have known how the drink's unpleasantness grew as he neared the liquid's bottom. The gentle pressure of her hand on the cup did not waver.

"I should like to have you taught," Sir Robert managed, after the last drop.

No, she shook her head again. This time, he was certain as to what she meant.

"You obviously are an **intelligent creature**," Sir Robert said, by way of urging her. To which she again shook her head no, firmly. ❀

❀ By the end of elementary school, it was obvious that I possessed enough **gray matter** to power my heart and lungs; and I even learned my left from right, and how to tie my shoes. In junior high, however, the powers that be viewed my skill sets, as well as my capacity to learn new tricks, to be of an entirely lower caliber.

My sister, unable to read fluidly or write coherently due to dyslexia, was deemed a genius sometime around her second-grade year. Despite her handicaps, she was burning up the road in mathematics, and special classes for both her disability and her talents were ordered. She got to take glass-blowing classes at Los Angeles City College (which we thought was quite exclusive at the time, although we were later to discover there were non-geniuses among the attendants); was instructed to play pinball to improve her eye-hand coordination; and sent to a camp, Clear Creek, where all of the "mentally gifted" children of the Los Angeles Unified School District luxuriated in their exalted status.

There were also weekly classes at the elementary school for her to attend, where kids who showed early promise in gobbling down the concepts of C.S. Lewis and M.C. Escher were given drama and creative writing workshops. I was in no way acquainted with such writers and artists and their subdural parlor tricks, and yet in fourth or fifth grade I demanded to have my intelligence tested as well, so I could have access to the same creative outlets. That was the biggest mistake of my academic career.

My intelligence quotient and I didn't quite make the cut, although my score was perfect: perfectly average. The results were ignored, for the most part, by all but one of my elementary school teachers (I am preparing a monograph on the one teacher who didn't). But in junior high school my lack of intelligence became amplified for all to know and revel in. Midway through my career at Bancroft, the tracking system changed from being based on something solid, such as socio-economic status, to how one performed on the Stanford-Binet: either one was "gifted," or an idiot. You can just bet which category I fell into.

Gone were my friends, Wendy first among them, because they were to be funneled into "advanced classes." I was banished to the wastelands of wannabe gang members, the spawn of single-parent households (although they weren't labeled as such back then), apartment and duplex dwellers, and latchkey children. There are idiot celebrities, I suppose, but there is no such thing as an average one, and I was stranded among the nameless, faceless rabble re-learning multiplication tables and the function of a comma in a sentence. Such was our preparation for the rigors of vocational education. The gifted/ advanced classes were swept up in learning the rudiments of data entry, keypunch, pre-Algebra; and reading *The Catcher in the Rye*. The gifted group also turned out to be a more socially advanced bunch too, with the two sexes communing with one another at lunch and recess, and a myriad of other, non-school functions. I was restricted to single-sex bench on the playground, and single-sex sleepovers on the weekends.

All of this—the information and its implications—was embossed onto my family's collective psyche. We all knew my younger sister was special, a prodigy bound for great things (our parents never ceased to remind both of us about it); and I was a high achiever who would never quite achieve as highly as my sister. Still, my mother and father suspected that I was not entirely worthless, so when I was exiled to the idiot classes, they were determined to do something about it.

I must give credit to my mother, who somehow saw through the fog of her depression to figure out what to do next. She told me to ask my counselor to transfer me into the social studies and English classes—there was no hope for me in math—and if I didn't get them, I should just sit in the counselors' office until I did. "Tell them your mother said not to move," she said, and I suppose she was in a position to put her pluck and stubbornness on the line here. The eighth-grade counselor was the wife of our pediatrician, and by extension, an acquaintance of my uncle, the doctor, and former chief of staff at the hospital where any self-respecting doctor had privileges. It didn't hurt that while I was resolutely engaged in this sit-down strike outside, Wendy's grandmother had dropped in on some other matter. I was never told what her business was there, but she volunteered to the counselor that I was of fine academic character. A few minutes—or was it hours, days, weeks?—into this act of civil disobedience, the school administration folded, and I was admitted to two of the gifted classes.

After eighth grade, it became an annual battle of wills between me and whoever my academic handlers were that particular season, to see which classes I could worm my way into, and which special assemblies I would have to be barred from. I won't get into the aftershocks this all had on my self-esteem (of course they were horrendous), but at least the whole thing gave me a goal, something to overcome, in my dawning adolescence.

"It would give you a way of speaking," he tried, but the girl did not shake her head no, as might have been expected. Instead, she shut her eyes as she raised a hand to her throat. She might have swallowed then, but Sir Robert could not see, owing to how her hand concealed that space. Her eyes remained closed for another moment, and when she opened them, they were wet.

And then she bolted.

Without her the room fell more fully into silence. Sir Robert used the quiet to reconsider what had just happened, whether her actions could be translated. He hadn't the chance to merely attempt some remark, or secure an expression on his face. And yet she had left, without waiting to be dismissed, before any tears had properly fallen, before she could have dispensed the last stages of this treatment.

Sir Robert considered calling after her, summoning a chambermaid, sending for her at some later instant. But she would not so soon return, he knew. In her own way, she had made her final statement. She was not an outcast because she did not speak. She was an outcast because she knew something. She had ripped out of his room as though she had in fact spoken out of turn, committed an act of treason. Her resolve, he realized, was all that shielded her from a more dire fate.

If this girl knew something, though, Sir Robert also found himself in possession of equally precious knowledge: he knew of her. Any other man who had his head rightfully split open by some fall, he knew, would likely be either delirious or dead by now. This girl knew something. Of treason, of healing; there had to be more, or perhaps these two were one in the same. And Sir Robert had discovered, that afternoon, one other thing. If the death of his wife, the current war, his relations with other nobles had sapped his ambition, this girl restored it. Not that he was so moved by her plight that he felt he needed to perform some great act; not that she cried out for love, or for rescue. But she showed him a possibility. How a man might be made immortal, with her help, to fight his battles and lose, and perhaps to fight again, until he was winning.

chapter three

Samuel had never made anything this delicate before. His hands, arms, and mind had been trained on much sterner, steadier objects: hammers, anvils, and the hooves of horses. But his mother had also taught him to sew, because she said any man who could not sew his own clothes—or his own skin—was an infant. He had never sewn with these particular materials, and if he pulled at the parchment too hard, it might tear; if he left the leather stitches too loose, they would unravel. He always seemed to be left where he started, at the beginning. He would have rather have forged a bracelet, even a ring, than put together the gift he had in mind for her, but nothing of his usual talents would be suitable for the occasion.

Samuel had been drafted. In two days' time he would be marching off with untold numbers of other young men into the Queen's Service. **Conscription** did not come as a surprise to Samuel. ❀

❀ Many were registered for **the draft** in my neighborhood, and I assume that some were even chosen, but I also assume that many also wriggled their way out of it, because that was the kind of neighborhood it was: white, moneyed, and above all else, educated. Self-educated also counted. One boy, with whom I became friendly at the end of my ninth-grade year, managed to stay out of the draft by virtue of his amateur work as an orthodontist.

When this boy (from the canyon, although his mother was very friendly with my own) first reported for his physical, he was still wearing his braces. The brass told him to come back once the braces were taken off. A freshman at UCLA, he was an ingenious sort, and knew there'd be no female freshmen in his future with all that metal in his mouth, so he took the braces off himself. A year later, his number came up again, and he put the braces back on. This on-and-off thing continued until 1973, when the draft was finally called off.

I have no other intelligence about any particular person sent to Vietnam or having to be retrieved from it, although the draft was a real concern to the moms of the neighborhood, according to one conversation I overhead in my eighth grade.

My new, gifted social studies class in junior high school had taken a day trip to the state capitol. Late at night, on the way home from the airport, all of the day-trippers had fallen asleep in the back seat of one of the chaperone's automobiles. All of them, except for me. I listened in as the driver of the car told of her family's close brush with the Selective Service System. Her older son, whom I barely knew, had luckily drawn a high number in the draft lottery, and then, miraculously enough, the draft ended. I was tempted to tell her that based on my experiences with her younger son, who was now sleeping beside me, she had nothing to worry about in terms of her progeny surviving Vietnam. Her younger son was a supremely vicious character, and I can enumerate all of his offenses—emotional and physical—against me if given the opportunity. But I was in the gifted class now, and I was smart, so I just kept quiet.

I wondered how much of this woman's near miss with the draft board story was meant for public consumption, considering how the family that lived next door to this woman's was home to that much celebrated P.O.W. from a M*A*S*H unit.

He had been watching his elders fall under its aegis since before he

could walk on his own power. Every solstice and equinox, Samuel was made to sit on his father's shoulders and wave at the departing, soon-to-be soldiers. As a boy, he was deposited at the front of the parade to shake hands, to congratulate them in their promotion to manhood. When he was made an apprentice, his father ended this requirement, because it seemed more essential that Samuel should learn his craft; develop the control and eyesight that would enable him to one day inherit his father's business. He was still required, by his age, to attend the lottery, and there came to be boys younger than he who were sent off on the conquests the Queen deemed vital to the health of the populace. Although unacquainted with the duties of soldiering, Samuel still became familiar with their return: sometimes in acceptable health, sometimes in pieces, and most often, only in the imaginations of their bereaved parents.

Perhaps Samuel's absence at the farewell ceremonies blunted the realization that he might have to go off some day. Perhaps his surviving that illness made him feel a bit too protected—if he had escaped the forces that once tried to yank out his breath, forces as determined and vicious as dying, rabid pests—then surely he could outwit the odds of being snatched by the Queen's Service. Just after his name was called earlier that week, it seemed that his hearing halted, momentarily. He had been stunned into silence. No other names registered and his father said nothing congratulatory or of consequence. Instead he clamped down his strong hands onto Samuel's narrow shoulders, as if Thomas was trying to forestall a desertion. Lucy and Grace looked up to him with the same foreboding question in their faces. They suddenly seemed too small to him, to be in such a crowd. Their mother pulled them closer, into her apron, and then led them away, as if that would have to satisfy for an explanation.

By the time Samuel and Thomas arrived home, his mother had found an old satchel Thomas had likely used during his time in the Service. She set to mending it with the help of the twins. Another mount needed re-shoeing, but first its hooves needed to be re-filed. Samuel nailed in four new shoes on that gelding and then re-settled it in its home stable, a half-hour's walk down the road. When Samuel returned from that errand, his father had him douse the fire and sweep and bury the ashes. Samuel did not think of Jenny, whether and how the news might affect her, until he was at supper, the warm cup of mull placed in his hand. Jenny was still missing from his table. He was seized by an instinct to run to her quarters and bring her back to the house, restore her to her former position. She could take his place, now that he was leaving.

"Every night we shall have boar and pheasant and cream and berries, whatever our Samuel desires," Thomas proclaimed as his mother placed a dish before the new soldier. The girls clapped their hands as if they had been instructed to do so. Yet there was no delight on their faces. Their hair had been placed under matching bonnets, as if they were too soon ready to end the evening. Samuel saw now that his mother also had not taken her usual seat and that there was no other food, beside his own, on the table.

"Girls: to bed," Thomas commanded, and there was no brooking this authority. His mother left him a kiss on the top of his head, and withdrew with the girls clutching both her arms. Before Samuel could question or object, his father had stood up and walked over to him.

"Yes, sir," Samuel said, rising from his chair and taking the hand his father offered.

"You have business to clear before taking your leave?" Thomas asked. Before Samuel could lie and say no, Thomas elaborated: "You have had **business** these past few weeks, after nightfall." ❀

❀ Owing to the location of our house, far, far away from any means of public transportation, I could not just sneak out to carry out any **mischief** that I wanted. That was something only kids from the canyon side of the neighborhood could do, and besides, they must have had the encouragement and chauffeuring services of their parents to aid them. One of their favorite activities was the Friday Night Ride, which was probably nothing more than a horseback ride in the dark. But to me it was another one of those rites of passage, like attending Cheech and Chong's Halloween Party, or the Clear Creek Camp for gifted children, or going to the Renaissance Pleasure Faire that were being denied to me, because I was ugly, unpopular, and ungifted.

Sponsored by the cooler, classier Sunset Stables, the Friday Night Ride was a mysterious, cutting-edge prelude to what I was sure was a weekend of romance and rebellion. I can't tell you what happened on those rides; all I know was that people rented horses and in one large group, explored the wilds of Burbank after dark. My ballet teacher, who tried to initiate a cadre of hill and canyon girls into some kind of culture beyond what was on television, had a daughter my age. Call her Polly. Polly and her canyon friends regularly attended the Renaissance Faire during its spring run, and they were habitués of the Friday Night Ride. Aside from any restrictions my parents put on me, I knew I would never go on a Friday Night Ride, since you had to be invited, and there was no way Polly or anyone else within any quantifiable distance of her, me, and a ten-foot-pole was going to let me in.

So for a good while, my instinct for anarchy had to be carried out literally under my father's nose. In his bedroom is where it in fact took place; from where he reigned over the lone television set in the household, a small black-and-white Zenith that often broke and just as often left my sister and I bereft. Hell would freeze over before my father would relinquish the remote control, which we called the "click click;" the television practically stood at his feet, on the dresser opposite the king-sized bed.

My father slept voraciously when I was a child, because he worked nights, as the owner of a stall in the downtown wholesale produce market. Apparently, though, he could never quite pull a profit out of the operation (he inherited it from his father), and he quit the night shift sometime while I was in elementary school. Its circadian demands, however, have remained with him to this day, and he easily integrated them into his next job, as a self-employed wholesale Christmas tree broker. In other words, he worked on his own schedule, and really for what amounted to only a few months of the year. When he wasn't working, he confined his hobbies—reading, drinking tea, and resting—to that giant bed. Nowadays people would explain his behavior away as the result of depression, but given my needs and interests of the time, I thought he was doing his level best to deny me that valuable TV time.

And I needed the TV—to watch *The Midnight Special*, or *Don Kirshner's Rock Concert*—if I was to know anything of what the kids would be talking about on Monday morning. They, of course, were actually at the clubs on the Sunset Strip—Gazzarri's, the Roxy or the Whiskey-A-Go Go—after finishing up the Friday Night Ride. If there were age limits at these clubs or other restrictions, I didn't know about them. All I knew was that something was happening and not only was I not in on it, I would never be.

So I satiated my risqué desires with the television set, and yes, sometimes sleepovers, and one night, when Wendy was sleeping over, we heard that David Bowie was to be that evening's entertainment. I suppose if Bowie were on *Midnight Special* or *Don Kirshner* or some other network-sanctioned outlet my parents would have been more understanding. But this was supposed to be "raw footage," on one of those cheap, local channels and there was absolutely no way on God's green earth that my friend and I were going to get anywhere near that television. "Your father is sleeping," my mother said, which is what she said whenever I needed something from my father and he was unable to provide it. And he was the only one who could provide such dispensations and permissions, for my mother's illness had defanged her of all authority and initiative.

Wendy and I were not particularly big Bowie fans although there was not a girl my age who was not somehow entranced by him: the way he looked and the whole Ziggy Stardust mystique, and the not-so-subtle lesson he taught about reinvention. "Bowie shows," where young girls in red shag wigs and Mylar body suits lip-synched to Bowie tunes, were *de rigueur* during junior high talent fests. The best bar none was Cherie Currie (of The Runaways all-girl-group fame) and her twin sister's at Mulholland Junior High. It was the stuff of legend. (The daughter of my father's best friend went to Mulholland and was my primary source for this information.) So we just had to watch the Bowie broadcast lest we turn up at school on Monday, ignorant as usual.

As my father lay in the bed like a huge mound of hibernating, molten aggression, we crawled into his room and situated our necks to take in the rock 'n' roll spectacular. Despite my father's deafness, we were fearful of rousing his consciousness, so we kept the set at a spectacularly low volume. It didn't really matter though, because what we wanted to see was the part when Bowie got down on his knees and bowed before Mick Ronson's shredding guitar, i.e., the famous fellatio simulation that drove audiences around the world into a frenzy. We didn't really know what fellatio meant, but just as Supreme Court justices have an instinctual knowledge of pornography, we knew what we were seeing once it was put before us. Wendy was out of her mind with giggles as this rotoscoped around the room; the walls flickered and the transistors in the set buzzed whenever the audience screamed. And I was quaking in my booties to think that my father would wake up to take it all in.

So his father had known during this time: Samuel had been sneaking outside, two to three times each week, to check on the girl who had once been theirs to worry over, to provide for. He took to her gifts: an **obsidian blade**, ❀ or pieces of flint he swept up in the shop; the ends of bread loaves the twins wouldn't eat; quarters of sewing material his mother could not notice missing; old underclothes he boiled and hung to dry, when his father was out. Anything she might make use of, he took to her, because she had nothing. Samuel had known never to ask beyond what his father would tell him about Jenny, so he had known never to pursue the matter of her departure. But since that night he visited her after Sir Robert Drake's accident, he had been unable to leave the matter alone. Seeing how the girl lived now, without a proper bed or a wash basin; seeing how she collected scraps from the servants' tables as if she were a rodent, hoarding; seeing that thing she had found in Sir Robert's riding gear, and how she could neither hide nor rid herself of it, Samuel worried.

❦ Both the canyon side of the neighborhood and the hills were pocked with fire trails, narrow dirt roads the Fire Department supposedly once used to trim brush and fight spontaneous fires that plagued the Hollywood Hills. These trails were filled with **arrowheads**, or so I was led to believe, based on the reports of my elementary school companions. With my crossover canyon friends—ballet dancers like the daughter of the linguistics professor, who lived on a "private" street that dead-ended at a trail—I searched for arrowheads, but never found one, although my sister did. But she was gifted and hung around with a smarter crowd more adept at unlocking the secrets of Laurel Canyon.

She also was a tomboy, and a skateboarder, and committed the illegal act of trespassing, I'm certain, to gain access to the storm drains where she and her friends could practice their skateboarding moves, long before the Z-boys were doing it in Dogtown. At any rate, arrowheads were among the most coveted items of the canyon experience. Sometimes they were brought to school, at great peril to their bearers, because they could be stolen, or confiscated. They certified that whatever had happened the day before, you experienced a real, true, adventure, and you didn't just go on some silly hike or nature walk with the Girl Scouts. Instead you had faced down garter snakes or potato beetles or spiders of indeterminate breeding, and quite possibly poison oak. To find an arrowhead meant, ultimately, that you were living somewhere that was truly wild, uncivilized, and not just another dumb suburb. I don't think any of us would have put it in those terms, but with the benefit of hindsight, I think that's the best way to frame it.

Jenny was as **strong**, ❀ certainly stronger than himself, and as strong as any of his contemporaries; she could pound out a horseshoe, a bit for a bridle, the armor for a nobleman as well as he could. Thomas had made certain of it, having apprenticed not just Samuel, but the two together. Jenny was as deft with a clinch cutter as she was with her flowers. Thomas had said once, in passing, that her father had wanted this: his daughter should know something of a trade she could earn a living with, should her speechlessness make her undesirable as a wife. It was that possibility for Jenny, that she would be left alone in a world where Samuel had already found so much happiness, in his home, his parents, and the twin darlings, that might have made him worry.

❀ Among the many honors I was denied, due to either my attitude or inability, was the President's Council on **Physical Fitness** badge. This was a patch, with the embroidered seal of the good U.S. president as its focus, which stood as the gold standard in physical agility. It could be sewn proudly onto one's backpack, for the rest of the world to marvel at. To win one of these patches, you had to pass the physical fitness test, a blistering routine of sit-ups, skip-steps, pull-ups and other treacherous tasks. Everyone in Bancroft Junior High had to take this test, except for those in "Corrective P.E.," a haven for cripples and athletes too precious or promising to risk their limbs on the dangers of conventional physical education.

One of my dancer friends was diagnosed with scoliosis (the mandatory test for scoliosis was performed by the junior high school nurse each year), and was placed into the corrective class. I don't know what they did in there but I'm pretty sure it wasn't much. Another dancer, who studied at a different studio, was also in there, owing to the possibility that she could be injured in regular P.E., and her career put at risk. Yet another girl from my dance studio, who claimed she was similarly committed, got in with the help of her parents. But the rest of us, including one associate who was merely a tap dancer, were stuck in regular P.E., that life-scarring fifty minutes every student had to undergo once a day, five days a week, nine months out of the year.

When the test for the badges came around, I performed miserably. I took horseback riding classes twice a week, ballet three times a week, and spent most of my weekend days rehearsing for future ballet performances, or actually performing at convalescent hotels, community centers, or children's hospitals. But I was a mess, physically, and the more I danced, the more of a muddle of orthopedic problems I became, to say nothing of my allergies (to perfumes, make-up and certain foods) and stomach ailments (too many to mention). Once, during the gymnastics retinue that made up the P.E. torture routine, I failed to perform a back bend, and my tap dancing associate proclaimed, "Oh my God, I can't believe you're a toe dancer. You are a weakling."

It was not her silence that made him worry, he told himself, because he had always known that silence in her; he did not know how to consider it strange, or as some said it was, despicable. Indeed, he found himself more concerned after Jenny when her silence verged on breaking: when there was some outcome, some object, she desired so fiercely that her eyes, if not her throat, seemed on the precipice of speaking. An all-white kitten was one such interest, when they were children, and the white-orange core of metal his father withdrew from the pot the first time they were in his shop together. More recently, when Samuel tried to remember it, the only other such occasion was as Jenny hovered over him in the nights that he and his parents doubted he would make his recovery.

"I had to see her," Samuel said contritely. "She has nothing, no one—"

"Except for you," Thomas finished for him. "It may not amount to much now, with your leaving, but you must realize the danger you could have brought upon yourself, brought upon us all. Samuel, if you think nothing of me and your mother, then think of your sisters."

"They would have gladly accompanied me given the opportunity," Samuel said.

"And yet you did not present it to them," Thomas said, "because you knew."

"Yes, sir," Samuel relented.

"What do you now propose, given your new position?"

Samuel watched his father with a new urgency. He did not find him stooped, scarred, or with any defect. But he sensed now that such imperfections would expose themselves soon enough, perhaps as soon as he left. When he returned—if he returned—Thomas would be a substantially different man—older, his hands and back stiffer, his aim on the anvil no longer so precise. His father was giving up a portion of what had made him strong all these years, but Samuel doubted he had the power to carry that strength forward.

"May I go to her, then, if only in these last days?" Samuel asked of his father.

"I'd think that my permission now is irrelevant," Thomas said.

"It was never my intention to jeopardize any—"

"I know, Samuel," Thomas said, and he put a hand to his son's shoulder, to guide him back into his chair. He balanced himself in one of the twin's seats to sit beside him. "I know why you did it. It is unjust, what has happened to our Jenny. But it is what the Queen calls on us to do, just as she has called you now, into her Service."

"How can my seeing to my own family—"

"Samuel," Thomas said, the weight of his voice conveying just how much he needed to interrupt his son. "I'd like to think there is too much we do not know—of the heavens, of our world, of the Queen's good governance. It is not always for the best, but it is the best we can expect."

"Yes, sir," Samuel said, reluctantly, because his own breath felt uneven, undependable, as his father explained all this; it felt as though there could not be enough for him to live off.

"Now you eat this meal your mother prepared for you, and all the rest she'll prepare before your leaving," Thomas instructed. "And then go to our Jenny, and take care in your travels. She'll need to know of your new position, and that in our hearts we cannot abandon her."

"Yes, yes, Father," Samuel shook his father's hand, and he beamed, the air that seemed so strained and distant moments ago now streaming through his chest, opulent, and golden.

❀ ❀ ❀ ❀ ❀

It seemed too early, after his supper, to make his way to the stable; he had become accustomed to stealing away there in the dark, when owl and opossum, wild cat and raccoon were awake and just beginning their business. Whatever use they made of the roads and trails at night, they scurried back to their hovels and branches once Samuel appeared. He carried with him only a walking stick; no sword, or knife, or bow and arrow, a prospect his father would have likely protested. But to carry all that, to have to gather it together before he left, would have awakened his sisters and his parents; it would have served as some kind of notice the next morning that he had been out in the dark, without even a thought of obtaining permission. So he walked as softly, as invisibly, as he could, and he had come to delight in how well he was able to manage it; he thought of how he was able to weave himself into the trees, the grasses, the dark that moved all about him, as though he were meant for such tasks, such demanding silence.

He missed that as he took his walk this evening, with his father's approval. But he also knew, as the dusk gathered around the exposed roots of trees and paws of small animals, that the adventures awaiting him in the Queen's Service would require so much imagination on his part. They would be all too stunning, and crucial. Having to tell Jenny of his call to service; having to tell her of her own duty in this situation, was, he told himself, a kind of practice. Samuel was not so profound as to think his childhood was over, but he could not help but recognize that he was leaving Jenny in a situation all too precarious, if not unsettled.

"Good evening," he said slowly, afraid that his voice would catch considering all he had to tell her. "Jenny," he said as softly as his excitement would allow. To say her name then: to simply say it, it offered him some measure of calm and confidence.

Her hair ❀ looked almost red in reflection as it caught the light and fell over her shoulders. She nodded her greeting and then rushed to him, her arms occupied by two burlap dolls she had obviously made; Samuel could smell the jasmine she had used to stuff them. For Grace and Lucy, he assumed, but the dolls also gave him a less comforting piece of information: if she had made those dolls and presented them tonight, it could only be because she feared losing all contact with them.

❀ Before my mother had her nervous breakdown, she would sit on the edge of her bed, my father watching television behind her, after her shower at the end of the day. She'd take out the bobby pins and a plain rubber band (the kind that is used to hold up a rolled up newspaper, no cloth-covered substitute, even though plain rubber bands were said to be deleterious to human hair, the cause of tangles and split ends) that held her French bun in place. I'd watch **her hair** tumble down her back and fall to her waist, and try to count its colors—black, brown, red, and inevitably gray—as she combed it out. She really yanked on that hair, as though she could always count on more of it growing back in to replace what she so blithely disposed with her comb in her fist. My mother had the most marvelous hair when I was a girl, although she never showed it off, at least not in my presence. I especially loved those red strands; my sister was a redhead, but we called her strawberry blonde. My mother's red hair was rich, enigmatic, a trait I thought only I knew of.

After her illness, she took to wearing a simple ponytail, and she stopped brushing my hair, which became a ball of knots, tangles and snarls, a jungle of hair offenses. There was a boy in elementary school whose hair was similarly neglected, and we used to call him "Rat's Nest." By the time of ninth grade I carried a rat colony on my head. I know my mother was oblivious to my condition, because these were the days when she was having cigarettes and coffee for breakfast and going back to bed until dinner. My father complained that we looked like ragamuffins, my sister and I, but he was also indisposed to doing anything about it. I wasn't moved to improve myself until a boy in my Spanish class asked me, "Who does your hair?" I took it as a compliment and beamed, "I do." He answered, "I thought so."

"Jenny," Samuel heard himself say again. "You must know I have news."
She took a step back, as if to make room for his announcement.
"You have heard the details?" he asked.
She nodded, and offered him the dolls. Her face was in shadow, now, and he was grateful, not having to see what her eyes might have reflected.
"You have spies for ears," he said and Jenny shook her head, no, but again lifted the dolls and placed them in Samuel's arms. Then she put out her two hands as though she were measuring the twins' height. If she had spies, their names were Lucy and Grace.
"So they have tried to make it easier for me, for us," Samuel said, and he was moved then to grasp onto Jenny's hands, worked rough by all her chores but amazingly small, soft, and willing in his palm. "You know what this means then."
He felt her trying to pull away, as though sashaying in a Morris dance, executing a separation that would be only temporary
"But there's more than that," Samuel said. "Jenny. You must let me see it."
She could not have pretended any doubt as to what he meant. It was close to becoming a ritual for his visits, that she show him the thin metal plate, sharpened into a dagger, that she had discovered in Sir Robert's saddle a fortnight earlier. Showing it to him—removing it from its hiding place beneath the hay where she slept; peeling off the handkerchiefs and scarves that she used to conceal it; allowing him to run his fingers over its strange, unintelligible insignia; these had all become signs for the two of them. They did not communicate that all was right with the world, anything but; they told of unfinished business between the two. She had to reveal what she knew and

Samuel need convince her, before another such instrument was found in Sir Robert's tack; before she herself could be blamed for it.

Most importantly, though, they told that another visit was necessary, and Samuel and the words and love he brought from her former home, would return soon enough. Their ritual was to end once Samuel handed back the object to Jenny, but on this night he grasped it firmly through his gloves, refusing to relinquish it.

"You must make this known, Jenny," Samuel said as sternly as he could manage. "Now. Tonight, if possible."

She did not shake her head no, in disagreement, as he had come to anticipate. And her eyes did not widen in protest. Instead they changed almost indescribably, the whites and the irises more vivid, as though shining with some new force that came close to bursting. Samuel thought he saw Jenny raise a hand to her throat, but he couldn't be sure; he shut his eyes to any of her gestures, because now there could be no more excuses. Once he was gone, there would be no one to interpret for her.

"I will speak for you, if I have to," he said.

He opened his eyes to find her arms crossed around herself, as though she were holding objections, along with her fear, inside her.

"We must. We must do this," Samuel said. "You cannot stay here, alone, in these circumstances. I refuse to allow it. If you cannot make this plain, then I will, tomorrow, without you."

The night that had been crawling into the stable now suffused all time and space between them. Still, he could see that she was staring openly into his face, her eyes quickened into a kind of terror. He could have been asking her to betray the Queen, and he was so shaken by the possibility he took her into his embrace, to comfort both of them.

"Jenny, Jenny, Jenny," he chanted into her ear, and his hands contemplated moving up and down her long hair. She smelled of the jasmine she had stuffed the dolls with, a flower that blooms at night, when it is not watched.

"We will put on our best appearances," he promised. "I will find something for you among **my mother's things**, ❀ if you like, and something for myself too, from my father's. I will walk in there with you on my arm, and I will stand by you. I will not abandon you to him," he declared. His hands dared a brush against her tresses; smooth and straight they were, as though she cared for them with the same attention she paid to her horses. "I will make this right, Jenny. I promise," he said, and when he released her from the embrace, the verdant clarity that he had always counted on in her eyes had returned, even stronger through the darkness.

✿ Aside from my subsequent discovery of cream rinses and hair conditioners, I also learned, in junior high, how to **borrow clothes** to overcome my fashion deficiencies. In this department I had the help of two particular dancer friends and with them I was able to surmount if not the social and academic barriers junior high presented to me, then at least the ones my parents had in place. But first, onto fashion:

Owing to my status as a granddaughter of The Colonel in the neighborhood, my fashion sense was dictated by the tastes of the U.S. Army and its commissary on Terminal Island. That was where I was taken each year by my mother to be outfitted, probably in the previous years' cuts and patterns stashed as surplus in the warehouses of Middle America. My mother's secret passport to fashion was all the more humiliating because I was growing up in a neighborhood with a significant number of dads in the *shmata* business, who made certain their daughters looked like anything other than Russian peasants. They handed their children off to the name designers and trademark products they could find at Rudnick's, while at the PX, I was always in between sizes or tragically too small for anything.

I yearned to dress like my contemporaries, in a style that could best be described as mid-century slut. I wanted to wear halter tops and French T-shirts; platform shoes or high-heeled sneakers; and jeans, very tight jeans, preferably the kind with studs, embroidery or rhinestones traveling up and down the legs. Sometimes, my mother took pity on me, and brought me into the living rooms of these *shmata* men. There I would go through the samples of what they had to sell, precisely because I was so small, and was the only girl for miles around who could fit into these discards. But if anyone was to ask, I wasn't supposed to tell. So I came away with a couple of hand-painted T-shirts to add to my plaids and elastics and polyester.

It was those disdained daughters of single harlot moms and underemployed fathers who enabled me to break out of this rut. They loaned me their clothes: hip-hugging jeans with studs down the legs, and a pair of platform sandals; a halter top with some character on it from a Hallmark greeting card. The best was a wrap-around dress, Diane von Furstenberg style. The dress was horribly ripped in any number of places, so to extend its life I taped it up with the same First Aid tape we used on our toes during toe class to prevent blisters. One day, my efforts earned me the attentions of a boy in my art class. "You look…. different," he said. It was just enough.

I never borrowed from the wealthy girls in my ballet classes, nor my horseback riding friends, like Wendy and Polly; these poor kids were the ones who knew how to look good, and they knew how to get around my parents. Their names were Lynn and Inez. We began planning Friday night sleepovers at Inez's apartment; she was one of the better dancers in our troupe, so all the better to get to ballet class early the next morning. And we always made it there, if not in prime condition. For the night before, we would put on our costumes, suitable for traipsing up and down the Sunset Strip one block away from Inez's; sometimes we had some dope to smoke, but more often than not, we had nothing, and had to act as if we did. (Once we tried smoking crushed up Vitamin C, because some other Strip minion told us it would have the desired effect.) Either way we'd set out for adventure, as though we were pioneers in a brave new world.

Our rounds included Tower Records and Licorice Pizza, which were entirely appropriate forums for girls like us, but we got bored there, especially since we had taken a pledge among ourselves that there'd be no five-finger discounts. So we'd walk by Filthy McNasty's in our high-heeled platform shoes and tried to look as though we belonged in a strip club. Once we took the elevator to the top of the 9000 Building, where the Playboy Club was, but we were too afraid to actually go inside. We tried out a lot of elevators and a few stairwells but hung out mostly at the Sun Bee market, or Gil Turner's Liquors on Sunset. The liquor store attracted a lot of other kids who were turned away from the nightspots.

But what I liked best were the nights we gave up on the Strip and went back to Inez's apartment, where she had a stereo, her mother's records (all kinds of Texas psychedelia I didn't recognize, like Delbert McClinton, a real oddity to us big city girls) and a black light. We'd turn on the black light, strip down to our tighty-whities, and dance to the music. Not exactly ballet practice. Our eyes were focused on each other's nether regions—solely to enjoy the black light's effects, naturally. The next day, during class and rehearsals, we were giggly and spent, having had the times of our lives—the best times I can remember of the misery that is supposed to be adolescence.

❦ ❦ ❦ ❦ ❦

They made a confounding pair, Jenny the outcast, and her escort: he was blond with blood-brown eyes, his skin well scrubbed and his body well dressed; Jenny was also outfitted in a new suit, simple but much too large for her bones. The boy, meanwhile, could not keep it a secret that he was frightfully uncomfortable in his dress; his shoulders and arms shifted as though trying to adjust the sleeves and his collar; his legs paced as though he was not confident his trousers would stay up. It must have been a borrowed costume, Sir Robert believed. Jenny's face also looked borrowed, smeared clean, probably with the boy's single handkerchief; her neck and hands were green with hay and turf. She was a good head smaller than her escort, requiring her to look up at him, even though it was abundantly clear she was the hardier, the more tested, of the two.

"Good morrow, child." Sir Robert tried to smile at the girl. He was as pleased as he always to receive her.

Jenny curtsied quite properly; the time and attention she invested in such manners had increased in line with Sir Robert's recovery. As she rose, she swept one arm in the boy's direction, to suffice as an introduction.

"And what might be your interest here?" Sir Robert asked the boy.

"I," the boy began, but he dallied understandably, Robert thought, as he had a moment to consider exactly where he was, and to whom he was speaking. He bowed stiffly, and his eyes wandered nervously about the room, until they settled on Jenny for an instant, and her encouragement.

"My name is Samuel Bright," the boy finally decided on saying. "My father is—"

"Yes, yes, yes," Sir Robert stopped him. "But what is your purpose here, with this girl?"

"I, I speak for Jenny," the boy said, with what Sir Robert ascertained was as much finality as his slight age and frame could muster.

On whose authority, Sir Robert was prepared to ask, but he found his answer in the girl's posture. It had not profoundly changed from their other encounters; she had become easier in his presence over the weeks she was treating him, so much so that she had gathered the strength to ignore suggestions that once had her scurrying out of his chambers. Now she was quick to apply her balms and salves and possibly even to smile, briefly, at his words. But she bore a new confidence, as she stood beside this boy; her eyes did not switch so quickly in fear, and she stood and breathed as though she had found a place in this world, on his arm. But she could not have taken full stock of the mettle of this protector, Sir Robert was convinced, because Samuel Bright weighed no more than eight stone if he had been dragged out of a river. His stance was as rickety and unnerving as that of a rangy colt. He was all enthusiasm, and no discipline.

"Obviously, you do," Sir Robert said. He sat himself down at the table where a bowl of fruit had been placed, according to the girl's instructions, earlier in the morning. Red grapes, hard green apples, and globes of citrus:

they were to help him somehow in his recovery. Beyond that she could not explain. Now he pushed them toward the pair, whether to test their resolve or prove his loyalty to her, he was not quite certain.

"But it's a bit of a risk, shouldn't you think? You're being here with—"

"This concerns your Lordship." Samuel Bright released himself from the girl's slack embrace to step forward. He would save the world, Sir Robert saw, if only given the opportunity. "We have come with news of your safety."

"Oh I'm sure you have, for you to make this kind of call."

"Jenny has found something." The boy removed that something from his belt—flat, circular, but with the sharpened borders of a dagger. It might have cut through the boy's skin if not for the thick work gloves he outfitted himself with. Still his hands trembled with the object's importance. Once in his palm, Sir Robert immediately identified its insignia and relevance.

A pair of snakes armed with swords and shields, unnecessarily baring their venomous breath: the mark of Sir Matthew Payne. He was not one to believe in cloaking his message.

"Where did she find this?" Sir Robert asked.

"In your saddle," Samuel Bright said. Sir Robert noticed how the boy had drawn himself even closer and that he now spoke in a harsh whisper. "On the day of your accident."

"So," Sir Robert said, to pace his thinking. He stood up and walked the few steps needed to stand along Jenny, to see her face reflected in Sir Matthew's deadly missive.

"You said nothing of this for, how long has it been?" he asked her directly.

"She told me that night, " he said hurriedly, and then amended: "In her fashion, she told me. I've been trying to convince her ever since to come to you herself."

Sir Robert angled the metal plate so that it might catch the sinking sunlight in his chamber, and be sent off to illuminate the girl's face. "And why now, does she choose to expose herself—to expose both of you?"

Sir Robert neglected his watch on Jenny's face to record the boy's eyes seeking out Jenny's, as if he were asking for some type of permission. But the girl had shifted her glance away. She no longer appeared as brave as she had moments earlier.

"I am to join the Queen's Service, at week's end," the boy announced.

"And Jenny will have no champion," surmised Sir Robert.

"Yes," the boy said, and he cast his look downward, as if to mourn this personal failing. Whether it was his intention or not, the boy was beginning to make known his true sentiments. There was to be some sort of exchange for this information, even if Jenny had never consented to such a bargain.

"I'm sorry, but this girl is an outcast," Sir Robert said, standing up to signal the end of the conversation. When the boy did not pick up on it, he continued, "She is an outcast because she—"

"She was not always so," Samuel Bright interrupted.

"No?"

"My family—my parents—we raised her as our own," he said, both too quickly and too proudly. His eyes were no longer on the floor but on the girl's face. "She—Jenny—is like a sister to me," he continued, and he might have said more, but whatever it was, caught in his throat, and he took a long, almost tortured swallow. "I have two younger sisters, twins, and Jenny has been a second mother to them."

"Is this true, girl?" Sir Robert asked Jenny directly.

She assented with a nod of her head.

"This you also concealed from me," Sir Robert admonished her.

The girl stepped forward; whether it was to catch up with her protector, or to make known her intentions, neither man could tell; Sir Robert thought he could hear the boy take in a raft of air as though something momentous would issue from her lips. But silent she remained, and she reinforced that silence by grabbing onto one of the boy's arms, and hiding behind it.

"Please, your Lordship," Samuel Bright said. "She had no way of telling you, and we do not know why she was made to leave us."

"She was made to leave your family?"

"Yes, sir," the boy said, and it must have pained both of them to recall this episode. The girl bowed her head and the boy moved his focus away from Sir Robert's, as though he were postponing a realization he knew was inevitable. "This winter past, after she helped me recover from a severe illness, just as she has helped you. We had news that she was no longer to live with us."

"And how did this news come to you?"

"My father. My father told us. He has always dissuaded me from asking further," the boy admitted, and not without a bit of shame, Sir Robert thought, upon reflection. "Please believe me, sir. Jenny is a fine girl. She was orphaned when I was just a small boy, as my parents have informed me. Her father was said to be a friend to my father. We took her in, and she has brought only love and joy to us. We learned all of our chores together, all of our letters."

"This outcast is lettered?" Sir Robert asked.

Samuel did not answer until he spied for instructions from Jenny's grassy eyes. "I learned my letters; she sat beside me," Samuel Bright corrected himself.

"I see," Sir Robert said. "So **this girl has never spoken**."

"Never, sir," Samuel assured him. ❦

❦ I know the **physically damaged female** as dramatic inspiration is terribly retro, but I have an excuse, to wit: As an aspiring ballerina (when I was not an aspiring horsewoman), I became well acquainted with the trope of the female in distress. The ballets we practiced were dominated not just by humans disabled by the depth of their emotions, but also swans, dolls, sylphs, and Willis (the ghosts of girls who die before their wedding day in *Giselle*), all done in by vicious social systems. There were indeed few empowering role models for my young self in the oeuvre I was presented with.

So where was I to go for much needed positive reinforcement? Surely not to look to my mother, a mad housewife pounding away on her old Royal not to keep a diary, but to sabotage the PTA minutes, or unilaterally change the PTA by-laws. The mass media offered Mary Tyler Moore and Helen Reddy but they were too accessible, and therefore too conventional. My mother in those days used to taunt my dad about his supposed attraction to Gloria Steinem, who would have made a fine example for anyone, but she was neither in the movies, on album-oriented-rock radio, or on television, and I didn't rightly know who she was.

I got my dose of the various strains of cultural venom about every Saturday night after ballet class. I had a regular babysitting gig with the parents of a kindergartner who lived on the hill side of the neighborhood, within walking distance from my house. They paid me seventy-five cents an hour and all the pop culture I could absorb. They had a cache of Beatles albums that I poured through incessantly, especially the albums with bonus photographs. When I was finished with those I would turn to their subscription cable television service, known then as the Z Channel, the legendary movie channel of 1970's Los Angeles.

On the Z Channel I could watch everything I had heard of but was prohibited, by my parents' equivalent of the Hayes Office, from accessing. As I stayed up into the wee hours so as not to miss my abundant babysitting paycheck, I saw Antonioni's *Blow Up* and *Zabriskie Point* and Richard Dreyfuss in *Inserts*,"commercial-free and unexpurgated. I tried watching *Last Tango in Paris* but I either was bored or could not understand what Brando was saying; it sent me to sleep. Jack Lemmon movies were numerous on Z—*The Prisoner of Second Avenue* and *Save the Tiger* I watched because I remember my parents being obsessed with them. I had no idea what I was watching.

When *Wait Until Dark* was on, I could not keep to my seat. I was off the couch, digging through the carpet. I had to get closer to that television. I was trying to throw myself into it. Every girl wanted to be Audrey Hepburn at some point, I know. But I didn't want to be a thin, fashionable, sophisticated Audrey Hepburn, but the alone, hobbled, threatened and blind Audrey Hepburn. I didn't want to be intelligent—even if it meant not being in the gifted classes at school—but spontaneously, surprisingly smart, showing my talent for heroism only when it was most desperately called for.

Much has been made about the damage this romanticized image of handicapped women has done to gender relations and women's liberation, but for me that flawed Audrey was a much more practical role model than, say, her confident Sabrina, for it was one I, with all of my deformities and disabilities, had a realistic hope of someday emulating. It was also a much more malleable fantasy, for unlike the one other blind woman-in-peril movie I had ever seen, *A Patch of Blue*, the end of *Wait Until Dark* was never resolved for me. My clients returned home before I could see the triumphant ending.

If *Wait Until Dark* was the template of my daydreams, *A Patch of Blue* was their inspiration. Elizabeth Hartman's illicit and racially risky relationship, her helplessness, and her wretched circumstances all conspired to make her, in my eyes, more romantic than Emily Dickinson. She was so fragile, because of her disability, that she was more feather, or flower petal, than a person; she required constant attention, lest she curdle or collapse. She lived in a tenement in Los Angeles according to the story line, but to me she was a princess. My father's mother, Grandma Eva, introduced me to this fairy tale: while my mother was ill, I spent many nights at her house. At much too late at night, she would allow me to watch with her the movies broadcast on the farthest reaches of the television dial. Not that such fare was inappropriate for children, but a two-hour movie would be stretched, with the addition of commercials, into an all-night marathon. As I dozed off, my grandmother watched on, and was always willing to explain a scene I had just missed, such as when the girl is blinded by her tart of a mother and one of her johns.

In fairness to my mother, and to maintain fidelity with the facts, my mother never treated me as Shelly Winters treated her daughter in that film, not even metaphorically. The worst that could be said of my mother was that she was "unconscious," an expression my parents used for women in the neighborhood they believed didn't know what was going on around them. My father used this particularly in reference to women who ignored their husband's affairs; my father didn't have affairs, but my mother was similarly knocked out of it, and otherwise absorbed in the repetition of her scathing, self-loathing thoughts.

When I was older and could understand such things, my mother explained the true meaning of my father's use of "unconscious," which therefore classified her in the category of my father's other oft-stated critique of the neighborhood's women: she was another "crazy broad." For once she came home from the hospital, her mania having been arrested, she was in the thick of a major depression, and my sister and I were not to touch her, or talk to her, or ask too much of her, or pretty much interact with her in any way beyond the most necessary mother-daughter functions. Our father reminded us of her illness often enough that my mother became a kind of warning signal to us. Only through straight A's and the right extra-curricular activities, could we, her daughters, avoid her fate.

Elizabeth Taylor was one my father's favored visual aids in his task of saving us; in high school he had entered a contest to win a date with her, and sadly for all those involved, he lost. When *Suddenly Last Summer*, Tennessee William's mini-play about homosexuality, cannibalism, and a mentally damaged female, was on television, he had me and my sister watch. He did not hesitate to describe the situation involved, how Ms. Taylor had undergone an experience so horrendous that it had to be literally cut out of her mind. (Lobotomy would become a favored topic of discomfiting questions at the dinner table afterward, and in ninth grade I read *One Flew Over the Cuckoo's Nest* and tried to adopt its psychedelic episodes as my own, without much credibility.) But when it came to *Suddenly Last Summer*'s Hollywood ending for the offending—and anonymously depicted—homosexual in the picture, my father was at a loss. For, across the street from the Wonderland Avenue Elementary School, where the green line between canyon folk and hill people was laid, sat the home of one of my father's old friends, a known homosexual.

My father's friend was another Jewish kid from Hamilton High School. Much like my father, he was a guy always on the make. There was a lot of Duddy Kravitz in my father when he was a young man, or so he said, and a little of Duddy Kravitz in every one of his friends. This friend enrolled at the U.S. Naval Academy after high school, but was discharged for reasons mysterious and unmentionable. Then it was onto another service academy—the Coast Guard?—but nothing became of that, either. Over the years my father would try his hand at selling citrus, potatoes, Christmas trees, tires, Real Estate and Coleman campers; this man eventually wound up selling cars, and he helped us snag a discount on a pair of Volkswagens. But my father was disgusted by his friend, bemoaning whatever the state of his household arrangements. His rented digs were a known safe house for neighborhood homosexuals, and my father's friend, in my father's own words, was as "queer as a three dollar bill."

Long after my parents' divorce, long after this man's death from AIDS, my mother told me not to judge my father's homophobia too harshly. He really was ripped to pieces when his friend died, she said; it was not a grief that she witnessed herself, but she had heard about it, loudly and clearly, through the grapevine of connections that continued to ensnare them after their marriage.

So there you have it, proof at last, even at its most discursive: of the deleterious effects from gender stereotyping the mass media perpetuates; particularly on impressionable girls, dissuaded from the need to become powerful, self-sufficient feminists.

"And yet she is a font of knowledge: potions, roots, draughts, medicines," Sir Robert said. He had begun to pace around the pair, circle them, as if to improve the locus of his observations. "The magic that follows when alchemy fails, perhaps?" Sir Robert teased, but for the moment Samuel Bright chose to be resolute. "For both humans and horses, she is nurse, surgeon, and doctor. But from where did she trawl all this wisdom? And all without the facility of speech, the power of repeating," he mused. "She must be very intelligent, to have to act like such an imbecile before her betters."

"She—" Bright began, but then he stumbled upon sensing the narrowing space between himself and Sir Robert. "In my life, she has always possessed this acumen. If it pleases your Lordship, may I say I—we—neither of us has hidden anything from you that could possibly be of use."

"And what is not of use to me?" Sir Robert persisted.

The blood of the boy's blood-brown eyes seemed to thicken in his irises. There were too many holes in this boy's account, and they had not seemed to matter so much until this point, given the urgency in his relaying it. Sir Robert could see the material in that boy's eye color, condensing into something close to embarrassment.

"'Your Lordship, please," Samuel Bright insisted, and he fell so quickly to one knee that the girl found she had to steady herself ungracefully."

"I'm afraid you overestimate my influence," Sir Robert said. "Both of you."

"Please," Bright continued. "Jenny, I—we are without influence. While I'm away, sir, if you—if I—"

"You are not suggesting to be relieved of your service, Samuel Bright."

"Never, sir," the boy said humbly. "But Jenny—"

"Would it not be better to leave this to your father?" Sir Robert asked, but the boy shook his head, as he did to any number of people—friends, helpmates, members of his father's guild—Sir Robert suggested. As much as this girl's powers were a secret he hoped to use, Sir Robert understood, this girl herself was Samuel Bright's secret, a mystery and a power that he possessed on his own.

"I would be pleased, Samuel Bright," Sir Robert said, motioning for the boy to rise, "to have your trust placed in me."

❀ ❀ ❀ ❀ ❀

Samuel did not consider himself a scribe, although, as he had told Sir

Robert, he was lettered. He knew how to compose a letter, a bill of order for his father's shop; and he was teaching his sisters rhymes and psalms. For it was the position of his father to instruct all the children in the alphabet and sums. His mother, meanwhile, told him of the Bible; she could not read, but had committed the gospels to her heart. And it was Jenny who sat beside him as he learned, copying passages from Genesis or the columns of his father's accounts. It was Jenny who traced out the letters Samuel seemed to be having trouble with, or small, urgent words—hot, cold, warm, soon— to report in the ash and soot the most pertinent news of the shop. So if she could not completely read or write, she could most assuredly draw; figures, symbols to remind herself of what she had seen and done; and he had seen her read maps and their legends, and follow directions plotted on a page in pictures and arrows. Together they might build a record, then—for his sisters, or the children he might one day raise, or the family of cousins they might one day be blessed with.

But the work of making the physical book—two books, in fact, for he would also have one with him—was far more delicate than he could have anticipated. If he should work too quickly, he might lose the needle in its pages, or the leather thread that was meant to bind the pages; he might tear those pages when he meant to sew them together. These were books that would have to withstand all matters of climates and the carelessness of Jenny's stable mates. It had not occurred to Samuel, before his meeting Sir Robert, that the contents within those pages could be as treacherous as the process of making them. Should an outcast be found to have knowledge of writing, of what the mind and spirit were capable of creating, then she might no longer be an outcast. Would those who disenfranchised her see their own authority threatened? This would not have displeased Samuel, although he spent little time wondering after it. While he was not an apostate as to the wonders of Heaven and the Universe, God's representatives on Earth were not nearly as persuasive to his thinking. That they might have erred where his family was concerned, and be publicly called to correct such an error, was a satisfying possibility.

Thomas having freed Samuel from his regular duties, Samuel devoted his last day to his bookmaking, allowing Lucy and Grace to try their hands at some of the stitches. They demonstrated an immediate acumen for the work; their fingers were so small and docile, they did not protest or corral themselves into awkward, disconcerting knots and needle pricks. But he could not let them finish, he explained, if these books were to ever truly contain the gifts he had planned. He and Jenny would complete a fabulous story for the two of them, and the girls did more than smile; they jumped and danced together in a circle at the prospect. At dinner they brought to him a tankard of buttermilk and a plate of carrots, bread, cured beef and hard cheese. He worked through the meal so Lucy and Grace could run their hands over the suede cover of Jenny's volume, as though they too were writing messages with the trails their fingertips and palms trying to embed themselves in the material.

❀ ❀ ❀ ❀ ❀

"Tomorrow," he said by way of this last greeting; so anxious he was over what was to occur during the next few hours that he had somehow discarded the manners called for.

"Tomorrow," he repeated, now as if he had to convince himself that he actually was going.

Jenny bowed her head rather than nod, as if according him the respect due a soldier. She kept her eyes set on the ground once she completed her gesture, as if acknowledging the custom that upon his initiation into the Queen's Service, he would forever be considered her better.

"Jenny, please," Samuel said. "They say there's a hundred-mile march to start off. To pull the wheat from the chaff, I've heard. Then you might avoid my glance, but now?"

Jenny shook her head, and returned to grooming the horse in the stall. A black mare with cream stockings: a new mount for Sir Robert, Samuel speculated. Jenny must have been working on its coat for some time; it glistened in a high tone that seemed to illuminate the dusk in which they all stood.

"She's beautiful," Samuel said, to which Jenny smiled, as if accepting a compliment. She ran her hand from the horse's ears, down its neck and onto its back, directing Samuel's attention to the animal's conformation. Then she reached down toward a bucket in a corner of the stall and lifted out an apple, which she passed over the horse's back to Samuel. She moved toward the horse's mouth and put out her hand: her instructions for Samuel to pass the apple onto the horse. It was to be their introduction.

"You are a lovely," Samuel said as the horse took the apple from his hand. "Jenny will take the best care of you, I'm certain."

Jenny seemed to bask in the endorsement he offered; although her smile did not widen so much as it sunk in more deeply, permanently, into her cheeks and lips. She brushed the horse's forelock and kissed it on its nose; Samuel might have left without another word, and he had no doubt she wouldn't have noticed.

He did not savor having to lure her out of this mood, but tomorrow: the sound of that word, the sounds that day would summon: they pulled and needled at his consciousness. He would not sleep a moment this night, and for no reason: watching Jenny in her element, communing with that horse as though it were her own offspring, Samuel felt sheepish. All of the spectacle of the last few days, and she was in no more peril than any other stable worker. It was also possible she was more at home here than she had ever been with his family.

"Jenny," Samuel said, hoping his reluctance did not register in Jenny's ears. It did not seem to; she returned her attentions to him eagerly, her eyes and smile still vibrant with contentment. "I have not come only to bid you farewell. I have another request to make of you."

She nodded and walked over to where he stood, as if to offer him all of her concentration. Samuel pushed one of the two books he had made into her hands, and showed her the second one he had kept for himself.

"See, I have made one for myself as well," he said, and he rippled through the blank pages of his book proudly. Jenny did the same thing with hers but now provided Samuel with a blank, puzzled look, as though she still did not understand. "You can **write it in each day** ❀ as I will in mine; and when I return, we can trade and read what has happened to each other."

> ❀ Oh yes, I was quite **the diarist** in junior high school. It began in summer school, before seventh grade. We read a portion—for we were not gifted, and therefore could not be

exposed to texts in their entirety—of *The Diary of Anne Frank*, and I thought I'd like to keep a diary too, considering that I lived in a Jewish family with a secret, in the midst of a war (or wars) I could not explain. I had often harbored the ambition of becoming a writer, owing to two incidents from my elementary days. The first occurred with one of the Jenny-mothers; I was telling her about a sunflower I had seen, and how tall it was, and she replied, "Oh Janey, you have such an imagination!" I latched onto this compliment with a fierceness that has yet to desert me, but at the time I was also confused, and thought perhaps she had never seen a real sunflower, as I had.

The second incident occurred in fourth grade, when we were putting together a class/school newspaper/magazine project, for the teacher we thought was ironic, the one who punished us with marching. This man was full of ideas on improving our education, and for weeks we worked on articles for this project. I wrote about the family of stuffed elephants I nurtured, as well as the copious conversations I had with the baby of that family, whom I dubbed Convenient. This must have been a very big word back in those days, for it really impressed the teacher. When he criticized how I spelled the name—C O N V E I N Y E N T—I explained that because I was using it as a proper noun, I could spell it any way I pleased. I have no idea how I knew this, but the teacher was floored, and from that day forward was forced to consider me something other than the daughter of that crazy mother up the street.

When my girlfriends—Wendy was the head contagion in this instance—had me listen to Elton John, I knew exactly what kind of writer I would be. If Bernie Taupin could write songs without knowing how to play an instrument, why couldn't I? I wrote scores of lyrics about injustice in the Los Angeles Unified School District and other weighty topics, until I found a book of Bob Dylan's lyrics. It was in the gift shop beneath my ballet studio, and after I read that, I was finished.

Once I crossed song lyrics off my list, I continued to write: novels cum horse operas with cowgirls rather than ranch hands; plays that were a kind of wish fulfillment involving certain boys at my school; and poetry, finally, venting at the various outrages around the world. Poetry is a predictable, if not fraught territory for teen-age girls, as the product tends to lean toward the morose and maudlin, and occasions great competition among those inspired by the emotional paucity of their home situations.

I could have written about my mother, although acting as though I was also nuts, and telling everyone my premonitions about winding up like her some day, was much easier than rendering my fear through language. (Blabbing about her also was a much more efficient route to ensuring my own celebrity, which was, of course, of utmost importance.) So I wrote about my crushes and the landscape and whatever other nonsense I could drag out of my mind, and stewed at the slavishness of my work compared to others. There was one girl in particular—she is quite the prominent lawyer now in Los Angeles, so she shall remain thankfully anonymous—who turned me into a green-eyed monster.

Our poetry sometimes shared the same concern with the inaccessible opposite sex, although the opposite sex was far more accessible to her, given that her eyes were often compared to Elizabeth Taylor's. I considered this a particularly tart injustice, given it was the Elizabeth Taylor of the "National Velvet" period, but what could you do. Her hair was long and well brushed, and she was sweet and needed to be rescued, it seemed—her father was an alcoholic. She was also in that eighth-grade gifted-English class, reading the great works that I was not smart enough to understand, let alone decode, into my own eighth-grade experience. It came to be known that she relied on Neil Young's "Tonight's the Night" for inspiration, as her father shared the same weakness as the people Young sang about. And how did it come to be known? For the eighth-grade gifted unit on poetry, one of the boys devoted his oral presentation to her life and work. Now that's the kind of fame you can't buy. That's golden.

So while I was holed up in my spacious, suburban bedroom, reading my copy of *Lennon Remembers* from the Ivar Street library again and again, I remained an underappreciated and under-producing poet, while she squirreled away peace and time from her father's alcoholic binges to produce really stunning verses and stanzas. We believed she soothed herself with the attentions of the boy Wendy and I mooned over for most of junior and senior high school. The truth was that she had the attention of all the boys, so what did she have to complain about? When she broke her tooth due to an accident in ninth grade P.E., the entire junior high campus limped about in shock, shock, that such a stunning face could be suddenly made so pedestrian. In other words, she was transformed from a touching, delicate magnificence into something more like the rest of us: pubescent and awkward, if not horribly flawed.

In both junior high and high school, she left behind a significant number of broken hearts which I could all too easily catalogue; I can't speak to what happened in college, although I know that she didn't get the kind of financial support I did for that endeavor: my parents paid every last cent of my expenses, both necessary and frivolous. For her father, however, it was a particular point of pride that while the family financed his son's education at the University of Notre Dame, for his daughters there was not spent a single dollar.

Over the years, her younger sister and my own became very good friends, and as a journalist I briefly worked with her Notre Dame-educated brother. Through these channels I collected enough information to form either insight into, or sympathy for, how this girl was forged in a particularly grueling crucible. Still, I'm pretty sure I wouldn't have been any nicer to her then given what I know, because the bottom line was that her poetry was far superior than my own, as this little ditty of mine should prove well:

Georgie Porgie
Pudding and pie
Kissed Patti Boyd
And made her cry
She cried so much
She went to Eric
And that's why we have
The Dominoes and Derrick

Suddenly Jenny's book was just under his nose; she had shut her eyes tightly, wanting nothing to do with it.

"Why?" he asked, but she did not change anything. Indeed, she seemed to shove her book even further into his face, if that was possible.

"You, you need not—confess anything," Samuel spoke haltingly, because he was nowhere near certain as to the nature of her objections. "It'll be like writing a letter, although it will have to wait to be read, that's all." Her book waved in his face, now, as though she could not make her rejection of it any clearer.

"You—you need not set it down in words, " Samuel begged. "Pictures will do. Your horses, and the Market, and my little darlings, of course. Who will watch them grow up for me? How will I recognize them when I come back? And maps—maps of where you've been. Please, Jenny. I—I must have something of you."

It surprised him to hear himself say this; he had not thought of his request in these terms, but they were true to what he was after: some proof, assurance that Jenny would go on as she had been doing while he was away, and that he would not have to miss that much of it. Precisely why he found himself in such need of this accounting was also beyond his comprehension in the moment; but he did understand, for himself, at least, how having her keep track of her days alone would give him a way of reliving those days with her, should he return back to her.

"I must have something of you, to look forward to," Samuel said as gently as he could dispense it. "I must."

Her green eyes were first to return his favor, with a tentative flash upon re-opening, like the first leaves of spring. She then pulled the book back and held it to her chest, promising to keep the diary with a nod that resembled prayer.

"Thank you, Jenny," Samuel said, believing that she just must not have understood, in the beginning. "I promise you will receive no less from me," he said, and he found he was nervous in making this pledge, because it was quite probable she had not the slightest interest into whatever he might pour out into his pages. "I will read it to you, if you will grant me the patience."

There was another object placed before him now: a package: another doll, like those she had made for the twins. It had no face stitched upon its head, however, and it did not smell of jasmine. With one of her fingers, Jenny demonstrated how the folds on the doll's back, arms, and legs opened. Inside she had filled the doll with sachets of flowers and seeds; small vials of particular essences. For each sachet, she pointed to her heart, head or stomach, as if to explain the purpose of the medicine each contained.

When she finished with foxglove for the heart, arnica oil for aches and pains, aloe juice for wounds to the skin, and a goldenseal mixture for digestion, she stopped gesturing with her own body, and used his. In particular, she pressed her single hand with the force of two against his chest. It produced a sensation Samuel only loosely recalled, possibly from his illness; for now, it communicated that these red swaths of velvet were for his breathing. He already knew of the caraway seeds; the marshmallow root and chamomile flowers that were boiled into his mull; and the jar of honey that now made up the bulk of the doll's body. But there were other substances he had not seen before: petals a rugged yellow; a pumpkin-colored powder, and slivers of a root that resembled sliced almonds.

With her fingers and palms Jenny showed him how to use these new medicines—whether to be dashed into water or brewed into a tonic; added to food, or chewed on slowly, in the smallest possible proportion. Then she pressed on his chest again but Samuel could not comprehend; it was as if she was trying to push something out of his lungs, but since his recovery there had been nothing there to trouble them.

"But I am fine, now, I promise I am," Samuel said, but Jenny disagreed, shaking her head as she jammed one of the sachets into his palm. His fingers she forced into a fist and then directed that to his chest, and when she pressed down there again, with both their efforts, Samuel again sensed a peculiar commotion, one that he could not quite describe and sent him looking for words in the haze of his former sickness.

"Only at my worst, am I to use these," he guessed, and Jenny nodded. That explanation would have to satisfy him for the moment. Her hand rested lightly where she had last pressed it, and Samuel wondered how much longer she might keep it there; it fit so keenly in the arrangement of his bones, as though they had been carved to provide a home for it.

"You may understand now, why I need so much of you," Samuel said, because he had always known, even if he had not stated it to himself, or out loud before his parents or the likes of Sir Robert, that Jenny had saved him in some way while he was ill. He had always known this, but now this insight took on a weight he was not sure he could balance. Jenny, however, must have always perceived this, for she seemed to be following his thoughts without error when she took his hands, slack at his sides, and raised them to her lips to gently kiss them.

"It is late, for both of us," Samuel said, with a bow of his head. He loved Jenny as any man might love his sister, but surely he owed her so much more. She had released his hands to allow him to take a grand step back, so he might say his good bye with the proper gravity and flare. "Good night, then," he said, and as he walked away, he wondered at how deep was the debt they held together, and whether it would ever be possible to measure it.

chapter four

If Sir Robert was anything, he was a man of his word. As soon as he saw the boy's battalion march off, he found himself a spy among the royal stewards, and assigned him to the girl. Every morning and every evening, he received reports that she had been sleeping, or exercising or massaging horses, where she had been to supper and any visitors she may have had. The reports those first few days were not what he expected: pedestrian. He had wanted there to be patients, a long line of peasants and merchants seeking cures for their bent fingers and tilted backs. Or perhaps the other stable urchins summoned her to their charges, to deliver a colt or soothe a spooked mare. Instead there was nothing, and no one, and if she was lucky enough to eat in a day, she had no partner. If she was an outcast, she had accepted her sentence, with too great an ease for those casting her out to be comforted.

Sir Robert again described the girl to his spy in greater detail. He went on about her clothing, and the apparently stolen costume she had worn to his chambers days earlier: a stiff pomegranate dress that did not require a bodice; with Union Roses constructed of ribbons at the breast, and a skirt that did not twirl, but floated. He wanted to know if Samuel Bright had left her with something before his departure; whether she would take some action of mourning—cut her hair, fashion a necklace out of some thread of his, or scar herself, gently, in some manner—so he might gauge her depth of feeling for him. But there was no such consequence to her appearance. Her old clothes—and they must have been used by any number of persons until she managed to inherit them—returned to her frame and at night, she surveyed them for damage and patched them over. The only thing the spy was able to report was a brown suede block—a satchel or a book, or a simple swath of cloth—that she attached to a strap of leather, and wore across her chest like a shield. But she buried this object, whatever it was, beneath her blouse, so the spy could not be sure of what its true nature and purpose was.

His primary goal in assigning a spy to her, Sir Robert led himself to believe, was to resolve her mystery. Of course one had heard of outcasts. In childhood they were a kind of threat, an admonition for every act of impertinence. If parents and pastors did not wield the specter of becoming an outcast, then for children they were a kind of secret disease. One suspected himself of harboring the potential to become one, crippled or deformed or so essentially sickened that outcast became an inhuman form of God's favored being. Sir Robert did not feel himself to be an outcast, literally; but among the Queen's court, given the nature of his entrée and his stubborn beliefs, he could sometimes sense he was becoming one: a foreign, incomprehensible creature.

The mystery of this girl could also be significantly simpler, he knew, if he could catch her speaking. The spy was instructed to listen for any sound, no matter how slight, that might progress from her lips. To the horses she adored, Sir Robert instructed, there had to be coos or clucks or absent-minded humming: he would take any evidence of communication. The best of the Queen's equestrians instinctively made such commands or coaxed their mounts. She would have to do the same, Sir Robert was certain. Or perhaps she purred like a stable cat as she rubbed salve on their legs and balms on their hard mouths. But his spy swore he heard absolutely nothing in all of his surveillance. She was dedicated to her silence, if nothing else.

That made her all the more alluring to Sir Robert.

"She is profoundly dumb," the spy announced after a fortnight of his monitoring. Since coming into Sir Robert's employ, and his sovereigns, he appeared a bit more ruddy in the nose and mouth, as if only his eyes had been spared the rush of wealth. "She will not even beg for an apple if she is starving," he asserted as proof.

"She is not dumb," Sir Robert insisted. "Does she not understand what is said to her?"

"So little is said to her," the spy went on, "it's difficult to know if she understands, or if she is just responding to some—if she has been domesticated, to a point."

"She is not an animal," Sir Robert said.

"She lives as one."

"And is that her choice?"

The spy seemed shamed to not have taken this road in the investigation.

"Find out," Sir Robert instructed.

"Yes, sir," the spy answered with a predictable enthusiasm.

"You would also do well to affect a silence as secure as this girl's," Sir Robert reminded him. "Lest you be exposed, without endorsement."

❦ ❦ ❦ ❦ ❦

She slept under the roots and flowers she had hung from the top of the stall, upside down. Her bed was a bale of straw, sculpted in the shape of her body from her tossing and turning. In the eaves of the stall, she stored what passed for her possessions: a saddle cloth she likely used as a blanket, and her bed clothes, which might have been sewn from white muslin at one time, but had since taken on the tinge of stable mud. The spy said he had to climb onto the struts and low walls that separated the stall Jenny slept in from the others, to see if she had secreted anything else: there were bottles and vials, some empty, some packed with bright powders, and others with oils and liquids he could not begin to name. He expected to find cooking implements, a mortar and pestle at least, where she composed her ingredients; a raft of recipes, written in her own and possibly illiterate code: something to explain how it was at all possible. But there were no such items to be discovered, the spy insisted. Sir Robert, with all his **comforts** ❦ inherited through marriage, had become incapable of conceiving any other kind of life.

    ❦ **Poverty** was one of the seven dirty words you could not say either in Laurel Canyon or Laurel Hills, and although I thought I knew much about it—for I had seen *Oliver!* and there were, from time to time, money problems in my own household—I didn't know squat. The closest I came to impoverishment was the potential loss of the class genius from my elementary school, an instructive tale for our day and protected age.

The class genius was a blonde girl, the baby of a family that lived at the top of a very steep and exclusive-looking driveway in the Laurel Hills section. I don't know what her parents did for a living, but due to some economic misfortune, we children were informed one day that she had to move out of the neighborhood. We children were often informed on this girl's doings, as she was the class genius from kindergarten on, and special arrangements had to be made in terms of our behavior, her schedule of activities, and the respect we—parents, teachers and her contemporaries—had to give her, that was her due, lest we all suffer the consequences.

That she had to move away was no big deal, since with the rising tide of divorce and other issues, we had a recognizably transient student population. But this girl was going to have to move to a school that was far inferior to our own, cloistered gem of public education. If this move went through she would have to rub elbows with the apartment residents and dregs of the Wilshire District, which our parents solemnly intimated was a neighborhood much darker, and more diverse in complexion, than our own. A pall was cast on our classroom as we anticipated the removal of our best and brightest, until someone prevailed upon the mindless clerks of the Los Angeles Unified School District, and she was permitted to keep coming to our school and associate with the likes of us, even though she was no longer one of us.

If this didn't offer the spoiled brats of Wonderland Avenue School a clear lesson in the consequences of poverty, it certainly woke us up, if only for a moment, to the implications of class in our society. And was this girl really a genius? She wound up graduating from UCLA , although in all fairness, she is now a full professor in the hard sciences at a major research university (and I am only an adjunct professor in that wishy-washy world of the humanities). Yet the genius-girl was also very hip in fifth and sixth grade to get all us Jewish kids to read C.S. Lewis, so how much of a genius could she have been, really?

Yet she was the closest my cohort, at least, would come to confronting the falling economic expectations of the 1970s, until we were shipped off to that junior high and forcefully integrated with the less advantaged kids of metropolitan Hollywood. A growing portion of Wonderland kids, year after year, in fact refused to be part of this exercise, and their parents somehow secured their children transfers to the San Fernando Valley and the more desirable Walter Reed Junior High School.

Within the borders of the Bancroft Junior High School attendance area was prime *Day of the Locust* territory; it was populated by all the filth and degradation that my father always harangued against after his daily walks down Hollywood Boulevard. This was the land of movie extras and TV cowpokes; they scrounged away in their bungalows and flophouses, running from the jobs that waves of Hispanic, Asian, and Armenian immigrants clamored over. Wendy's house was situated deep within in this grid, although her house was well appointed, with a screened-in porch, and antique furniture we were afraid to touch in the living room, just like my grandparents'. Indeed, the girls interested in horses seemed better situated, geographically and economically, to avoid the nightmares of mental illness and cock fighting that Nathanael West described, and that my father had me commit to memory (it was one of his favorite books, naturally). But my friends from ballet class, living on the outskirts of show business as they did, were, in my father's mind, truly living out West's apocalyptic scenarios, although to me their circumstances seemed absolutely romantic and inspiring.

My favorite hovel belonged to Inez, one block below the Sunset Strip. At Inez's, the carpet had been run down into nubs; hot water was a precious resource, and the shower couldn't be run at the same time as the toilet. There was a kind of low grime in the entire place that hovered about our ankles, and the sounds of the Strip's nightclub patrons, strip club bouncers, cruising automobiles, johns and God knows what else was out there were rude and persuasive. Whatever went into that apartment came out not smelling like the dope we smoked, but ammonia: it must have been in the water, or in the solutions this girl's mother tried to apply to the walls and the mattresses.

The girl who joined us in these Friday night sleep-and-stoned-overs, Lynn, lived in a duplex in what was then a staging area for drug dealers and streetwalkers. Nowadays it is quite the fashionable spot, securely within the neighborhood that inspired *Melrose Place*, and re-populated and renovated by young Hasidic speculators. Back then, though, this duplex was ratty, depressed, and most of all, overcrowded: there were five children in her family, two underemployed parents, and only three beds for three bedrooms. Her parents and youngest sister slept in one bed in one room, and my friend and her two other sisters—ages 10, 12, and 21—were similarly arranged in the other. The only boy in the family, a teenager, had his own bedroom, which was heavily protected. When I asked why he had this room all to himself, with a stereo on top of that, Lynn explained, "He just took it."

Despite the warnings and restrictions plastered on his door, we sometimes went in there to gape at his stereo system and shuffle through his Black Sabbath albums. When her older sister was away at work, we'd go through her things, a treasure trove of make-up, Tampax, costume jewelry and an occasional packet of cigarettes. Sometimes, this sister could afford a weekend out of town. She'd go to San Pedro and stay in a hotel with her girlfriends, an activity that seemed wonderfully risky to me, even though I still associated it with my trips to the commissary and the PX, and not with the likes of Charles Bukowski.

We did not spend very much time at Lynn's house, as there

wasn't much in the way of snacks there, or privacy. But even with its drawbacks I found this slum so much more interesting than my own home in the Hollywood Hills. Its doors were thick and carved into them were all sorts of ornate details; the doorknobs were crystal or glass, and the windows were similarly old-fashioned. In the living room there was a build-in seat beneath the bay windows, and if you sat there, you might make believe you were on a boat, or a terrace, somewhere with an unlimited view, so that you might feel you were outside, in the crude and delectable ghetto, without ever having to actually commune with its elements.

Sir Robert himself slipped into the stable one night, because he wanted to see her sleeping. All young girls should look like princesses as they sleep; his wife had when he first saw her, in the hunting camp her father had set up. But in this girl's white, abandoned face, she did not appear to be dreaming of better circumstances. She was braced against the cold in the fraying blanket, and she had twitched and shivered as though trying to escape from a tongue-lashing. Sir Robert, on his knees in the stall across from hers, and desperate not to wake either the horse in the stall or the girl he was watching, worried that she might talk in her sleep. Whatever was hectoring her, he could see, was insistent if not persuasive, and very, very loud. But she fought it off—the voice or the monster—probably with rue, as the scent from that plant, swaying above her, was the only one that seemed noticeable around her.

Perhaps it was the rue, or perhaps it was an effect of some other root she harvested, but from what Sir Robert could glean from his own and his spy's intelligence was that there was nothing else to be drained from the girl's activities. Not only did she not have a lover—by definition, an outcast would be denied one—but she also seemed to have no need of one. She did not stare after the young courtiers who arrived to dance and converse with the ladies-in-waiting; nor did she exhibit any interest in the other stable workers—the slaves, the stewards, the Queen's horsemen. She was just as uninterested in her fellow girls, from the scullery maids to the seamstresses, to the wet nurses to the consorts, who streamed in and out of her surroundings. Perhaps the only tangible particulars the spy was able to reap was that the girl's father had been a blacksmith. The spy's report on this piece of speculation came without a name for this blacksmith, or a source for the information, but it made sense given what Bright had told Sir Robert earlier. It did nothing to further an explanation as to why she was separated from Bright and his family; or whether his silence was a refusal, instinctual, or a natural calamity.

If the spy was useful in any aspect, it was that he kept all this far and away from everyone, most essentially the Queen. To involve oneself with an outcast was more than unseemly, and lent itself to questions about one's respect for morality and order. If taken far enough it could lead to charges of treason, the disregard of the Queen's law. Especially in the case of Sir Robert, who was known to meddle in the affairs of state, protesting to the Queen about this campaign or that military action, even when no meddling had been called for. Sir Robert also had been mindful of the Queen's reaction when he first raised the subject of this girl: the depth of her pallor, as though she were being forced into an act of betrayal, even abdication. That the Queen favored him at all was beyond fortunate, for Sir Robert knew he had done little to earn it; that favor was the source of everything he had, in material goods, security, and title.

So Sir Robert waited. He kept out of the way of Sir William and Sir Thomas of Glencord, that Beechum fellow and Sir Gaines, although he continued to speak with the Queen as he regularly did, against the adventures these men and Sir Matthew Payne recommended. He planned to confront Sir Matthew but he was waiting for the right moment—both to show Sir Matthew just what he knew, and to summon the girl to his chambers. She had saved him from infection, from hallucinations and nightmares and a delirium in which he would have wasted away, and once his enemies understood the power this girl afforded him, they might come around his way.

The solstice was approaching, although the Queen and the best of her guard had temporarily retreated to the summer palace, when Sir Matthew called for her. She curtsied as well as she knew she should, and was no more filthy or disheveled than he had seen her earlier. But her eyes were restless—distrustful, even. They glanced about the room as though the walls themselves were moving.

"We have my dresser here, as a witness," Sir Robert offered her. "And I have only a favor to ask, not demand." Sir Robert stepped aside to give the girl a clear view of the dresser, who nodded as if to confirm his master's statement. "If you decline, no harm will come to you," Sir Robert said, because he was that confident.

"We ride tomorrow to the estate of Sir Matthew Payne," Sir Robert said, and to remind her of Sir Matthew's significance, he opened his palm to display the rounded dagger she had discovered. The girl immediately drew in closer and placed her hands on Sir Robert's shoulders, and turned him so she might see the back of his head, the site of his injury. She lifted her fingers up to the scar and traced it with her fingertips. "I would like you to accompany us," Sir Robert said, grateful that his back was toward her at that instant.

Sir Robert felt the girl draw away then, as if she carried a raft of air with her. When he turned around, she was on her knees, shaking her head as if begging.

"We will ride in a large company, and you will be treated as any other member of that company is treated," he promised. "I will see to it. Now take my hand, child," Sir Robert said, and he offered his free hand to her, where her bowed eyes would register it. "Rise and tell me what you are afraid of."

The girl did as she was instructed, but her eyes firmly set on Sir Robert's face. He looked for himself in her eyes, but she kept her distance, and his reflection away. Within the net of his fingers hers felt tender and graceful, without the nubs and calluses he had anticipated. As if to answer his question, she nodded toward the weapon that had been used against Sir Robert, and then shifted her focus to her skirt and other clothes. It was not clear whether she was referring to her person—her status—or its consequences: her appearance.

"Our time there will be brief. I have only to say to him a few words," Sir Robert said. "Now come here, child," he said, and he led her to behind a screen that his servants had set up on one side of his room. Behind it there was a fresh bed and bedclothes, and hanging from the screen, a noblewoman's dress.

"You will **sleep here** ❀ tonight," he went on, so that she might not have the chance to shake her head in complaint. "You will be fed, and cleaned, and rested. And if that pleases you, you may sleep here every night, and there will be warm milk and honey, and wine, and whatever you require, should you say 'yes,' and possibly even if you say 'no.' I am already so much in your debt."

Her mouth was open, although not quite in a smile: she was amazed, as he had hoped, but when she blinked, it was as if whatever he had managed to fill her vision with had shown its flaws. She shook her head in a firm no.

❀ The primary attraction in **sleeping over** at Inez's was neither the company, nor the location of the apartment. It was smoking whatever dope we could get our grubby little hands on, and it became harder to get that dope the more we enjoyed smoking it. The first time we "blew some pot," as one of our sponsors in the activity put it, we were in fact supplied by a sympathetic adult— well, she really wasn't an adult. She was a 19-year-old runaway from Texas who had somehow made it to Topanga Canyon, which we didn't know too much about except that it was like Laurel Canyon By the Sea, and that was good enough for us.

No one supposedly gets high the first time, and this adult, space cadet that she was, made it real fun for us. She hid the dope somewhere in the apartment, and once she had left (she was visiting Inez's mother, a space commander for the entire planet), we tore through the place like gangbusters. I don't remember who found the packet or where it was, but we gobbled it up like greedy little munchkins and I don't believe anything happened.

As the weeks went on, however, there were other packets from other adult sponsors, and God, how I did love smoking dope, how it literally erased the sensation of the skin I was in, and turned me into a floating bowl of ridiculous gelatin. I also appreciated the numbness it visited upon my face, the drowsiness in my eyes that were otherwise hyper-turned-on, and most of all I enjoyed having an excuse for being so out of control, stupid, and loud, which was how I always was. It was oh so much more acceptable, however, to have a pharmaceutical excuse for what was happening.

I harbored no hope of ever losing my virginity at that stage, but smoking dope was the next best thing to it. I knew quite well that I was being initiated into an adult practice, or more accurately, an adult practice of the canyon, and I felt as though I had gained access to a secret society of knowers, sages, cool teenagers and cooler adults. The only problem was that no one could rightly witness my entrée into this mighty society, and besides, they really had no interest in doing so. And they—that interminable they that determines who gets what of the social resources in our developing years—wouldn't even have believed it, even if my arrest for possession was on the front page.

And please, please, do not blame my foray into illicit drug use on peer pressure. The only pressure came from me. I was deathly curious about it and probably would have done anything to have had a shot at transforming myself. You must remember that my psyche was a festival of self-centeredness and self-loathing, and once I got the hang of dope smoking, I could not get enough of that sensation of being able to dance forever while still being able to get my homework done—and all with straight A's, you know, so my square parents would remain oh so unsuspecting.

"Your young man—" Sir Robert began his argument, but she had already began shaking her head vehemently. "Your Samuel Bright," Sir Robert amended, "would rest easier, knowing you were under my supervision." To this the girl could not object, and with her eyes at their feet, she relented.

It would have been impudent, he thought, to have spied on the girl as she slept just yards away from him, but he did listen. She neither snored nor sighed in her sleep, and if she yawned in the morning, he did not hear it. She awoke and dressed as soundlessly as she completed any task, and when Sir Robert awoke from his dreams, the girl was preparing him breakfast.

At supper the night before, she ate slowly and carefully, as though cognizant of being under observation; but she ate everything that was offered, and took with her to bed a small cup of buttermilk. Now she appeared polished and gleaming: her black hair braided and set in a bun and the shade beneath her eyes gone. Yet she still appeared unsuited to her surroundings in her noblewoman's dress. It matched her eyes but gathered in strange places and her décolletage was blank, vacant; not only due to her small size and likely malnourishment, but the color of her skin, fresh now after bathing, so blazingly white, whiter than marble with its imperfections. She would need jewelry, he thought, and he would give it to her: dark stones, rubies or sapphires, as dark as the blood and secrets that held her together.

Indeed, because the mud and dust had been scrubbed off her cheeks, chin, neck and knuckles, Sir Robert could now see so much more of her expressions. Her conversations with the hot water she poured over an unfamiliar set of leaves; the cream she whipped into butter; in the fruit she arranged on a plate, were all in her eyes. Her lips pursed for an instant when effort was required. How vigilant all her expressions were, but they had to be, since her each and every move was open to so much interpretation. Once she was finished she disappeared behind the screen for a period, and re-emerged with a strap of leather across her chest. It was attached to something she had secreted in her bodice.

He watched her pack a few indistinguishable roots and cloths into a satchel as he ate his breakfast; he watched her soothe the horse that was later brought out for her, a youngish animal that was not familiar. It tried trotting away as she attempted to mount it, but the steward had its bridle in hand, so it could only rear. She approached **the horse** ❀ head-on, kissing it on its forehead and rubbing it under the chin. Her hand did not leave its body, his neck and shoulders, as she walked toward the saddle, and then successfully raised herself into it.

❀ Where I did, admittedly, succumb to peer pressure was with the **horseback riding**, a subculture I was also initiated into during a sleepover. My father's best friend from high school and UCLA had two daughters, Shelli and Kari, who by the time they were in junior high were expert horsewomen. When I was not below the Sunset Strip, or babysitting, I was participating in some sort of illicit confab at their house, a lush palace of diet soda, an adjoining swimming pool, and a seemingly infinite number of televisions. The Koszdins (as we called them, collectively by their last name, since it was a form of Cohen, the most storied of the Twelve Tribes of Israel, and the smartest) were thick with affluence, and when the girls were old enough, Jack bought them their own horses, Mesa and Pebbles.

Shelli and Kari were not drug users; Kari had her own, resplendent social circle at the vaunted Portola Junior High School to assuage whatever crimes her parents committed against her self-esteem. Shelli was too smart, stubborn to be talked into anything. Her clandestine activities took a different form: At Birmingham High School she collected intelligence (arrest records, parental income and profession as well as amount of divorce settlements and child support arrangements, SAT and ACT scores) on everyone. But she spoke to practically no one, it seemed. Both girls also had a hearty collection of plastic model horses and subscriptions to horse magazines, and every month or so I was treated to marathon discussions on horse etiquette, breeding, and gossip among the equestrians.

Since there were also quite a few girls in my school who would consent to only having a horse as a best friend, it was easy for me to get swept up in the fervor. Remember, I was not one for striking out on my own, at anything. I took lessons, once or twice a week, at that stable for squares. But I was no horsewoman.

I always felt ridiculous, talking to horses. My friends like Polly and Wendy confided to their mounts—owned, or rented—about their hopes and fears, perhaps the goings-on at school, but I had no real relationship with horses, other than basically fearing them. That was probably why I was such a lousy rider, my arms flapping about as I rose on my toes in the stirrups. I was afraid to even canter for the longest time, and when I posted during trots, I was always on the wrong post.

My favorite horses at the Pickwick Stables were Spot, a brown gelding who had hard mouth; and Foaly, a bay gelding that set his ears back whenever someone entered his stall. So I let the Mexican stable hands handle him in the stable and with his tack. Wendy assured me that when Foaly set his ears back, he did that to everybody.

Once I made the mistake of drinking some milk before a ride around the oval, and I was thankful for the stomachache that made me relinquish the horse—that's the beginning of another story of ulcers and other ailments, but it fits in here nicely. Another time, I was bucked off a Palomino that was really out of my league to rent, but I asked for him anyway, to impress one of my friends. He threw me off right in front of the entrance to the Sunset Stables, as fate would have it, and I had to walk back to Pickwick to find the horse waiting for me there, to have his saddle removed. I was in tears. The following days in ballet class, after having fallen on my head, were no picnic either.

In one facet, however, I was able to keep up with my fellow traveling: we horse lovers had our own language, our own topics of gossip, and a system for summing up the entire world in a few choice horse metaphor associations. The blond boys were Palominos, and the ugliest boys we called geldings. I was also quite adept at collecting the plastic model horses that were so much more easily loved and admired, given their superior countenance.

She must have surprised everyone, for it surprised Sir Robert, when she chose to ride sidesaddle. Still this show of civility by an outcast was not enough for the rest of the riding party, and men and horses parted as she and her mount strode past. She was a confident horsewoman, her back erect but her arms and wrists relaxed; when launching into a trot she showed no need to adjust her seat, and no discomfort. All of his actions—the spying, his invitation to sleep in his quarters, this journey to Sir Matthew's—had been undertaken at the greatest personal risk. And yet, so far, they seemed to bring him no closer to who she was, or what he hoped she could do for him.

The ride was pleasant enough, before the onset of the summer. The sun provided more light than heat; the trees and grasses, puddles and stems seethed only scents and breezes, without the whip of temperature and humidity. Sir Robert led a company of eleven—bowmen, stewards, weapons handlers, himself and the girl—along a well trod path that posed no danger of obstacles or highwaymen. But the girl, perhaps because she was without an assignment, steered herself toward the back of her group. Sir Robert was unable to watch her at any length without becoming too obvious. The colt, from what he could hear behind him, was not an easy mount; the rhythm of its footfalls clashed with spurts and halts, but still there was not a trace of any guiding voice to calm him.

The fortress the party confronted upon arriving at **Sir Matthew's estate** ❀ did not surprise Sir Robert. He had come to expect the grandiose and imposing from a man stupid enough to engrave his weapons with a pair of snakes. Sir Matthew knew they were coming: a drawbridge awaited them, to ferry them across the moat that separated the road from the first of the estate's pastures. But as they approached the main house itself, ringed by iron pikes and mace-like adornments, the horses circled their ears, as if to read an approaching storm, and their riders tilted in their seats. Sir Robert had his excuse, to check back on his men, only to catch the girl unmoved by the scene.

❀ There was **money, money, everywhere**, but not enough for me to feel it, or to brag about it. It was old money too, or old for a Jewish mercantile family, yet I did not see any evidence of it in my own house, or my uncle's. It was there, though, copiously intermingling with my father's own earnings, my uncle's doctor salary and the triple-dipping pension of my grandfather. I hated the house I lived in because I thought it poor, shabby, second rate. The houses of my friends were adorned with knickknacks telling the story of their families; my next-door neighbor had a soda fountain in her living room and the Ladefogeds had a room dedicated to the African musical instruments the professor collected on his travels. I attributed my house's deficiencies to my mother's craziness as well as her military brat background; as a dependent she had to be ready to cut and run at a moment's notice, and could not own anything. The house she and my father built together was the only home she ever really had, and she just couldn't handle the responsibility of decorating it.

I despised my room most of all, with its cheap balsa wood furniture and linoleum floor. The couch and easy chair with an ottoman in the living room were shoved into corners, leaving a huge, blank space in the middle. As toddlers my sister and I had a ball dancing to my mother's Broadway recordings there, but as a teenager I found that space intolerably boring. The houses in the canyon had candles and incense and beaded curtains; alcoves and misshapen rooms, arches and exposed staircases, places where kids could hide out and away from their bogeymen. But everything in my house—the bedspreads and upholstery, the perfectly square and rectangular rooms— crushed the human imagination.

In truth, I know now, my house was really an overly tidy museum; it was especially adorned with my grandfather's plunder from World War II and the post-war occupations. From the U.S. adventure in Burma, we had Oriental rugs in the bedrooms, hallways, and dining room; and from the U.S. occupation of Germany, we had demitasse, Meissen figurines and Dresden china in the china cabinet, and charcoal and pastel art works on the walls. We also had wooden carvings, silk paintings, and hidden in the closets hats, kimonos and silk umbrellas my grandfather collected while he was helping to introduce democracy in post-imperial Japan. My grandfather, who faced his share of hardship as a Jewish officer, caught malaria during his time in Burma, and still he managed to do a good deal of damage: his home, which was just around the corner from ours (and actually belonged to our uncle), was similarly stocked with carpets, tchotchkes, and miscellaneous, international treasures.

The inventory around the corner also included whatever else my grandfather picked up during the Korean War, his Meissen collection, some Wedgewood, and the family heirlooms from turn-of-the-century Pennsylvania (my grandmother was the daughter of a silk merchant, pre-Depression), as well as the goodies my uncle had accumulated. In my uncle's bedroom the shelves ran from floor to ceiling with Ham radio equipment and the latest in Swiss and Japanese electronics. In the hallways the walls displayed his cache of framed, antique maps, and the backyard hosted, along with a swimming pool, a giant antennae to pick up Ham radio signals as well as the UHF channels. My uncle's house had three televisions!!! Two of them were color!

My uncle's home office, where my grandfather and mother kept the books for his private anesthesiology practice, was chock-full with issues of *National Geographic*, rare editions of German medical books and Gunter Grass. My uncle traveled everywhere and often. He had gone to medical school in Switzerland and therefore had friends everywhere. For many years he dated a nurse (my sister and I were to find out years later, upon his death) in Sweden; he brought me back presents from Thailand, Greece, Australia, and New Zealand. In addition to his regular buying trips to Switzerland and Japan, he went to Israel regularly, and volunteered as an emergency surgeon for the '67 and '73 wars. His closest friend there said he had to come, because unlike the rest of the doctors, he was unattached, and therefore expendable.

Once, he told me, his passport was temporarily held hostage by the Soviets. He did not give me any details beyond a few nail-biting days in a hotel, waiting for his passport to magically rematerialize. So it makes sense that among his most precious possessions in his home office were his samizdat texts of Solzhenitsyn. My uncle was always complaining that

American children were spoiled brats and that my parents would do better to raise pigs: at least those could be sold, he said, and slaughtered. Eventually he would literally throw at me a paperback copy of *The Gulag Archipelago* and said, "Read it. Maybe you'll learn something." He sounded skeptical, and with good reason.

All of this was maintained by an African American maid (although I shiver to tell you what my father called her—no, not that N word, but the other one—and would still would call her, if she were alive today) named Audrey, who occasionally filled in as a baby sitter. All of the other kids had "Spanish" maids (that's what we called them, although they usually came from Mexico or Central America) and learned to say, "May I please have more milk?" and other such phrases in Spanish. I felt deprived of this opportunity. Audrey moonlighted as a Pentecostal minister, or so it seemed, because she was constantly singing to herself or reciting Bible verses as she worked. The Spanish maids were usually live-ins, and they had their own rooms in the houses where they worked; but for Audrey, my parents, grandparents and uncle only bought a car, a 1968 Dodge that she kept in impeccable condition. We were a downscale lot, dragging down the neighborhood Real Estate values.

Inside, he offered her his arm, for he did not want to call her out, when he spoke to Sir Matthew. But she gently declined his offer, as though she knew what he had in mind. Again she kept to the back, behind the stewards. As they were lead to the room where Sir Matthew would be receiving them, Sir Robert reminded himself that at the moment, there were better uses, than speculating on this girl, of his time. He listened to the echoes of this house, measured the height of its shadows; from the soft, wet smell that clung to the halls and the slate on the floors, he realized that it contained a dungeon. He could hear it in the hollowness of where he walked, and he could see it in the moisture that crawled up the walls. Outside the world was green and languorous, but inside Sir Matthew's home it was musty, a winter that had stayed long past its invitation.

Sir Matthew had seated himself on a massive marble chair built apart from the wall but seemingly of the same material. He was not known as an imposing man but he had achieved a rather imperious look on his throne at the foot of a red carpet. He was not armed but on either side of him he had arranged for a guard: five men on each flank, in chain mail, holding shields and wearing breast pieces with that ridiculous insignia. Sir Robert bowed as deeply as he could, not so much out of respect, but also to keep himself from laughing.

"And your retinue?" Sir Matthew directed Sir Robert to make all the introductions before he even acknowledged Sir Robert's greeting. "This one, I demand to have removed," Sir Matthew ordered, once Sir Robert finished with the stewards, bowmen, and other servants.

"Come, come child," Sir Robert commanded the girl to him; she advanced cautiously, as if traversing a cliff. He took her hand in his so there would be no question as to her status, as far as he was concerned. "This," he heard himself say proudly to Sir Matthew, "is Miss Jenny."

The girl curtsied, and as she regained her posture, she cast a look at Sir Robert, as if seeking his approval for her behavior. Sir Robert nodded to her, and allowed her to step back, in line with the bowmen, so as not to be so directly within Sir Matthew's curdling gaze.

"And what is her purpose here today?" Sir Matthew demanded.

"That will be discussed, soon enough, " Sir Robert promised.

"I've heard something of this wench," Sir Matthew said, his voice rushing toward the high ceiling and its chandeliers, then threatening to hush out the candles. "Although I doubt, for the sake of the gentle people in attendance, that I should speak of what I've heard," Sir Matthew continued. "Does the Queen know of this association?"

"To a point, yes," Sir Robert said, and he enjoyed registering at that instant Sir Matthew's reaction. It marked the end of his smug self-assurance. "Her Majesty, should you dare to disturb her rest, would understand both my method and my purpose."

"Then on with it," Sir Matthew clambered.

"Not yet," Sir Robert said. "First, I have other business." With those words, he felt Jenny drift back, possibly out of Sir Matthew's sights, closer to Sir Robert's armed men. Like Sir Matthew they were likely unnerved by the girl's inclusion, but he had made it plain as he could his position about this girl, and they knew well enough now was not a time to challenge their patron. Sir Robert stepped closer to the throne, and lifted his voice, let it surround and suffuse the rafters.

"The Queen's troops have made no progress since the equinox," Sir Robert said. "Your men, Gaines', Beechum's, even a measure of my own. Their welfare will not be any further served by this escapade. "

"And how do you define 'welfare?' " Sir Matthew asked. "Their fields are being planted, their crops are being sowed, and their share of their profits are under my protection. Their women and children are provided for."

"At what cost to them in currency, and in their well being, the sanctity and survival of their families?" Sir Robert retorted.

"Your impertinence shows how little you understand about this affair," Sir Matthew accused. "Better minds than your own have determined that the threat from the Gongols still exists, and better minds than yours in particular are still administering for the health and safety of their soldiers. If you have problems providing for your own, you should transfer your custody to someone better equipped."

"You know—and you knew—that the Gongols would not last through the winter. They have been in retreat for months now; **there is no threat**, and there never has been, apart from the one you manufactured," ❀ Sir Robert said. He enjoyed the way his voice echoed in this room, although it was such a waste, its newfound size and grandeur, debating such a mean little person. "You constructed this conflict, " Sir Robert continued, "and you can disassemble it. Begin when the Queen holds her first council after solstice."

❀ In the eighth grade "gifted" **English class** from which I was exempted, during the fall semester the students read two complete books: *The Catcher in the Rye* and *A Separate Peace*. I was to read *The Catcher in the Rye* many times on my own, and in graduate school, where students of creative writing read it far too much, as if they were divining Salinger's address in New

Hampshire from it.

A Separate Peace is an entirely different story. Among kids today it's largely forgotten, from what I've gathered, having been replaced by the likes of Maya Angelou and Sapphire. But *A Separate Peace* lives on in the annals of the Internet, which are written by and for baby boomers. Technically speaking I could be considered a boomer, although I was not, as I've indicated earlier, deemed mature enough to handle such literature. I did not read John Knowles until I was twenty-three-years-old, and stranded in Israel. My three-month-long experiment with Zionism was largely a disaster, and I spent most of the time seeking out English language texts to read from my father's cousin's library of Yiddish, Hebrew, Aramaic, and other reincarnated languages. I turned up a copy of *A Separate Peace* that had probably belonged to one of the cousin's three "gifted" daughters, who had gone on to become an artist, a lawyer, and an archaeology and classics professor, in that order. I don't know how those girls did it, understanding the complexities of an East Coast prep school, when they were raised debating the differences between Herzl and Jabotinsky. But I suppose this is what "gifted" kids do, traverse such boundaries.

Maybe I just didn't get the Christian imagery the book's triumvirate of characters suggests—and I seriously doubt the eighth grade English teacher, a Jewish mother in waiting if there ever was one, got it either—but I resented the idea that the "war" at the prep school was equivalent to the war America's soldiers were fighting in World War II. But it also made sense for Bancroft's best and brightest to be reading, for the war at the East Coast prep school was unlike the war we were warned against on campus.

Bancroft Junior High was thought by many to be ground zero in Los Angeles' eternal conflicts among youth gangs. At the very least the school looked like it: its bungalows were painted over with gang tags and gang graffiti. The names and ranks of gang members covered our lockers and stairwells. (In all fairness to the youth gangs, I must admit that the bathrooms were the exclusive territory of the regular school kids, who wrote such timeless aphorisms as 'Jane con Roger Daltrey (or some other rock 'n' roll cutie; we thought Daltrey looked like a boy on our campus we stalked relentlessly) por vida' on the walls of the girls' room or 'Jane Rosenberg is a gay transsexual whore—call her at (insert phone number here)' on the walls of the boys' room). In homage we imitated this gang script on our notebooks. Yet this war for us was mostly abstract. L.A. gangs were not interested in nervous, affluent, college-bound white girls.

According to the official histories perpetrated by the Los Angeles Police Department, various rap groups, the Internet, and an HBO documentary, the main conflict in those years was between African American gangs. Most of the kids we thought to be gang-related, however, were Hispanic. They wore their blue jeans too long, and rolled up at the ankles; blue bandanas and blue pilot's jackets with fake blue fur on their collars. Should you come to school with your own pants rolled up, you were inevitably approached to be asked which gang you belonged to, or to be told to take your pants off.

I'm convinced that this is the closest many of us had to any actual gang activity, although when I was in elementary school, and *West Side Story* was shown on television, a bunch of kids organized into Jets and Sharks and threatened to have a rumble one afternoon. It never materialized. In eighth grade, however, the junior high administrators planned a carnival that had to be canceled because it was heard somehow that the gangs were going to crash it. Our junior high carnival was thought to be the perfect backdrop for their wanton bloodshed.

I don't remember what I thought of this, but I was probably too self-centered to be affected much by it. The girls around me, however, were petrified. I thought they were hysterical as they cried and hugged one another, afraid to walk home their usual routes even the day before the scheduled and quashed carnival. The gangs were out to get them and they didn't want to be got. The entire episode made me wonder if there was something wrong with me, because I was so unable to feel for them, to feel anything from all this upheaval.

At the time I attributed this insensitivity to my ugly, evil appearance and intellectual deficit but now I am wondering if it had something to do with the education I received, one proscribed for those of average intelligence, or less. The gifted kids got to read *A Separate Peace* because of their profound ability to feel and articulate *more*; to me a gang war was just a gang war, but to them, it was an assault on their adolescence, or more rightly put, their innocence and childhood. They were rewarded for understanding they had a connection to these people who were so different from them; a connection they made by virtue of all the esteem they had been fed about their essential humanity. Someone like me did not deserve to be fussed over with fancy books and big ideas because my capacity for feeling was as limited as my intelligence. Inside I was a gurgling mass of love, hate, jealousy and confusion, shame and longing, much like my peers, and yet there was something innately wrong with my combination of emotions and how I processed them. I did not know how to be afraid of anything more than horses.

Sir Matthew's response was far more measured than Sir Robert could have calculated. He found himself bending, leaning toward that throne, as though a humbler posture would enable him to better hear his adversary.

"Are you threatening me, good sir?"

"Of course not," Sir Robert said, straightening up. "I've stated my aim. Now onto other concerns."

Sir Matthew nodded—if not granting Sir Robert a longer audience, then to his guards, perhaps, who seemed to draw in closer to one another, and to Sir Matthew.

"Something of yours has been found," Sir Robert said, and, as he had previously arranged with his party, waved his hand for his minion to gather more closely around him. The girl, he saw, took the opportunity to shield herself: she found a spot behind the line of men flanking Sir Robert. The bowmen and weapons handlers stepped forward; the chief steward, as he had been instructed, handed Sir Robert the object that had seemingly been defanged: its surface had been buffed to a blinding finish, and its edges gleamed in the last gasps of sunlight that Sir Matthew consented to allow inside his castle.

"We merely wish to return it to you," Sir Robert said, and he displayed the dagger-like object by rolling it out of his palm. Sir Matthew said nothing. "Do you not recognize it?" Sir Robert asked.

"No," Sir Matthew lied.

"It bears your insignia."

"It must be a forgery. The Gongols have perpetrated—"

"It is no forgery," Sir Robert said. "It is named and dated: the signature of a craftsman on this estate. How many others have you had made to be slipped into guts of your enemies, or their saddles—"

Sir Matthew rose to his feet, but his hands remained on the throne's armrests. "I demand to know," he began, and then he paused, as though he could not decide whether to display his resolve, or his temper. "Where did you obtain this counterfeit?"

"Miss Jenny discovered it," Sir Robert said. With those words, the line on either side of him parted, as if his men wished to expose the girl to more of Sir Matthew's scrutiny. But she did not appear frightened, as her earlier behavior might have predicted. Nor was she composed, but within her demeanor, the stillness of her position and the determination of her gaze, a recognition of who she was, or perhaps better put, what she was capable of.

"She discovered it in the hide and blanket of a horse that threw me," Sir Robert added, "so that I would be gravely injured."

"But you were not," Sir Matthew said, and he began descending the steps that led up to that seat where he dreamt himself a king and commander of armed men. "Or you would not be here with these impetuous accusations." Sir Robert's men took a step for each Sir Matthew took, but Sir Matthew's guards remained stationery; a rehearsed bit of business, Sir Robert knew, deigned to increase the appearance of Sir Matthew's bravery. "Now I want this 'child,' as you call her, removed from my sight. She is a witch."

"If she is a witch, perhaps she could tell us, how such an object came to be in such an inopportune place," Sir Robert suggested.

"She is a witch, and nothing she says can be trusted."

"Yet she has not said a word."

Sir Matthew stopped his advance. He was not only a little man, but also a **deformed one**. ❀ He could stand straight and lead with his chest, but his greed and dishonesty squeezed his face further back into his skull, accentuating his nose and leaving his eyes crunched and beady.

❀ Now we come to the heart of the matter. For not only was I **deformed** in my emotional make-up, but in my physical one as well. And I am not talking about the braces on my teeth. I'm talking about my nose, which was outrageously large. It hosted a bump at the very top, and then it snagged in a different direction from where it should have gone. Finally, as it descended the slope of my face, it turned inward and hooked. I appeared as if I had no skin between my nose and lip, a kind of muted harelip. Oh Lord, was I ugly, and there was no hiding it—not with the make-up I used in my ballet performances, or the various personalities I tried to outfit myself with.

If there were times when I thought I might forget about my looks, I always had someone around to remind me. People gave me nicknames like "Big Nose" and "Pointy" and I walked home to a cacophony of rhymes and jingles extolling the vices of my copious nose and nostrils. Given all of the feedback I received, I would often go to my mother as a kind of reality check. Her response was that I was beautiful, but given her condition, I tended not to trust her. So I'd ask my father and he'd give it to me straight. I do not wish to start an argument with him over the exact phrasing he used, but even today, when we reminiscence about those simpler times, he'll say, "God, you were awful homely-looking."

You might think his answer cruel (pronounced by my father with a special emphasis on the second syllable), but my father's acknowledgment of my aesthetic challenges led him to agree to do something about it. One of the many experiments conducted on my father and his asthma included a nose job (to correct a deviated septum), something that wound up working none too well; my mother, for purely cosmetic reasons, also underwent the procedure. As I grew up but not into my nose, it became slowly apparent to everyone that if I was going to have any piece of my mind left after I was finished looking at myself in the mirror, I'd have to go under the knife, as well.

"If you knew as much about this girl as you claim, you would know that she does not speak at all," Sir Robert said. "Nevertheless, her discovery was made known to me by another."

Sir Matthew's lips straightened. "This, this is slander." He could barely speak, so set was his jaw and mouth in anger.

"It could be, were it not the truth," Sir Robert said, "and it could be called by another name."

Sir Matthew's mouth loosened into wonderment and fell into an open-mouthed frown.

"Extortion," Sir Robert said. It took longer than it should have for recognition to spread throughout Sir Matthew's ashen face. "For a most noble cause, of course," Sir Robert added by way of explanation, and his words must have worked, for then Sir Matthew swelled with color, a sickly pink of complaint, as if he was a baby with the colic.

"This war was begun at the behest of you and your allies, for the purpose of personal enrichment," Sir Robert said. "You can tell the Queen you are withdrawing your men, and Gaines' and Beechum's and the rest will follow; or you can continue plundering your own people, and I will continue with my accusations, my slander, my extortion, and," Sir Robert paused to hold the weapon up to Sir Matthew's eyes, "my evidence."

chapter five

It is the same thing **every day**, ❀ and yet it is not. We wake, but we do not wash; there is never enough time; and then we march. I believe we are marching in circles; the terrain is a confusion of hills, springs, and rocks, so we know not our destination. We simply wake when we are told to, lift our knees and feet and hope we can propel ourselves forward. For another day, another six days, until a day of rest, supposedly. Then we flop and lurch all over again.

❀ If I had to, I could still perform the entire routine we went through **every class** at the bar, from the *por de bras* and *demi pliés* to the *rond de jambs* just before a break, and stretches. Perhaps I wouldn't perform it very well, but I still remember the routine each of my classes went through. When we first started, the teacher performed the steps for us until we could link the name of each step to the movement. Eventually all she'd have to do is dictate the steps, and watch the subsequent demolition of the art of ballet. We were supposed to be concentrating, of course, but I think we spent most of our attention on whose butt was sticking out, and whose sickle foot was acting up; each girl worked harder than the girl in front of her, and probably no more than that. A true mark of our progress came when she would tell us to warm up on our own, and we could complete everything without prompting; this, I must admit, took my group quite awhile. We were in no hurry to grow up.

After bar work we went through our positions, combinations of steps, and the first bits of choreography in our upcoming productions; we kept one eye on our feet and elbows, and the other in the mirror. This is not how it is supposed to be; Michael Jackson, at the height of his powers, was always accused of dancing too much for the mirror, for his own satisfaction. We were probably not much different. Perhaps this is what made the end of the class the worst part: *chaine* and *pique* turns. You could not look in the mirror and do them; you had to spot, keep your eyes on your destination, and whip your head so the rest of the body would follow. I dreaded this. I dreaded all sorts of turns, *fouettés* and *piroutteés*, because I had to come up with some other method that approximated the turn's correct appearance. I would simply fling myself in the correct direction and then I prayed.

After class came rehearsals for whatever production was in the offing; every June we had a gala recital, and in the fall we went touring the charity spots—old folks' homes, community centers, children's hospitals—of Southern California. The workshops before the June recital were the best, with long stretches of eating and socializing as other dancers worked on their solos or kept their muscles limber. My friends and I, meanwhile, played jacks during our breaks or read racy novels to one another or talked all too much and all too loudly—so loudly, in fact, the ballet teacher would yank a curtain that stretched from one end of the studio to another to divide us from the really serious students. She did not want them distracted.

The schedule kept stars firmly fixed in our eyes most of the year, since there was a role to prepare for, the promise of an audience and the purchase of a costume from the Taffy's catalogue. But during the summer, it was all drudgery, because there were no performances to worry over. Summer was the time for conditioning, technique, and it was frightfully boring.

But we had to get through it if there was to be a part for us in the fall, or next June. The ballet teacher must have had the patience of a saint, although to marry her husband, she had to convert to Judaism.

We breakfast. The best that can be said of the food is that it is not horrible. It is just the same: cheese flavorless and soft; fruit that is sometimes too sweet, it is nearly rank; and milk, flat and a few days old. We don't know where it comes from.

We clean our weapons; march again; march again, find a new location to set up camp. There are days when we march to no particular destination, only for practice, and once we find a camp, we build, or dig, or hunt. The camp always needs to be fortified, with more supplies, or deeper moats, or embattlements that when we leave, we just as soon tear apart. We store our catches and whatever else we manage to forage high in the trees to keep what is nocturnal away, and we burn and bury what we cannot use, to dissuade those animals that might walk in our waking hours.

We eat again, a leg of something, or if the livestock run low, the body of something snared by our arrows or our traps. A cup of mead we might enjoy if the next morning is for the church; there is no church to take us to, of course, but each regiment seems to come up with a man who appoints himself rector or deacon or invests himself with some such authority, and he leads us in reciting hymnals and verses. There are no bibles or prayer books. After this gathering, our recess is over, and we return to our tasks. We do not march unless there is some crisis, or belief that some crisis is imminent, but we clean our weapons, we look for, store, or dispose of food, and we sleep in a pile of our own sweat and loneliness.

❀ ❀ ❀ ❀ ❀

I do miss you, Jenny. There are no other words to frame my feelings. It is the same for everyone: my parents, my sisters, the men my father and I shoe horses for, branded livestock, forged and pounded without enough of a payment; I dream of them all, particularly the boys who left long before I did, and here I should find them, in the better regiments, but I do not. I am with men who come from all over the country, and not one of them from our village.

But I can send word to my parents and sisters, even to my father's customers, and I have no way of knowing if Sir Robert is keeping his promise to us. Does my father look after you in some fashion unbeknownst to the authorities? Do you see the twins, the darlings, with my mother on their errands? I believe this is why I feel so strongly for you in particular, because I cannot know how you are faring. I am so confused as to the treatment you have been dealt, and I cannot picture the day-to-day of your life, despite all my efforts.

And as I write to you, I remember how we learned this together: the shapes and sounds of letters and words, practicing their composition until my hand and arm cramped and froze. I thought my fingers would never surrender the quill on some afternoons, and I would spent the rest of my days clamped around its stem, while you and your agile fingers so nonchalantly spun tales in the dirt: another family had absconded with our garden tomatoes, when my mother went looking for them; I remember your telling her this in a single word: "raccoons." When my father said he would hunt them down, you wrote, "fairy raccoons." I remember the map you drew leading to a litter of new rabbits abandoned by their queen, and the warnings of storms on their way, or horses that were hurt and required a house call. In the ash you wrote of the ore that had boiled over, a fire you started or had to put out on your own; it was as if you were born to transmit such bulletins, of the natural world on its regular rounds. And yet I struggle to put down these few sentences every once in awhile, these ordinary thoughts.

My class of conscripts is lucky, we have been told, to have missed the coldest nights; that we have had this time and training to fortify us for the next winter. But it is spring that ushers in the most intolerable evenings, the Earth so much more in a rush to expel what during the day it had hungered. The blades of grass on which we sleep seem to slash inward, up to my lungs, and when I awake, I feel as though I am being strangled. I rub the salve you prepared for me, Jenny, on my chest. Beneath my clothes, I wear a capped vial of it, and inhale it through the nose in my private moments. The scent reaches down my throat to untangle its hold. I do not think I could survive without it.

❀ ❀ ❀ ❀ ❀

Can you still write, Jenny? Do you remember how? Do you remember the orthography Thomas plowed into me? You must have. Otherwise you would not have been so quick to blow out the words you inscribed in the cinders. You must have known your fate, what being lettered would mean for it. It was never my intent to put you in any danger, Jenny, with this gift. But I see now that I must have. It was never my intent to expose you to any kind of risk. But you and I: we must fight against this sentence, this penalty you are paying, for what crime you have committed, no one can say. No one can say because you have done nothing, Jenny, other than perform your miracles that are part of your being.

You are nothing less than life to me, Jenny: the giver and guard of my life. When I was ill, and now through this interminable spring frost: why did I not recognize this earlier, when I could have told you so simply, so directly, without the hazards my writing presents now?

Is this why you have been cast away from us, Jenny? That your talent is the source of your punishment pitches me into anger, into distrust for the people I should love. But we will right this, somehow, when I return, I promise. I should have begun such a quest earlier, the moment you were taken from us, but I needed to be reminded, I suppose, of what my family and I lost. I was reminded of your courage when you had to present your case to Sir Robert. Yet he was gentle and just, as far as I know. And when I return, when I tell him what I did not have the temerity to point out before, I know he will help us further. He called me your champion perhaps in jest, but he will see that I can live up to that designation.

Will you forgive me, Jenny, if I have erred in hungering for you so much? If we cannot correspond, then I will have to catch up, seeing your pictures, reading your bulletins, recreating all the time that I have lost. What you are seeing, sensing, what you know that no one else has the ability to perceive, to shape into knowledge.

❀ ❀ ❀ ❀ ❀

My father tells me to be proud of our work: that when we walk through the village, or to the Market, or perhaps at court one day, we might see the results of our labors: A horse carrying the Queen herself, or those that brought food, or clothing to Market Day. The horses that we see plowing fields or powering a mill. Or horses that brought back news of this war or some other conquest; the spoils they might bring, piled into carriages or carts. We will be able to point to these achievements, count them. Yours must be left to your imagination, although you should know I have my memories. Being away from home, from you, has taught me the importance of remembering—remembering for you, Jenny, if you cannot for yourself.

Here, we have no achievements to point to, to boast about, to remember once we are returned to our villages and households. **Our cause** ❀ is our country, or so we have been ordered. I have no objection to this. I am more than willing to believe in it. But if our cause is our country, what are we doing to advance it? We are to beat back the Gongols, who threaten everything we admire and adore; we are to eliminate them at all costs, and yet we neither spy nor see any evidence of them. They are said to be amassing on our borders, invading our forests, infiltrating border towns and hamlets. It is imminent, the danger they present from these clandestine fortresses. It is clear and focused. But none of our searching and scouring produces even a trace of the enemy. Sometimes I believe we are chasing phantoms.

❀ Sometime in junior high school, we began to take up **causes**. Call it "*A Separate Peace* syndrome." Children are much like adults in this need to find something to organize against, if not something to organize around. In this early period of adolescence we were beginning to organize around potential identities. I, however, was the only cause I was interested in, ultimately; and dance is not a cause. It might possibly be a calling, although I'm not sure that my attraction to it was that elemental. I liked pretending to be being something I was not: beautiful; I liked the way I looked when I posed in front of the mirror. I liked the camaraderie of working on a production, and I loved the costumes and of course I liked the association with celebrity: Elgin Baylor's daughter took dance at my studio, along with a host of aspiring actors and actresses, whose faces I can well remember but whose names have been lost to all of us.

I might give myself a bit more credit: When Elton John broke up his band to form another one, my friend Wendy was traumatized, for how would she ever see her beloved Nigel Olsson again? I was truly shaken by how upset she was, as though she had been conscious of losing her mother and what that had meant for her life. I wanted to help her, but had no idea how I could. I wound up calling MCA Records for her later that day and talking to some operator there, only to confirm the worst.

In high school, we learned to spread our empathy beyond our immediate surroundings. A neighbor from the canyon side, whose parents were of an Old Left bent, arrived for journalism class one day in a Mao jacket and hat and told us all to quit school to work in the rice fields. One boy pinned "I am a Zionist" buttons on us in the school bus. Two others (confirmed heterosexuals, believe-you-me) obtained minor celebrity for painting their fingernails black to protest the Briggs Initiative. That's the same California proposition remade in infamy in the movie, *Milk*. It would have outlawed the hiring of gay teachers throughout the state, but thanks to the efforts of Harvey Milk and company, it failed. We also had a riot in my senior year to protest the closing of the campus smoking area. We were kids then, of course, and didn't know what was good for us.

But the biggest cause of all, I remember, was my sister's. It was born during the summer after my friends and I graduated junior high school (she was two years behind us). Most of us were going to Hollywood High School, but a few were to go to Fairfax. Fairfax was imagined to be a tougher school, in both academics and social dynamics. The class genius was destined for Fairfax High, for example. And Fairfax gangs were unfamiliar to us—they were said to be mostly African American, not Hispanic, as we had become accustomed to.

I spent that summer first at summer school with Wendy; and then hanging out at the Wonderland Avenue playground with the playground director; the twenty-some-year-old who got out of the Vietnam draft; the class genius; and a few other heroes and villains. As for my friend Lynn from the ratty duplex with whom I played dress-up and smoked dope: her home was only two blocks away from Fairfax High School, and in that attendance district her fate was sealed, practically at the summer's start.

Lynn did not go to summer school as I did, but hung out with another up-and-coming Fairfax student, one of her neighbors whom we all knew from junior high. But this girl was not one of us. She didn't ride horses and she didn't dance. She was the bushy-haired stranger, when that cliché was at its most active. Make no mistake: she was white, and her hair had no aspirations to feign an African American natural. But it was wild, big, and tangled, and her bangs were seemingly trimmed with a razor blade. She scared us, plain and simple.

I hadn't spoken to Lynn for about two or three weeks when she began sleeping on the beach at night, switching boyfriends at a furious pace, and leaping beyond the gateway substances we practiced with to the big stuff. Then Lynn dropped out of ballet class. Her new friend was introducing her to all kinds of enterprises, which inspired our curiosity and our ability to shun. My sister, however, had no such ability and set out to retrieve this girl from her downward spiral of sex and drugs. I can't recall specifically what my sister did, only that she hounded me constantly to do something.

I knew, for some reason, that this was just something I should stay out of. I was beginning to take my college prep courses and was taking my dancing more seriously. But my sister would not let this go, and threatened to tell our parents about my own experiments. She didn't, and sometime during my sophomore year she arranged a meeting between Lynn, me, Inez, and some of Lynn's former comrades. Lynn looked the same, and sat in her duplex dressed in a bathrobe. She was drinking water constantly because she had some kind of infection (I guess I know what kind of infection that was, now that I'm an old married woman).

When she was not dangling the specter of having my parents torture and exile me for all my moral shortcomings, my sister took each and every opportunity to remind me of how I had abandoned Lynn to a sinister drug underworld. I'm sure I rationalized my actions though. I had long since dispatched with the boundary between me and six of the seven deadly sins. I wasn't damned—my theological systems were limited to the here and now back then—but I was doomed to be "a fluke of the universe," as the novelty song put it. This situation with Lynn represented to me just one more thing to be afraid of, fear being the primary motivator and shaper in my life: fear of my parents, of spicy foods, of failure and impoverishment; of breaking my bones and not being able to dance, or of missing school and homework assignments and the latest gossip; fear that I would never grow up, or that I would grow up to be like my mother, or that I would feel like this forever; and finally fear of just about everything else there could possibly be, to be afraid of.

Eventually Inez drew up a certificate for my sister and awarded it to her for "caring when no one else did" (although her wording was nowhere near as delicate). This recognition seemed to quell my sister's ambition. At Fairfax High School the pranks and partying kept going on, and one of the last times I saw Lynn, she was trying to explain the difficulty of conducting a mock trial in social studies when she was on an acid trip.

❀ ❀ ❀ ❀ ❀

The Gongols are not said to be human, although we know they must be; otherwise why else would this fear be so inspired in us—not fear of them and their weapons, their cunning, strength, and audacity of their forces, but fear of killing them—killing something so like ourselves. The Gongols are said to have a claim on these lands, but a false one. I have no reason to dispute this: in the homes we search, in the churches, markets, and shops we inspect; indeed, in this war we are making in our own land, we find nothing but our own people.

There are no Gongol ex-patriots. We descend into villages that the Gongols are said to have infiltrated, but we find not even villages: settlements of a few families, castaways from some other town, forced to move away because of debts, or broken marriage contracts, or an accusation of heresy. We surround acreage that the Gongols are said to be farming on, or hunting in, and we find no evidence of their presence, past or present. Their retreat has been total, and their claims are not active. We have swept the frontier that divides us and we find them solidly on their own side, and we, with our torches and arrows and numbers, our horses and our weapons, and our new contraptions, are on the side against our countrymen.

But if Gongols are not human, then why are we told of their tactics and motivations: their need, like our own, for crops, for grazing space, for timber, for a destiny that must be fulfilled? Why are they prone to the same influences— the heat, the cold, the dampness that weds into our skin, that consumes our feet and calves, our fingertips and knuckles—the same weaknesses?

Do they panic as we do? Panic is our enemy: panic and fear. They threaten to consume us. They tempt our nerves, and then our weapons. We are always to be on guard for the Gongols, for they do not fight like men, fairly, we are told. But each time we are prepared for a fight against the Gongols, it is fear and panic that we encounter.

A fortnight ago, a Sunday, we lazed about as we are permitted but should not truly be doing, a rain of arrows met our eyes and we shot back in the direction we believed they were coming from. We were heartily astonished, having no embattlements to hide behind so we simply fell to the ground, rising only to shoot blindly our poisoned tips and sharpest measures. The rain of opposing arrows continued and to this moment, we do not know who was responsible; it might very well have been a collection of disgruntled rogues whose homes and livestock we plundered in the name of inspection.

The shouting of men, the flurry of arrows, the sounds of arrows sinking into the flesh of my fellow men: if I was not shooting blindly in the beginning of all this, like everyone else, I was eventually, because the chaos around me drew in closer, closer, until it was blur of white and red and men's tears. I do not know how my aim was, and I am afraid to know, to think that I killed or wounded some man simply defending himself. There is such a satisfying noise made by a bow once an arrow is released; there is a sound in tandem, the sinking of the target into skin and the material below, down to the bone: I am not sure I have ever heard anything before that frightening. You would hear this thump and sink and then fall to the ground, lest you were not hit with a similar note. Beside you, you might find some of your fellows, permanently felled, or merely on their way to a similar destination. Then it was over. The realization did not fall over us soon enough. The arrows in one direction ceased gradually and yet we continued shooting at ghosts. It was as if we were in twilight and refused to recognize nightfall, or dawn and we were holding back the day before us. Those among us who could still stand, or hold a bandage, were then directed to repair our compatriots. The shooting was over, and the screaming was just beginning.

I held pressure to wounds, as I have seen you do, with horses; I held wounds until my gloves were soaked through with their blood. Blood to blood, we were told afterwards; soldiers make a marriage more sacred than any officiated by God, as the blood of one soldier comes to be worn by all. It smells hot, and meaty, a feast for flies and hornets. They circle the injured, as if rehearsing the roles of vultures. When the blood was finished I applied boiling oil to wounds. Rarely had I the opportunity to **treat wounds** as you have, ❀ with your herbs and powders, but when I did, your recipes worked wonders. Some asked where they came from and I shrugged them off. Since they were so effective, in the long run, no one bothered further with their interrogations.

❀ Any psychologist or psychiatrist worth his or her consulting fee would likely say we teenage dancers indulged in dope smoking as a form of **self-medication**: if not for our physical trials, then for our emotional ones. We flew and spun and sashayed with much abandon, but we all considered ourselves secretly, if not deeply, injured in some way—by friends, family, boys; by life as we knew it. Illegal indulgences were not the only way out, but they were certainly the most convenient, even if we didn't know why they were so effective.

The actual form of our true self-medication was much more mundane. The problem we all faced with dancing was not in our backs and knees, but in our toes. Blisters and calluses have lead to the disfigurement of many a dancer's feet; they are caused by the friction between the toe shoe and the dancer's skin. Each *relevé* brings the box of the toe shoe into closer contact with the toes' skin. The newer the toe shoe, the worse the situation. Professional dancers might go through a single pair during a performance; we kept ours much longer, because we used (the now discontinued) Duro Toe (which, I have recently discovered, was created during the Depression to last longer and therefore be more economical).

Since our shoes lasted longer, we were spared a good share of pain. Yet as you may have anticipated with a group of teenage girls, the relative comfort of our situation did nothing to deter our complaints. We wrapped our toes in lamb's wool and toilet paper in addition to the foam toe pads Capezios gave us with every purchase. At some point, and I don't remember precisely when, someone discovered the wonders of First Aid tape. Lord, it was a miracle to our afflictions.

Nowadays anyone can buy Toe Tape, sixty yards for five bucks (cheaper on the Internet) at Capezios. It accomplishes the same effect as the Johnson and Johnson's we used to swathe each individual toe and avoid the blistering. Our teacher, however, considered such measures blasphemous. She said we were avoiding the toughening we would need to continue dancing, although she must have felt for us, because she did nothing to prevent our wrapping, our picking, our re-wrapping and other forms of toe-preening. With our First Aid tape we were somewhat invincible, except for when it slipped, and then with the blood and new skin formations revealed with the removal of our tights, we'd have adhesive mixed in. It made for a fragrant, easy-to-clean combination.

I had additional pain, given that I suffered from the same flat feet that kept my father out of the draft. As a young girl I had to wear corrective shoes, which did nothing for me, and the first time I took ballet classes, I had to quit; the pain in my ankles was close to excruciating. This experience prevented my ballet teacher from rewarding me with admission into the toe shoe class for some time, and then, once admitted, I devolved into a bedlam of severe cramps and other, unclassified maladies of the calves, knees, and ankles. It became so bad that my teacher marched me into Capezios (on the same Hollywood block as the landmark headquarters of Capitol Records) and had the store manager personally fit me properly, with a new kind of toe shoe with a pre-arched shank. I don't know if it worked, but I enjoyed the attention.

I stretched out my career as a toe dancer a little while longer thanks to a codeine prescription I obtained. No, I didn't obtain it; I earned it, by enduring the willful fumbling of my orthodontist. If the man wasn't a sadist, he was most definitely lame in his hands, which possessed not a shred of human feeling. He really did a few numbers of my mouth and as if to apologize, he provided medication. The prescription served me well each time my braces were tightened, when I needed to assuage my other, non-oral aches, or decided I wanted to heighten the effect of certain social engagements.

Eventually, though, the codeine lost its charm and Toe Tape could only take me so far, and in my junior year of high school, I announced I was quitting toe work. To be perfectly honest, I was not without ulterior motives, as I was beginning to cash in on all the hard work I had put into attracting a boyfriend and some measure of popularity. But it made no matter, what the reason was, because the ballet teacher was brutally disappointed, announced to the class that I had reached "the point of deterioration," when everything goes downhill for dancers because they have lost their will power. My reaction to this was much like my reaction to being bucked off a horse: instead of abiding, I just quit, outright, which my mother said was just heart-breaking.

❀ ❀ ❀ ❀ ❀

There are no surgeons among us, so we all became one: holding men by their shoulders while their wounds were dug out with knives and the burned points of our swords. We gagged them for amputations so that we need not hear their complaints. Otherwise we would have lost our nerve. A man here, a potter in his home village, taught us how to make one particular oil by boiling the needles of certain trees. This ointment did not prevent wounds from bubbling over but it did keep the men from scratching at them and opening them up, curtailing whatever progress they had made toward healing and having to begin the process anew.

❀ ❀ ❀ ❀ ❀

When I write to you, Jenny, it is to quell my fright. It is to know that you are not just a dream, and that my mind, my perceptions are firm, not apparitions born out of what I so desperately need, amid all this sickness and blood. I try to remember your hand on my forehead, or in my palm: what was it exactly that you did for me, Jenny, when I was so ill? Which combination of herbs, the strength of the tea you offered, the content of your thoughts? If I could remember, perhaps I could do something for these men. But I cannot remember, and I cannot save them.

It is not the Gongols who would do us the most harm, but Mother Nature and our own clumsiness. It was one task, to lug ourselves through melting snow, and I protested too much at the coming spring. Now we are truly having water.

Summer blossoms and we choose to camp close to water, where we might swim, wash our clothes, rest and cool ourselves—our bodies and our hunger. Yet when we sleep too close to a river, we wake to discover our faces and shoulders eaten, scratching and swollen. Some sprite has made a meal out of us; and I cannot imagine what it found in us, that was so appetizing.

Our joints burn after our swim, amid the coolness of the water: it is not decent for bathing or drinking, and where it has flowed over our skin, there are cracks and bubbles. Later some are taken in their bowels; they cannot stand and are afraid to lay down, and they cannot drink even what is boiled, what is mead or milk; they will die with their eyes and cheeks sunken in.

The camp is cursed, or sick men begat more sick men; we are told to burn everything. When we do not dispose of our ashes and embers properly, we find ourselves the next day chasing fire through the remaining weeds and firebugs in our uniforms. The summer rains bring ants, heat the termites, and the trenches and moats we do finish properly are no sooner overrun with rats and water snakes. This is to say nothing of the carpenter's bees in the wood we haul, hornets in our meat, and fleas in our horses. When they are done with the horses, they suck on our blood, or chew on our hair. Whatever comfort is drawn from nature for men is not enough, and whatever is allotted to animals is apparently less.

Sometimes I think I remember, Jenny, the days you kept at my bedside. How many days were you there? More than my parents, you must have been there. They told me later how they traded off in their sleep and their vigils. But you: you must have never left. Perhaps that was your trick. How could the Lord take me with you watching? When I remember, Jenny—and I must remember now, to keep up my bravery—when I remember, I see you kneeling, your hands on my chest, pushing and pulling, pushing and pulling, as though you were breathing for me, Jenny, when that dull ache turned vicious. I feel my head in your arm, your hands rising to my lips, to feed me broth and a tea with a severe fragrance. When I return, will you take me for a walk in the woods, show me what they were made out of? And sometimes, when I at my most lonely, when the day is too much like the one before, and the next one holds no promise, I dream of that time, when you and my parents must have loved me so much, and I hear your voices—all of them, Jenny. My mother's, soothing though on the verge of tears; Thomas', low and confident; and yours, Jenny. I dream you spoke to me. How might your voice rest in my ears, Jenny, as if it were more scent than sound, something I could always carry with me? Or would it flit away, high and delightful like birdsong, so that I may dedicate the rest of my days to pursuing its capture?

🏵 🏵 🏵 🏵 🏵

I saw a man **die** 🏵 today, Jenny. I must write your name now, the name of everyone I love—Mother, Father, Lucy, Grace and you, Jenny, because of what I have seen and how I came to see it. I have seen dead men before, and the dying, of course; I've seen them in other battles; I've seen them in the morning, when we wake to find one of our compatriots near death or long since gone, due to some malady that we ignored for far too long. I've even seen dead men and women, even children, in their beds at home, at wakes and funerals. But never like this.

> 🏵 In junior high most of us, me included, flirted with **death**, as both an idea and a reality. Inez liked to tell tales of screeching down steep hills in a stolen shopping cart and we canyon-hill people had stories of Suicide Swing, a tire swing at some undisclosed location that was only for the brave. I never went and so have no firsthand knowledge of it. As far as the idea of death, what I knew about it came from the nightly séances I listened to KLOS-FM deejay Jim Ladd conduct to summon Jim Morrison. Perhaps they weren't really séances, though, because Ladd enjoyed toying with the idea that Morrison wasn't really dead. Either way it made for a confusing morass of folk belief and warnings from my parents not to do basically anything, or else you might get killed.

Given that the driving age is sixteen, and that 16-year-olds tend to be in high school, and tend to get themselves killed in cars, we began to confront death more squarely at Hollywood High School, whether we wanted to or not. One of those who died was Dean Marto, a little brother-in-law to the famous Ladd; Dean died in a motorcycle accident, and I heard there was a giant photograph of Rod Stewart hanging over the funeral. Dean orbited in that universe of the ultra-cool, and so I had to rely on reports from the field, as I was not invited—and had no right to be. We kids from Bancroft Junior High, upon enrolling at Hollywood High, also learned of the mystery of an eighth grader from the other junior high feeding into our campus. Two kids from that other school sometime in the recent past had been fooling around with a gun in the basement when it went off in one of the boys' hands. The other boy was shot in the chest and died almost instantly, but not without saying a few words beforehand.

We Bancrofters had nothing in our experience to compare to this, and for all who came upon this story, it was the best horror story we had ever encountered. The players in it were anonymous for a long time, until I began to notice a boy in my math class, who paid a good deal of attention to me—well, to my jokes and attempts to distract the teacher. (He was fresh out of UC Santa Cruz and still wearing his Mr. Natural T-shirts. Said instructor would often lose lost his train of thought when addressing the bustier girls in the class.)

I had some familiarity with Tarot cards, owing to my days on the Sunset Strip, and I had begun a serious study of the art, or racket, in hopes of divining what had happened in this incident. What I saw in them confirmed no more than the rumors I heard in school, no matter the combinations of swords, wands, and Major Arcana cards I magically dealt out in my spreads.

So while death might be an experience I could never

comprehend first-hand, it was not necessarily a private process, one that had to be sequestered in whispers like mental illness or any other domestic drama my family was bound to fall into, sometime soon. In my junior year, my mother's mother—the Colonel's wife—checked into the hospital for what was to be the last time. She had already survived colon cancer and had been bedridden since I was a little girl, owing to the heart condition she picked up after surviving scarlet fever as a child. Had my grandmother been born and stricken twenty years later in the century, she could have easily overcome her defect with a plastic or pig's heart valve replacement. But in 1978 there were neither plastic nor pig's heart valves ready to step in for her own, and her illness had no resolution.

I loved my Grandma Stell as any granddaughter would love an affectionate, and attentive, grandmother. Although she couldn't get out of bed most days she spoiled me with her compliments and interest in whatever I was doing, and she loved to tell me jokes (sometimes racy) and teach me about her soap operas. She was a math whiz who read *The Ladies' Home Journal*, John O'Hara and Frederick Forsythe; and who spoke in her own aphorisms, such as, "When you own units, you watch the World Serious," but I didn't care that I never understood them. Although she was always sick, I only thought of her dying as a real possibility once before—when she tripped over a cement fixture in a parking lot and cut up her shin. That day, as my mother and I waited for an ambulance, then for a prognosis from the doctor, felt like the end of the world.

Now that she was in the hospital, I was determined to see her, although my parents didn't want me anywhere near her; they had kept the death of my father's father, ten years earlier, a kind of open secret. There was also the matter of how my father despised hospitals, owing to his father's death, and how my mother despised the Rosenberg side of the family's practice of camping out in hospital rooms when a relative was afflicted.

"Please, please don't be like your aunt and your grandmother," she was to beg me regarding future family ailments.

So when my parents refused to take me to the hospital to see my Grandma Stell, I had a boy take me. I'll call him Slayer, because that's what he did to me, man, slay me good and deep so I could only live on as one of his minions. I knew Slayer from the school newspaper, and he had a car, which came in handy at lunch, when we'd head off for sustenance at McDonald's. Although he had a rickety old Volvo, it got me to McDonald's each day, and it could get me to Cedars, and he began taking me there on a regular basis.

I felt drained, blank, stupid, and a little guilty once it was all over; by the time Grandma Stell died, I had finagled my way into transforming my chauffeur into a steady boyfriend. This was a real feather in my cap, since I finally had that nose job just before my junior year and while the results were not hideous, neither were they spectacular. My failure to obtain a steady date so soon after my physical transformation seemed proof of defects far more intractable and internal. Once Slayer was in place as my boyfriend, though, I would be invincible. Grandma Stell, meanwhile, was placed in a wall at the same Hollywood cemetery where I would later make a student zombie film; and we—my father, possibly my sister, and even I, for the briefest of intervals—fretted that Mom would be due for another breakdown, now that her best friend had passed away.

He was a Gongol, yes, and without horns coming out of his scalp, or fangs sprouting in his mouth. I knew better than to expect that. I knew he would look so much one of us, but this time, I was tempted to run to the nearest pool of water, to spy another look at myself. Is my hair matted and snarled like his, I had to know; is my beard a nest of burrs? I don't know how old he was, he was so run over with dirt and leaves and hair and something like charcoal under his eyes; our commanding officer said this is something they do, the Gongols, put this black around their eyes to deflect the sun. Only a savage would do such a thing, stop the sun from its natural course, we are told. The Gongols are not men but creatures that live in darkness, in an underworld.

But he was a man; the blood drying around his neck and jaw was the same color as our own. He was better prepared than we were to a degree. Inside the wool beneath his armor and mail he wore another layer, thin and soiled, but of an intricate texture. We had never seen anything like it. Had he not died, I believed, we would have tried ripping it from his body to wear it ourselves. But wearing a dead man's clothes in war is too much of a risk.

His eyes, though, are what shook me, how they remained open, as we ransacked his person and possessions. He lay pinned to the ground, mortifying before our watch, and yet his eyes were active, flicking, switching, blinking, begging God to save him, perhaps; or begging one of us to turn tail and rescue him. When his blood stopped bubbling from his neck wound; when his chest failed to rise and his skin plunged into the cold, his eyes stopped moving. But they did not close. They appeared more open, more susceptible to the light, more willing to answer and correspond than ever in his life. It made me wonder whether the dead do not stop seeing, hearing, smelling, thinking, feeling; it made me realize that the dead must still perform all these functions, but with an intensity and understanding that alludes we living dolts. They take too much in and cannot digest it, and they spend their death in this continual, excruciating amazement.

And then a murk began to pass through the pupils, like a swarm of something, a plague that suffuses the water, makes it unfit for drinking. This is not the true death, as I must have supposed before I saw this; this is not the soul's last and final notice to the Earth that it was departing. No, this was the eyes' message to us, as we rummaged through the scraps of food and repaired and broken arrows and all the rest that had to serve as his last will and testament: that there was too much to see in this condition, too much to comprehend, and even after seconds, just seconds of first seeing it, it was more than he could stand.

I felt as though I was falling ill again, as if there were stones in my throat and a smothered blaze in my chest. I imagined how this same murk must pass through the ears, the nose, through every inch of skin and scalp, every hair, and now I am afraid of what I never was before, what is necessary, even if its inspiration is sometimes unnatural.

Jenny, Jenny: I understand your power, now; the power you have to stop this. Not the power to stop death, but to stop my fear of it, the ache and tingle that begins in my windpipe, then settles just behind my stomach. Since I stood over that dying man, looted him and his fellow soldiers, I have swallowed back those sensations more times than I dare count, and only thinking of you, and your powers, halts the panic. You are my bravery itself.

❀ ❀ ❀ ❀ ❀

Now we leave behind us a garrison. A chain on the people, the links of which are alive and homesick, distracted and jealous, although after our marches and inspections, there isn't much left to guard against. This was not a fair fight; we had first spotted this settlement from atop a cliff; it was at the bottom of a valley. We were patrolling a frontier, we knew, and we also knew that to cross into that valley would be to cross into another man's territory. But still we complied, because we were cold, our toes numb and something like forbearance frozen on our lips, to satisfy our commanders. We practically ran toward where we could see smoke, smell meat stewing, and we swung and shot and stomped over anything that moved, and then we declared for ourselves the ownership of this deadened landscape. And we mean to keep it dead, which is why we leave our worst men: those who spit after the commander speaks, or piss on his armor in the night, or on his weapons. We have stretched our border, pushed it into another man's land, and killed some of our own and most of theirs to do it, and then we just leave it, to lay fallow, or rot. The prize is too abstract for morale.

❀ ❀ ❀ ❀ ❀

We are promised that we will stop when we find a river to cross, a natural boundary that can substitute for a deeper, legal one. Then we will have honored our Queen, and ourselves. Until such time there will be more injustice, more deviousness, more treachery in the name of honor, although not in the hand-to-hand combat. This combat is what keeps us honest, makes our quest true, and worthwhile: to prove yourself in the eyes of some monster that would beg to differ, that sees you as the abomination. But you can enforce a different truth, a more lasting one, the one that your God accepts, as well as your nation. If you can stand the smell of that creature's blood up to your wrists and ankles without retching, then you know you have conquered it, and that your strength is without question.

My father tried to tell me, as I left, many things about war. This is a father's duty, and he told me nothing that I was not to discover for myself. But there is one thing he forgot to omit: how humiliating it is, how shameful, how it leaves perpetrators and victims alike disgusted. My judgment is confirmed in every fire we set. We burn every place we've been, everything we touch, any thing that needs to be erased, forgotten. We would do better to salt the earth as the Romans did; there was trickery in that. This is just grief and its subsequent embarrassment.

🦋 🦋 🦋 🦋 🦋

Jenny, Jenny: your name is not magic. And yet I repeated it to myself as though it were a spell, a command, to bring me some confidence. How do you do it, dear girl? Is it in the tips of your fingers that you used to brush away my fever? Is it in the weight of your palms against my chest? Is it in the air you breathed into my ear, when I could not even hear my parents speaking to me; is it in the eyes that bore into my own, or in your heart, which you must have exposed to me during all those days, kneeling beside what everyone believed to be my deathbed. I need to know now, Jenny, because from these battles I may not return, and I do not want to die, without having understood that courage.

🦋 🦋 🦋 🦋 🦋

I could say that today was the worst, but it is a given that should I admit as much, tomorrow will plunge us down so much further. Our victims were gathered around a few fires and had linked their arms for warmth; now their carcasses rest alongside those of their privation: squirrels, chipmunks, raccoons, even skunks. Once they were pets, mascots, perhaps; then they were used for food, and now these animals, like their human masters, are scavenged by rats. War is not ugly because it turns men into animals; war is ugly because it reduces all of nature into wreckage. We were instructed that if we ran out of ammunition, we should throw rocks, use our teeth, attack with fingernails until there was no blood left—in either them or our enemies. But these men had no blood, only mud and ice in their veins. They were doomed before we encountered them, and now, for what we have done, we must also be.

❀ ❀ ❀ ❀ ❀

There is only one way I will survive this, I've decided, and that is to wear this book as close as possible to my chest. I would have it cover the whole of my heart as it was a shield, but I know it offers no such protection. But it contains what is left of my capacity to live as a human being again. It contains the instructions. It contains what I once eased into and swam against. Now since I cannot feel these things within my person, as I once did, then I will wear them where they once belonged, and if they are damaged—if a sword or arrow is driven through them—then perhaps they will mix with the internals of my body.

chapter six

Before Sir Robert had his title, when he was courting the sumptuous brown-haired beauty whose family would give him one, and make a noble of him, he would not allow himself to be afraid of losing her. He never had much to begin with—that was his reasoning—and when he fell asleep each night, even now, just before dreams and angels overtook him, he imagined he was in his first, original, and most familiar bed. A puddle of blankets it was, on the ground wherever his father could arrange it. **That puddle moved**, night to night, town to town, or more often than not, from barn to barn. 🏵

🏵 It wasn't until I was in sixth grade that I had any kind of confirmation that my father was also **a special case**. I always suspected as much, given that my father didn't have an office, or carry a wallet, or take us on real, out-of-town vacations. The only place we went was the Pacific Northwest and Canada, which he had to visit for his Christmas tree business (let's not even parse the irony of a Jewish Christmas tree baron). He was a real oddity, lumbering about the house with his Huxley, Maugham and Graham Greene (and sometimes Fitzgerald and Faulkner, and Eugene O'Neill, obsessions he shared with my mother); mourning the subscription to the Manchester *Daily Guardian* he was required to take out in college; and singing songs from old movies. He rarely bothered to get dressed for his in-house wanderings, and walked about most of the day in his underwear.

I got the confirmation I needed, oddly enough, from a teacher who delighted in reminding me and other children of average intelligence that we were *not* gifted and therefore not much would become of us. But that's another story. For this tidbit, it is important to know that she once tried to explain to us how Southern California was not like the rest of the country. Anyone who had ever lived here, she said, usually came from elsewhere. To prove her point, she asked every student where his or her parents were born, and they all had semi-nomadic backgrounds. When she got to me, however, she was somewhat stunned to hear that my father was born and raised in Los Angeles.

My father lived by a certain creed that to him must have seemed quite gallant, for he was so much more stable than other men: he was practically static. He was what he was and everyone else should have been that way too. You married whom you married and you did not go looking for better deals or extracurricular activities. You lived where you lived and you didn't take out a second mortgage, or move. (He, in fact, didn't even take out a first mortgage; the house was paid for with cash, every penny he ever saved since he was a teenager.) Jews communed with, and only with, other Jews, because gentiles were obtuse and mysterious; and any man who couldn't support his family was the devil incarnate, and his offspring would have nothing to do with his precious children.

Sometimes his motives were noble, such as his one-man battle to preserve the public school system, even if it meant integrating it with his intelligent and delicate daughters. We would be bused, and like it, and private school, the last scourge of scoundrels, was not an option. But just as often he sounded ridiculous, such as when he wouldn't let me go to the Bolshoi Ballet with my uncle because of the vast, anti-Semitic conspiracy that it fronted. The dancers were sent to America only to take money from rich Jews, he said, so that the Soviets could better imprison their poor ones. And that was the end of that discussion.

The power of his edicts was most acutely felt the night before The Who concert, when he declared I would not be going. No matter that I had already blown my baby sitting money on a ticket, and made arrangements to go with two friends. They, apparently, were the problem. I was supposed to go with Inez and Lynn: two prime suspects if there ever was such a combination. "We don't associate with those kind of people," he declared, and he clarified that he meant the divorced kind, although it could have just as well have applied to the financially impoverished. My father talked a good game of Skinnerian terms, pulling out his worn copy of *Walden Two* to firm up his arguments, but he really was a determinist.

I guess he had to draw a line in the sand somewhere, but that line became increasingly difficult to patrol once I enrolled at Hollywood High. Hollywood High: just one more way I disappointed him. Hollywood was the supposedly lesser of the two high schools I could choose but I was going there because the orphan was going there, and the place did not intimidate me the way the other school did. Hollywood also offered a school bus while Fairfax did not, so he could not argue; there was no way he was driving me to school each morning.

One of my first new friends at Hollywood was a girl who lived not with her mother and her siblings, and not with her single father. She lived with her grandparents because she was born out of wedlock, and to top it off, she was among those considered college-bound by the school administration. There she was, in my classes, expected to complete the same demanding work. And she was Jewish! Her grandfather was an Emmy Award-winning comedy writer for the Borscht Belt comedians my father admired. How did the same genetic material come to this fruition by such a tortured route? This girl put my father through some serious changes, which, while never discussed, I knew were broiling within. When I began failing math in my junior year, however, he quickly blamed it on her. "You've been talking too much to (that girl) and the other birds," he said, satisfied that he had laid failure where it belonged—at a doorstep in a different section of the Hollywood Hills.

If this girl's family tree was anathema to him, though, it was a strong, implacable oak compared to Slayer's. What were his parents' marital arrangements? Divorced? Separated? Did they themselves even know? Their father was definitely missing in action since Slayer, his mother and his baby sister emigrated to Los Angeles from New York. The mother was a graduate student at Immaculate Heart College (another sore subject for my father, since the nuns who ran IHC broke away from the church over the Vietnam War) and struggled to support her family. When she received some kind of fellowship or scholarship from the Bureau of Indian Affairs—she was a descendant of Native Americans—my father only kept his cool in the interest of not upsetting my mother.

Yet the list of offending characteristics, of instability and moral turpitude, only kept multiplying.

The only picture I had of Slayer's father was something approximating Burt Reynolds. Slayer loved Burt Reynolds movies and we saw plenty of them, because Reynolds reminded him of his father. Without Burt Reynolds I don't know if I would have believed that Slayer had a father, for not only did he not send money; he also did not call, or write, or provide any other intelligible sign of his existence. (And Slayer looked nothing like Burt Reynolds; that was part of his appeal, his unconventionality.) A friend of Slayer's father who lived in West Hollywood would occasionally play the role of Dutch uncle; and there were very, very small photographs of Slayer's father at the man's house. He wasn't exactly *persona non grata*, as Slayer occasionally pined for him and his mother indulged in a few vague trips down memory lane—like the night Slayer was conceived, although I tried not to listen too closely to that story. But Slayer's father did leave a huge abyss in the lives of his ex-family, which neither endeared him nor his survivors to such upstanding citizens such as my mother and father.

Sir Robert blamed this routine for the stiffness he experienced most mornings; his bones felt as if they had been split, like cords of wood, and stacked somewhere beyond his authority. More than once he had entertained the idea that Jenny could cure him of all this, but he was also grateful for the sensation, for what it reminded him of. He was being accused, more and more often in the current political turmoil, of being much like his protégé was: if not an outcast, then a man with no history, a usurper, a false prophet, an imposter. The cruel machinations of his bones each morning, he knew, was his proof that he fell anywhere but under those characterizations.

Sir Robert's father was an inventor, with no workshop, no materials, and no clientele. Something had happened to him, once Sir Robert's mother died, in childbirth, along with Robert's intended sibling. Whatever property or comforts the family had subsequently disappeared, much as Sir Robert's memory of his mother and the household she kept. Sometimes there was a cart for their travels, and an ass to pull it, but mostly they were on foot as they roamed, and they sharpened knives, dug privies, and repaired whatever they could convince people was broken.

Through this work Robert eventually rose to a position much like Jenny might have had, were she not an outcast: he served in the quarters of prominent families, wherever his father might sell, for a moment, one of his inventions. They were complex affairs, with wheels, chains, grease and pedals, and they bought Robert spelling lessons, bits of religious education, a quick apprenticeship in leatherwork and stolen moments for reading. One such invention, an assemblage for cannon shot that could be loaded into cannons with much less human effort, captured the eye of the Lord of Berwinshire. In the bartering for the rights to this device, the rootless Robert was installed in the Lord's private militia.

To Robert's mind there was not a single boy among them who had not taken an interest in the Lord's daughter. She was a swan; not the mature, white-feathered and aloof bird, but an adolescent, spirited and sometimes awkward, and compelling in the set of her polished blue eyes and splendid mouth. At her sixteenth birthday the Lord of Berwinshire had his daughter with him on horseback as he reviewed his troops, and she accompanied him most mornings afterwards. It became a badge of humiliation to be worn by Sir Robert's compatriots; more than a few wondered whether the Lord was actually accumulating a harem for his daughter, and they would all wind up becoming eunuchs. When Berwin's daughter was directed to Robert, so he might carry out one of her errands, she was none-too-convinced that he could complete the task.

"You, aren't you still a suckling at this stage?" she asked him. Her hand beheld an envelope that she wanted carried, presumably to a suitor, on another estate.

"I have not suckled for as long as my mother has been dead," Robert replied. His answer forced the girl to take a step back, as if to look him over from a fuller perspective.

Robert did not allow himself to think what she might have seen in him at that moment, but that same moment afforded him enough of an opportunity to study all that he needed of her. He could only win her, he knew instinctively, if he was bold, if not reckless; if it seemed not to matter whether she was to be his.

When she died, it was summer: Berwin wanted his daughter's room dark and she mourned for the light that could not curl past the heavy curtains. She said she would sleep so much better, under a canopy, if necessary, but in the breezes and birdsong of the garden; she did not want to be cut off from what had sustained her so much as a child, when she was the only sprite, the only life and love, in her father's castle. The surgeon said, however, that it was precisely this light, this air and its sweet murmurings, that agitated whatever had taken his young wife's breathing. Robert kept to her side as much as his duties would allow him, but he did not pray: his father had said it had not worked for his mother, and to take that risk—to pray and not to be heard—would have meant the loss of what others said was even poor Robert's birthright. He did not pray for his wife, and she died, holding the hand of her father.

He had lost her, and he had lost Jenny. They exchanged pleasantries, as much as possible in her condition, when she tended to his discomforts, or tried to prevent others. But she had long since abandoned the bed and other conveniences he had set aside for her. That single night, in preparation for the visit to Sir Matthew's, was all she would consent to. No sooner had they arrived back and Jenny took the time to cool down her horse, she retrieved her old clothes. The only traces of her remaining in his quarters were the sachets she had placed under his pillow.

He tried coaxing her back with offers of food and privileges: midwife a particular foal and it might be her own; riding in his company so she might stop off in some meadow or wood and collect whatever it was she required for her art; clearing out a stall to be made into a proper bedroom, or fresh bedclothes and more appropriate bedding. To all this she resolutely refused not by shaking her head or gesturing with her hands in some fashion, but by ignoring the subject. When the weather changed, when it thickened into rain and wind and finally into snow, he ordered furs and rugs taken to her in the stable, only to find them the next morning, still wrapped and folded, at his door. The food, however, she took without comment; at least that never reappeared, to his knowledge.

It occurred to Sir Robert, with increasing frequency, as reports from the war with the Gongols turned progressively more morbid, that the girl might have ulterior motives in refusing him. The Queen was gradually warming to his position on the war, particularly as her own Service and Payne's, Beechum's and Glencord's divisions lost men before they could be replaced. If the Queen had known—or if she had been forced to know—Sir Robert's entreaties toward the outcast, her ears would not have been so attuned to Sir Robert's appeals. Perhaps she was only working to ensure the return of her young man through Sir Robert's efforts, although Sir Robert preferred another possibility: She was protecting him outright, Sir Robert against a sea of enemies, out of recognition for her own unsettled feelings.

❀ ❀ ❀ ❀ ❀

In the cleft of February, when the dead, cold world outside the castle walls tugged and begged to be allowed within, the Queen consented to hold a council on the war, but not at Sir Robert's urging. Sir William had asked for it, now that his contingent was close to depletion. He had been asking Sir Robert for an alliance, but Sir Robert could only send his regrets; he thought it better for his cause should he not agitate, since his position had been clear at the beginning of the conflict. Locking arms with Sir William would only give his enemies what they wanted: proof that Sir Robert was up to something, a scheme that they could distort with their trickery.

Sir Robert refused an alliance with Sir William for one other reason: The man's past behavior. He had dallied and delayed when the Queen had asked him for men, and now, Sir Robert could predict, he would be asked to be relieved of his responsibilities, only to dawdle and postpone when it would come time for him to bring them home. Sir William may have turned against this adventure, but only when his military and domestic stores could be replenished would he act; he'd try to practice all his options at once, if he could. Sir Robert, then, prepared himself for any number of scenarios. He might offer to help Sir William, if Sir William would sign a blood oath to help him.

And if Sir Matthew was to challenge him—and he would, if not at the council, then in some other forum—Sir Robert would be well equipped. The dagger Sir Matthew had used against him remained in his possession, and the knowledge of what Jenny could do for him—for she never refused any request having to do with the safety and health of his person—remained in his head. To end this war single-handedly, to be loved by the present and future generations, to have his station forcibly accepted by those who would rather spit in his direction: Sir Robert was certainly not beyond harboring such **ambitions,** ❀ but he also knew, from Berwin's training, that to go as far as admitting as much to only himself would be one straw too many added to all his burdens. He shook his head and squeezed shut his eyes as if he could physically dispatch such thoughts. Yet they remained, behind his eyes, and over his shoulders, as he addressed the council that February morning.

✺ Many were the rationales for loving Slayer, and his **accomplishments** were among the best of them. He was the publisher and editor of his own news magazine, and he single-handedly started his own yearbook, to compete with the official Hollywood High School *Poinsettia*. We talked about starting our own publication as we exposed the dark truths of our campus for the *H.H.S. News*. He also had two jobs, as an assistant manager of one movie theater on Hollywood Boulevard and a doorman/usher at another, across the street. But he never had any money. Some of it might have gone to his mother, and the rest went toward gasoline and the maintenance of his frequently disabled fleet of Volvos.

Slayer and his pals loved Volvos. I don't know how this obsession began but it was nurtured through L.A.'s car culture and the Craigslist of its day, *The Los Angeles Recycler*. We traveled well beyond the boundaries of Los Angeles County in search of discontinued 122 automatics, 122 manuals and 122 wagons. One model continually evaded his grasp: the 1800. The 1800 was the low-slung and sexy sports edition and they came in coupes and station wagons (the station wagon had an all-glass hatchback). Their tail ends and lights looked like something out of *Close Encounters of the Third Kind*, which was playing perpetually at one of the movie theaters that employed him. We undertook other expeditions as well, to Disneyland, Dodger Stadium (which was verboten territory, owing to my father's perennial protest against how the City of Los Angeles handled the eminent domain proceedings thirty years earlier in Chavez Ravine); the once-famous Ice House nightclub, the Los Angeles Press Club—venues all that had been previously out of my reach—but always with the hope that we might spot an 1800 or some other irregular automobile ripe for re-selling.

Oh, I forgot to mention that Slayer played the flute in the marching band, and took a college-level journalism class at IHC for extra credit. He was a regular Sammy Glick, going,

going, going, every single moment, so that I wound up hanging out with his friends more than I ever did with him. My chief ambition was not to marry Slayer, but to get him to take me to the senior prom. The fate of the world depended on it.

"It is fine for you to suggest retreat, Sir Robert, given what little you have contributed to this cause," Sir Thomas of Glencord responded. "This war might have been over months ago, if not for your misplaced sense of honor."

"If you're referring to **my father's invention**," ❀ Sir Robert said, "and my refusal to have it on the battlefield, I will accept that insult."

"Perhaps you might honor us, good sir, explaining why you prevent us from using it," Sir Matthew called out.

"I would be delighted," Sir Robert said.

❀ **What did my father do** in high school? This is, in fact, a relevant question. My father had his own share of dastardly activities, mostly surrounding sports, for which his asthma and physique left him woefully ill equipped. His primary ambition in high school was to play football, but his father wouldn't allow it, until he reached 100 pounds, a veritably impossible feat for someone so sickly and adverse to the idea of eating. So he was relegated to the school newspaper, where he wrote about his beloved sport; and the track team, where he ran his way to blue ribbons, an All City ranking, a varsity letter, and other awards.

My father still managed to find a few pick-up games of football, however, in the park and on the streets of his neighborhood. At the park, once, he played so hard that he came home with a black-and-blue arm, Grandma Eva recalled for us, which wouldn't have been too alarming except that it wouldn't stop swelling. It turned out that he had broken a key blood vessel, but he lived to tell the tale. He also admitted to my mother once that he and his friends liked to play barefoot on the asphalt. This admission only came after he tried to re-create his glory days at a friend's New Year's Day party, as an adult, and he limped back home with the bottoms of his feet resembling a bout of smallpox.

When he was a track star, he told all kinds of little white lies to his parents so that he could travel to far-off lands for track meets. He went to the desert, Riverside, and San Diego, and told more little white lies about his credentials to get into the meets. All this trouble might be attributed to the little communist cell his parents sent him to in elementary school to round out his education. It was called the Arbiter Ring, or Worker's Circle, a Yiddish-Socialist curriculum for the children of immigrants. It also was a place to keep them safe, I guess, when they weren't in the cheder, or Hebrew school.

Being in the Arbiter Ring led my father to join the Grand Order of the Aleph Zadik Aleph, a Jewish fraternity, in high school. Anti-Semitism on his campus was vague but rampant, he said, and he and his best friend, Jack, tried to reorganize the student government elections. Jack was a refugee from Chicago with a plan to create a Chicago-style patronage system. Whatever the intricacies of their scheme were, they apparently flopped, and "Rosie" Rosenberg and his friend Jack and the other boys (one of whom wound up in jail during college, for stealing from the pawn shop where he worked) were reduced to playing the roles of dissidents. He finally did get to play football, though, in his senior year; he broke the 100-pound mark and made the C team, which is just one step down from junior varsity.

My father had a job or two as well in high school, working for his father's produce business, or as a bagger in a grocery store. Money wasn't the issue it had been for the family during the Depression, since they were beginning to benefit from the boom times. Yet still he worked and even held a third, more freelance type of job: doing the homework of other students. It was so much rewarding, apparently, than doing his own.

The rest of the council was sitting behind a table on throne-like chairs, although none reached the grandeur of the Queen's, who was sitting in the middle. Sir Robert, however, was standing before this group now submerged in winter shadow. He was there, in all honesty, to support Sir William's request, and make a case for abandoning the conflict, but he felt as though he were accused of some special deviousness, and without the benefit of being able to see his interlocutors, having to defend himself.

"That machine is an evil that would unfairly tip the balance," Sir Robert said. "All your honor, your devotion to fairness in all things, peacetime and in battle, would be shattered should you use it against the Gongols."

"You are denying your own countrymen a golden advantage," Beechum interposed.

"All I am denying is your romantic notions of conquest, " Sir Robert said, "and possibly the opportunity to kill more of our own conscripts." Sir Robert saw that he had the eyes of the Queen at that moment: they snapped and switched with his pacing around the room with an acuity that galvanized him.

"There has never been a clear purpose stated for this campaign, other than killing those we perceive to be our enemy, although I'm not quite sure if they have ever outright attacked us. Neither has there been a clear statement of goals in this campaign. There has only been innuendo and superstition."

"Superstition?" Beechum said. Another small man, Sir Robert had always thought, and seeing him leap out of his chair, in too-dramatic fashion, only confirmed Sir Robert's analysis. He was a miniaturized version of a man, all the proportions of his limbs and face somehow crunched. "You are likening this cause to a mental condition?"

"I am," Sir Robert challenged him.

"The safety of Your Highness' lands, her people, your own charges: a figment of the imagination?"

"The threat from the Gongols has always been imaginary," Sir Robert said.

"Only because you are afraid to think of them, to consider the consequences," Beechum accused. A small man with a small voice, Sir Robert thought; not even throwing his chest out could accomplish the effect he desired, so he began beating against the table, his fists with no more power than a child's. "Your cowardice, your selfishness, your unwillingness to aid and comfort those who have protected you, those who are unafraid to accept the price: these are not imaginary. These are the circumstances you have forced upon us. We have had to sacrifice that much more, open our eyes that much more, because you—"

"Because I can see clearly that which you wish to obscure and hide," Sir Robert said. "The land of the Gongols, the land that we now bleed over, is hopelessly fallow. Before we incurred on their lands, they had no interest in ours. None whatsoever. This is a campaign created to enrich those at the cost of the peasantry. They are the ones paying this price you speak of; they are the only ones, as you till their lands and extract every penny you can from them, so you can send them to this war, and profit from the favor of their wives."

"Your Majesty!" Beechum objected. "Your Highness!" Sir Thomas cried. "Again, with this slander!" Sir Matthew objected. "This creature should be silenced."

The Queen remained seated. Sir William might as well have been chained to his chair at the head of the table, for he had requested this council, and now he was terrified. No amount of candlelight seemed capable of lighting up the chamber, and with all the spitting and speeches a number of candles had been extinguished, enriching the night inside.

"War is always profitable to someone," the Queen said delicately. She must have been aware of the need to lance the silence even as the still quiet enhanced her authority. "Otherwise there would not be war, for it is always far too expensive for the other parties." Sir Robert hoped to find, in the postures of his opponents, recognition of the Queen's words, but a musty wind from the sleeting cold outside must have entered the room, and with it, the bend of his opponents' necks and shoulders were concealed. "Might I have my Chancellor of the Exchequer investigate this question: whose coffers have been most enriched?" she asked her counselors.

"All of you, obviously, have already checked mine," Sir Robert said.

For a response to the Queen's request, to Sir Robert's challenge, the council immediately said nothing. Instead they listened to the winds outside the council, it seemed to Sir Robert. Those winds would wrap the castle in a paralyzing chill that could strand them and their parties there for too long a while. If they could not come to an agreement on their situation they would be forced to live together, with it bubbling and boiling in every salutation, every supposed nicety.

"It is a fine thing for you to suggest, Sir Robert, given that you have contributed so little to the cause," Sir Thomas of Glencord finally spoke up. "We who have invested so much more than our resources, but of that brand of capital which you are so much less generous with."

"Your critique of Sir Robert's character has already been submitted, Sir Thomas," the Queen stopped him. "As for investigating the revenue collected off the backs of our countrymen, we shall set that aside for a moment, so we might get to the matter at hand. Sir William? You asked to convene this council, and we have yet to hear your opinion."

Slowly Sir William stood from his chair, as if he had aged just in watching the proceedings. Only the Queen and Sir Robert could have known the nature of his request, yet the others milled about distracted, as if daring him to state it.

"I am with Sir Robert," Sir William acknowledged. He quickly amended: "Not in all he says, but certainly in the outcome he desires."

"This is treachery. Appeasement!" Sir Matthew cried.

"Of the Gongols? Or of Sir Robert?" the Queen asked, the amusement noticeable in her speaking.

"Your Majesty," Sir Matthew said, rising from his chair. He slipped out in front of the table and unnecessarily bowed before the Queen. He was trying to be as grand as possible, in his puny frame and stunted voice. "If Sir Robert is permitted to succeed with his plan, if he and his cabal are to pull off this coup, he will only do so again for his own aims," Sir Matthew continued, and Sir Robert decided in that instant to just let him continue; let him drone and whine until his words melted into some hideous tone to which no one could listen. "Sir William," Sir Matthew addressed Sir Robert's co-conspirator, "you will be disposed of as soon as it is necessary and not kept for a moment longer; he will seek out other coalitions of convenience and then dissolve those just as swiftly for the next partnership of expediency. He will—"

"That is quite enough, Matthew," the Queen interrupted, and she nodded to Sir William, so he might recommence from where he had been halted.

"I speak only for myself, good sirs, when I ask for, if anything, a pause—not a cease fire, not a formal treaty, no bowing to some sort of understanding with these creatures—but just a pause—not a retreat—a pause in the fighting. To regroup, to sort out what we have done and how far we have to go—for a fight like this, a quest, no less, is never over. No. But we must pause, reassess."

He was pale when he was finished; all of his blood, Sir Robert was convinced, had run to his lips, to power his words. Into the seat at the table's head he plopped himself down, exhausted, for his final word.

"Sir William's losses have been, no doubt, the heaviest," the Queen informed her men of one fact Sir William was likely loathe to expose himself. "If no less than the Queen can vouch for him and his motives, then what say all of you?"

"I have no doubt as to Sir William's aims," Sir Matthew said, "only—"

"And your own aims are perfectly clear," the Queen sternly informed him.

"Your Grace," Sir Robert interrupted, and braced for the lie he was about to tell. "Please, I myself am not so sure of them."

The Queen nodded, perhaps out of indulgence, although to Sir Robert she looked weary; she had always found mediation distasteful, she had told him on more than one occasion, an unnecessary duty if a society was truly civilized, and therefore a reminder of how much more civilizing there was left for her to accomplish.

"This Lord of Berwinshire is not satisfied with his weapons, his land and livestock, with these mortal gains," Sir Matthew said, and he began to pace, as if he were careful to avoid Sir Robert in his path. "He has consorted with witches—"

"One witch," Sir Robert corrected him.

"Witches, I'm certain," Sir Matthew bellowed. "And outcasts."

"One outcast," Sir Robert quickly amended. "The outcast is the self-same person as the witch, you did not mention."

"One outcast, one witch: is it not enough!" Sir Matthew railed. "Into the bosom of this very castle! We—"

"We appreciate your vigilance," the Queen replied, but her response was two-pronged. In her voice, Sir Robert heard sympathy for his position, but in her eyes, he saw anger curdling, begging to be announced. "It will not go unnoticed. But I know of this particular case, and while it is not without its hazards, it can be explained. You have not heard of Sir Robert's accident, after this last council?"

"I have, Your Grace," Sir Matthew relented, and his voice shrunk, as if he were ashamed.

"In this case, this witch, as you call her, became a necessary evil, or would you prefer that Sir Robert not have recovered?" the Queen asked him.

"Of course not, Your Grace. But if he is finished with this abominable—"

"And I have no doubt that he is," the Queen said. "She does this—they all try, these outcasts, stealing their way into other people's situations. Now, out of your concern—" the Queen set the fire of her eyes on Sir Robert, the blaze of her concentration—"we will all do our best to ensure that Sir Robert's injuries and associations do not rise to the notice of this council again."

❀ ❀ ❀ ❀ ❀

The Queen did not have a habit of arriving unannounced, except, perhaps, when it came to calling on Sir Robert's quarters, for that was quickly becoming Sir Robert's regular experience. As he was settling in for the evening, he heard a knock and then a raft of air escape from his room; the Queen revealed herself in a robe securing her bedclothes, her hair loose and copious.

"Congratulations," she said to him, offering her hand. As he bowed before her, Sir Robert felt as though he were rescuing her hand in his own, lest that it should fall to the ground and shatter. He kissed her fingers, so fine but with a peculiar type of strength: resilience.

"You have accomplished your life's mission," she said to him.

"I wasn't aware I had one," Sir Robert said.

"Few men are," the Queen said. "That is why chivalry was invented. Now rise, Sir Robert," she ordered, and all at once all the playfulness of her voice was discarded. "Rise and tell me just how else you intend to write yourself into the pages of this nation."

"Your Grace," Sir Robert said as he complied with her first command, "I plead innocence as to taking your meaning."

"You might wish to save that girl—the outcast—with your interference in her situation," she charged.

"I might," Sir Robert admitted, "but not without your permission. She saved my life, Your Majesty."

"She saved the life to which you have been accustomed," she said. "Had she not taken her measures, you would have lived, although not as well. There would have had to been... adjustments."

Sir Robert had no retort to this. He could have anticipated her displeasure, even her outrage, at his continued interest in the girl, and that he was prepared for. Arguments could be made, arrangements for his decamping to his own estate, whisking the girl away from him: these were not alternatives he favored, but they rested in his mind, should they be necessary. But that the Queen should deprive him of his health, even his continued service to her: this he could not countenance. He might as well have been untended the day of his accident, or the dagger would have been more attuned to its target.

"Even I have had to make adjustments," the Queen said, but she must have known she was still being obscure, Sir Robert thought; he saw it in the furtiveness in her eyes as they searched about his quarters. She might have been looking for evidence of the girl, but he had taken care to eliminate any; there was no fruit on his table, no vials on either the nightstand or by his washbasin. The partition he had used to separate his bed from the one he had constructed for her remained, but the bed had long since been disassembled.

"Do you assume it a gentle task, a simple one, to reject what is essentially one of my own brood and breed?" she asked. "It is as if I am in err, in my soul if not in my body, by carrying out the sentence against this girl. As if I am undeserving of my own good fortune."

Sir Robert lowered his head, for what he was about to say could only be called impolitic.

"Then why not lift this burden from yourself, and from her, Your Highness? Why continue this disgrace against you both?"

"Because," she said softly. "It is the way of this world, a world of men and women and mortals."

"She could change that," Sir Robert said, his head still bowed, his voice, he hoped, kept in a tentative tone. "She could make one invincible, with her knowledge."

The Queen suddenly stepped back from him, as if to announce that all familiarity between them on this matter was closing. "I hope you realize the danger in what you propose," she said, her voice no longer slight and hesitant, but full, firm, and authoritative.

"Is there danger, Your Grace, in alleviating illness and suffering?" he asked carefully. "For this grace, this gift, she must be shunned and starved out of good company? For the very soul of her that God created?"

"God did not create this creature," the Queen said, in a blush that must have begun at her heart. It clambered up her breast, wrapped around her neck as though it might choke her, and then explored the rest of her face, stopping where her crown normally would have rested. "I can assure you of that," she declared, and even her hair seemed to darken.

"And should any one in my realm become invincible with her help, what might just be the result? All that strutting and squabbling, all that cock-walk and dancing I was forced to sit through this morning. That: that is the danger, Sir Robert, and I dare you to imagine it. A surfeit of men and their risks and their challenges, with nothing to keep them in check. I am certain, Sir Robert, you and your kind would put it all to the good, this invincibility, but what of your enemies and their offspring made invincible? The unnecessary dynasties born when no lord, no king can be naturally disposed of?"

"Your Majesty," Sir Robert said, and he bowed again, if only to give them both a moment to pause, for surely the threat the Queen perceived was nothing more than panic.

"Your Majesty," the Queen answered back haughtily, and she whipped herself away from Sir Robert, toward the table where some of the girl's arts were once practiced. "There is no majesty in mortality, in fallibility, in any human quality, by comparison."

"Maggers," Sir Robert tried. "You know there is no such comparison." He was speaking to her back now, and from where he stood, its shoulders and carriage appeared to be shaking. "Nor would anyone dare it. She is just a girl, without heritage, without even words—"

"Why does she not restore that facility to herself, with all of her powers and knowledge?" the Queen asked.

"Because even the smallest conspiracy must be spoken, " Sir Robert acknowledged, but only because he wanted to signal to the Queen that he understood where she was leading him. Yet Sir Robert had seen the grief and torment that overwhelmed the girl's face and neck, whenever she was forced to acknowledge her deformity. If her silence was just a ruse, as the Queen suspected, it was one with a horrendous capacity to dominate and devour her.

"So we understand each other," the Queen said, and she turned around to face him again, her pale complexion and superiority seemingly restored. "Whatever the level of your sponsorship, it must end. Now and forever."

"Yes, Your Highness," Sir Robert said, and he kissed her hand again, so that she might not completely see **his expression**. ❀

❀ Oh, the **terrible things** I was doing outside the sphere of my parents' influence, especially since Slayer was usually busy with some prior commitment. Slayer left me in the care of his two best friends, one the son of Chinese immigrants (and the brother of a semi-celebrated Beverly Hills police detective); the other a Jewish boy who was a couple of years ahead of us. This Jewish kid, Steven, enrolled at my father's other alma mater, Los Angeles City College, after high school. Steven wanted to be an actor, and sometimes he'd take me to a park where he'd recite lines from *A Midsummer Night's Dream* because he had the role of Puck in a school production. Other times he'd take me to his house, where we'd watch old movies on television with his father, a retired Real Estate agent.

Those times when I would actually get to see Slayer, meanwhile, were not much more breathtaking. For as he related to me the history of his sexual experiences, I began to realize that for him I was only a substitute, and a rather inadequate one. For alas, his heart truly belonged to another. She was far away by this time, taking classes and smoking cigarettes at a very glamorous junior college. She had her own car and made her own commute, having left the school bus and all of the other indignities of high school behind her for fools like us, so much younger.

When I remember the facts of her appearance—high cheekbones; long, straight hair; small, brown eyes—my own face comes back to me. But that may be because all teenage girls, especially white ones, basically look the same, their faces rash with hormones and ideals. To return to the facts, she was of the same thin build as I and was also a dancer, (we were even in the high school's Dance Production/P.E. class together for one semester), with aspirations to be a writer. But she was taller, smarter, prettier, sexier, and just about every other "er" that had been invented, compared to me. Plus, she communed with a much cooler crowd of Miss Pamela (Des Barres nee Miller) facsimiles—groupies, yes, some of whom had a real Laurel Canyon pedigree.

I believe Slayer and I eventually spent the majority of our relationship comparing me to her, without much success on my part, although he did take me to his senior prom, probably because she couldn't stand to be seen at such a puerile gathering. I considered this a real victory, akin to finally pushing that rock up the steep hill of relationship bliss, but a few months later everything changed. That first, best, and unforgettable girl consented without hesitation to his taking her to the Rolling Stones concert in a rare Volvo 1800 convertible he obtained just for the occasion. I was not invited. And perhaps a month after that, at a party he had escorted me to, Slayer reconnected with a blonde he had known from elsewhere and began, in a very demonstrative fashion, his next serious relationship. I watched even though again I was not invited to join in, and still, it was not over—but that's a footnote for some other fantasy.

chapter seven

Samuel had never bothered to count how many times he had entered the palace compound through its adorned main gate. Nor could he account how often he had marched through similar, but smaller fortresses on his way home that spring. Yet when he finally arrived, after a fortnight of drudgery, he felt as though he were seeing, smelling and tasting his home for the first time. Never had it felt **so brilliant**: ❀ from the crystalline water they marched over, atop the drawbridge, to the banners that had been unfurled from all the windows. If there were clouds in the sky, Samuel could not register them, for the canopy overhead rippled and twirled with silver, gold and green cloth, depictions of the coats of arms of the lords that had aided the Queen's Service. The names of Glencord, Beechum, and Gaines, people shouted, as they threw flowers at their men in congratulations. People Samuel could never have known foisted gifts upon him and his compatriots: cups of mead, jars of honey and preserves, kisses on the cheek, and mouth—Samuel gainfully avoided those. All around him it was raining elation, in songs and the vivid scents of yellow, white, pink and red roses.

❀ I did not make it to the **Renaissance Pleasure Faire** until it had been up and running for fifteen years, and how I finally gained admission to this Shangri-La for the senses wasn't exactly genuine. I was a "turkey," or, in a more polite way of saying it, a tourist, a paying customer who without paying had no access to the fun and games. And pay I did, for myself and probably for my escorts and the tank of gas it took to get us there. For I had friends now, friends with automobiles, and I was going to make use of them. Slayer was of course busy, but his mother and Steven, while financially bereft, were usually up for low-cost adventures involving traveling and free sightseeing. So storm the gates of the Faire we did, and a whole new empire was revealed—to me, at least—for co-optation or conquering, depending on how you feel about my chameleon-like ambitions. Whatever the Faire was by the time of my arrival—the old-timers complained each year that it wasn't quite what it used to be—it was J.R.R. Tolkien's Shire reconstructed, in real time and in live action. It was a fantasy burnished over so many times that it did not shine. It blinded. And what you saw is what you wanted to see, your own erroneous imaginings, if not from *The Lord of the Rings* than from fairy tales, Errol Flynn movies, and public television.

My first impression of the place was the dust—it was everywhere, on everything, and its favored resting place was at the back of the throat and in the crest of the nostrils. Yet this soothing yellow haze made me think of being in an apiary, and I felt the serenity that comes with being consumed by work you love. This was a dust that seduced, as if a drug, and as I walked the trails and paths of the fairgrounds for the first time, I felt high, transported, with the potential to transform from the "turkey" that I was.

It must have been a very prosperous era in both English history and Southern California when I first visited the Faire, despite stagflation and unemployment and all the other ailments that beset the national mood. Attendance at the Faire was so high that you did not so much walk through the fairgrounds as you were carried, by the over-capacity crowds that poured through the dust. They bought themselves costumes—handmade boots, bodices of velvet and suede—and weaponry—swords, daggers, shields, and heavy silver jewelry of a disturbingly Teutonic slant. And the food, the glorious food—heaps of meat in bread or driven through stakes, and giant turkey legs; ice cream on waffles and ice cream in cones and cakes.

I don't know what awed me the most, exactly, but once I saw through the dust, the merchandise and the scents, I was swept up in the Faire's shifting matte of colors. Close to the entrance, was a giant windmill of purple, green, blue, and yellow cloth panels. Those portraying nobles wore the rare, unadulterated hues: deep reds, gloaming golds, and pure pearl whites. The wardrobe for peasants was restricted to the duller tones, although among the vests and bodices and trousers and tights, there were plenty of intensely fused anachronisms— blues, greens, purples and pinks.

What I also took home with me that day was that it contained a vivid supply of men, more than willing and readily flirtatious. There were kids, teenagers, college students, dropouts and more mature specimens. Some played the lute, some sang madrigals, and all bowed and scraped to their female partners in the folk dances staged for the turkeys. Others owned the businesses they ran in the form of games and concessions, and many were there in hopes of obtaining some theatrical experience. All of them were fantastically attractive, and if not in substance, then in style, they bore a cool resemblance to the Ian Anderson of that era. What a fey, elfin creature Anderson was, a real Elizabethan boogeyman, and after that visit to the Faire, I dreamed that some day I would get a model just like him.

In the middle of this company strode the Good Queen Marion herself; she was carried in her throne by a detachment of the Service Guard. The previous night, she and the Guard had ridden out to join Samuel's regiment, so she might parade in with them this morning. Perhaps, Samuel mused, she might lead the people into thinking she had been fighting side-by-side with her men all this time. It was not the kind of thought Samuel would ever have allowed himself before. Now, however, the conclusion registered naturally, just as his feet rose and fell according to the time kept by others. What was harder for him to master, what he could not will himself to ignore, were any signs of his family in the crowd, and any sign of her. He was not afraid he would no longer recognize his mother or father, although the possibility entertained itself where the twins were concerned; they would have grown so much, he knew, but could they have grown out of love with their brother? Someone offered him a tankard. He threw its contents down his throat, savoring the cold and its honeyed bitterness; then he bit off a swirl of pastry someone else had set before him.

"Samuel," he heard, but he could not answer. It was his father, Thomas; behind him stood his mother and the two girls. He had to keep marching, the push from his companions behind him too insistent, but as he turned his head he saw they were marching with their families too. He reached forward for the twins, but they skittered away from him; he realized how different he must have appeared, like some beast that had slipped behind their brother's eyes, and into his clothes.

"Father. Mother. Darlings, darlings," he said, and he dove for the girls. They squealed and he scooped them up, in either arm, balancing them against his bow and arrows, his belt and his shields. Of course they were heavier than he expected, but he could not drop them. Lucy's nose burrowed into his neck; Grace fluffed about his hair. "Oh darlings," he breathed into Grace's ear. "Darlings," into Lucy's. They smelled so fresh, and he was a matte of mud, sweat, and rankness. "I did not forget how beautiful you are," he told them.

It was no longer a regiment, or a proper parade, but a mob that spilled through the streets; Thomas had his hands on Samuel's shoulders, as if to steer him through it. His arm he gave to her mother, whose eyes were brave, but blurred by tears. Lucy and Grace jumped off him once he could no longer move. It was not their combined weight, but their bulk, pressed against the other soldiers and their loved ones, that made continuing so difficult. Samuel was as tired as he had ever experienced, but with his family surrounding him, he felt as though he, like the Queen, was being carried.

Grace jumped around, to touch more of the beard he had acquired. Lucy quickly followed. Their fingers smeared and poked until he was laughing.

"You look a fright," his mother said, "a horrible, strapping fright," to which Samuel could only nod. "She'll fix you up," Thomas said. "At least they didn't starve you."

"No," Samuel said. "That they couldn't afford." His father had taken charge of the presents he was collecting: a bag of apples, loaves of bread, **a pint of cream and strawberries**. ❀ No one soldier could possibly haul it all. "Samuel, Samuel," Grace and Lucy sang. They picked up stalks and petals that had fallen to the ground before they might be trampled, and tried placing them in Samuel's beard. His father was talking to him, although Samuel could not place what he was saying; his mother was clinging to him so fiercely, he could not raise an arm to accept any more food. The girls were skipping, dancing about him as though he were a maypole. Now he never wanted this march to end.

❀ I've spent a good deal of my life having a **stomach ache**, owing to some condition which over the years has been has been mistakenly diagnosed as an ulcer, colitis, and spastic colon/irritable bowel syndrome. More likely is that I have a simple case of lactose intolerance. ("Blacks, Jews, and Asians," my doctor told me. "Don't take it personally.") Twice my pediatrician put me on a "bland diet," but I did not follow it, as it did not allow for a level of junk food intake to which I had become accustomed. So I just suffered.

I especially suffered when I was dancing, because man, was I hungry! I'd take a class, have my lunch, take another class or attend a rehearsal, and I would need lunch again. And the dance studio was located where a fast food eatery, a liquor store, a bakery, a grocery market, and a selection of and mom-and-pop drug and soda establishments intersected. Some might have likened it to a mall's food court, but it was more: a harmonic convergence of all the major food groups: fat, pizza, alcohol, M & M's and chocolate.

The fast food place indulged us dancers quite a bit, naming a burger for one of the girls. Much chili—it may not have been real chili, but grease from the grill jazzed up with other restaurant waste products—was heaped onto their concoctions. The lard from the French fries popped and fizzed in my mouth. The bakery was a famous for its cheesecakes, which were kept so close to frozen they were like ice cream. And they kept better than ice cream, of course, so you could nibble on them between bar exercises, rehearsals, and technique classes.

Of course I would end up very sorry for all this eventually. At the Faire, I discovered so much more to be sorry for. I still don't know exactly what is in a churro, other than the confectioner's sugar that covers its deep-fried skin, but those things dazzled my mouth when I ate them, and I ate a lot of them, a horror to me now. At Steak on a Stake, the cooks marinated the meat in some sweet concoction, and barbecued it over a pit with a hellish firepower. Then they either speared it with a stick or stuffed it into a French bun and sprinkled sesame seeds all over it. Toad in the Hole was all about roast beef sandwiches, and they were fine, but they did not compare with the cheese sandwiches I imbibed—the best ever, despite their consequences. They were made of two rather plain pieces of whole wheat bread and a ball of cheese, pimentos, mushroom and onions, then fried in a baroque-looking metal device, the George Foreman grill of the Renaissance, in a pound of butter per sandwich. Oh, the ecstasy and the agony—and if you knew anything about the privies (the Elizabethan term for porta-potty) at the Faire, you'd understand that much more personally. And then it was onto the waffles, the berries in whipped cream, the old-fashioned sarsaparilla...

It would have to, though, all the soldiers understood, as they wound toward the Market, where the route narrowed before it emptied out into the royal stables. Samuel and his detachment were placed behind the Queen's Guard, which meant they stopped short of entering the Market outright as the Queen halted the procession for her moment. He did not hear Queen Marion's speech and did not care to; her voice could not forge through the love and commotion he told himself he would never let go of. His mother kissed him on the forehead and his father took up the girls in his arms. They would be waiting for him at home, Thomas promised.

Now it was the soldiers who hollered; they spit out great spouts of mead, wine, and water. They sang and embraced, marching arm in arm with one another. They spread out into a single file as the road narrowed and dipped beyond the stable, before **a tunnel**. ❀ On the other side of that tunnel were the Guard offices and Service quarters for those men who were recruited from other lordships. On the side of the tunnel just before them, she was there, standing with her hands behind her back.

❀ **My portal** to the Faire was a girl who is now known as Sa Winfield, a ceramicist and most recently a seamstress to certain rock 'n' roll stars. In the old Hollywood High days, she was one funky chick, wearing her Faire costume to school. The rest of her wardrobe was every bit as eclectic; her Chuck Taylor sneakers in particular, which were always in unexpected colors. She was also a dancer and horsewoman and therefore known to me in that small gyre of horse and dancer chicks at Bancroft Junior High, but she was a grade behind me, so we were never friendly. At the time I forced myself into her web in high school, she was learning to play the harp. Her parents were old Hollywood hands: her father, John, a journeyman actor who turned to photography, and her mother, Jan, a descendant of San Francisco's civil engineering aristocracy. Sa's grandfather was one of the original builders of the Golden Gate Bridge and he was responsible for other civic accomplishments, most notably the fountain at the intersection of Santa Monica and Wilshire boulevards. Jan came to Los Angeles to study photography at UCLA, where there was no photography to study, but she stayed nevertheless, and my life has been so much the richer for it.

Sa's family included an older sister and her dog named Psyche; and a revolving cast of characters, mostly friends of her parents who as actors and carpenters and fortune tellers either worked on the various extensions to their home or lived in them. This was a kind of acceptably bohemian life as far as my parents were concerned, possibly because it took place outside the canyon, or because of Jan's worthy ancestry, or possibly because Sa's father worked for a living. Like a dog he worked, and he ran marathons and flew airplanes and was considered one of the city's premiere photographers of fine art. My mother remarked once that Sa's house reminded her of the play, *You Can't Take It With You*, and when I told this to Jan, she disagreed, saying it was more representative of the yet-to-be-written sequel, *Don't Leave it Here*. Over the years Sa would work for my father selling Christmas trees, and I would work for hers, developing film; and the exchange between the two families would include hand-sewn clothes and Christmas trees, joy and tears.

My sister had become friendly with Sa before I did because they attended The Alternative School together, a school-within-a-school program on our vast campus. But in my last semester of high school, when my father was convinced I could do no further damage to my academic record, I was allowed to enroll there, and I surrounded this girl, so that I might work at a dunking booth she was going to run at the Faire. Previously she had worked at the Faire's archery booth, with a few other kids from our school and some from the Millikan Junior High-Grant High School axis. I don't know whether it was my relentlessness or my enthusiasm that convinced her to hire me, but once I was in with her, I was in for good. After school we took dance lessons together. Sa had a thing for a boy who had a thing for Winchell's, a chain of doughnut shops, and sometimes we'd go to one of them, to be with him in spirit. Sometimes, of course, we would go nowhere, and sit on the mattress on the floor that was Sa's bed and listen to music—the harpist Alan Stivell and a couple of Jethro Tull albums because "they sounded like the Faire;" Queen (a favorite of the Winchell's doughnut guy); Yes; and *The Rocky Horror Picture Show*, both stage and screen versions. Sa was famous for her portrayal of Columbia during the weekly midnight showings of the film at the Fox Venice Theater, birthplace of the *Rocky Horror Revue* in particular and the movie cult in general.

She also showed me a Polaroid snapshot from her first year of the Faire, with a young, compact, blond kid with aviator glasses in the middle of a motley group. It was my first glimpse of Sam.

He wanted to run to her, to throw his arms around her shoulders, carry her away in his embrace, but he knew that even to say her name at that moment was too much of a risk. Just to say her name, so that she alone could hear it; but she lifted her finger to her lips, and with her other hand secured the book in his belt. Samuel reached inside his shirt to retrieve the volume he had made for her, and then handed it to her as she walked alongside of him. She was smaller, thinner, as though she had been pressed, shrunk; as though she were suffering the deprivations that were expected of him, the soldier. Her eyes were duller, from what he could discern, as she hid her face behind her hair in a way he was not accustomed to negotiating.

His face moist with drink, his beard a nest of crumbs and flower petals, his hair standing straight up—it must have been—with how the girls had been playing with it. He wanted to laugh at himself, to show her that he had changed too, and not necessarily for the better. But she slipped away as they entered the tunnel. He had only the book, which he now took from his belt so it would not fall, and clasped it with both hands. It was the only confirmation he had that he had actually seen her, and not summoned up an apparition out of his hopes.

❀ ❀ ❀ ❀ ❀

Once Samuel set his weapons and sack aside, his mother commanded him into the tub. Then she had the twins haul in buckets from the fire. His clothes filled with the warm water, and his mother denied him permission to strip them off; they were as thick with dust and grime as his skin, and she intended to slough it all off in one grand motion. Lucy and Grace splashed in his face and snickered at his soaked appearance. They said he looked like a hermit, or a silly, old, and **very dirty wizard** ❃ and he tried to laugh with them, but his strength lost out to his exhaustion.

❃ As I said before, a key ingredient in the Faire's appeal was its ability to animate the **daydreams** J.R.R. Tolkien's books inspired. Once I began working there, a year after my first visit, I discovered the cult of the Tolkien novels was stronger at the Faire than it was in my own high school, which was no slouch in the fantasy-science fiction-Dungeons and Dragons department.

I had read *The Hobbit* after ninth grade at the recommendation of an older guy, the local playground director on whom I had a mad crush one summer. He promised the book would take me away from my stultifying home life and help me understand all that Led Zeppelin I professed to love. To help me along, he wrote on my Wallabee shoes, "Jane alias Arwen," and "Arwen plus Aragorn." He also wrote, "How poor are they that have not patience," for many reasons; chief among them being I was fourteen and he was twenty-three. Every time he looked at me he must have seen (aside from my stunning good looks) my father with an Uzi (which was invented by an Israeli, don't you know; why else would my father make it his weapon of choice?).

I liked *The Hobbit* well enough and had a friend who was more familiar with the entire Tolkien oeuvre read the Arwen and Aragorn parts of *The Lord of the Rings* sequels and appendices. I tried reading the sequels myself, but when I got to the scene where the hobbits jaunt through a forest that begins to close in on them, I threw the book as far away from my person as I could. It wasn't a matter of patience: it was the suspense. I couldn't take it, and I did not open those books again until after my freshman year of college.

So it was not the Tolkienesque atmosphere of the Faire that

intrigued me so much as that atmosphere's vague connection to Led Zeppelin, which dominated not only the broadcast airwaves of my favored radio station but the air directly outside bedroom windows and car stereos in my vaunted Laurel Canyon.

Consider the figure of The Hermit we were supposed to be discussing here, and how legions of similarly wizened characters intermingled with the peasants and nobles at the Faire. The Hermit is one of the Major Arcana cards in the Crowley-designed, Rider-Waite Tarot deck, and is reproduced in full on the inside of one of Led Zeppelin's albums. I don't know which album it was—they never gave their albums names—but I used to stare at it, perplexed, for hours. At the Faire, I didn't have to stare at all. I could live in that mystery.

For at the Faire, beyond the stages and artisans, the food booths, armor and peasant fashion, there was the Witch's Wood, where you could have your fortune told or buy enigmatic scents and powders. A good deal of jewelry was sold there, of seemingly pagan origin: ivory carved into moons, and stars, and even other planets, upon request; agate, tiger's eye, quartz and turquoise set in rings, bracelets, and necklaces. You could outfit yourself as a belly-dancing gypsy, a concubine, or a Satanist with the frocks and pantaloons on sale; or you could turn yourself into a fairy, something not quite of this world, because the sight and scent of you would become all too fleeting, so blithe; too fragile to live among creatures as graceless as your fellow humans.

The message here, however, should not be misinterpreted. The Faire may have offered an opportunity for re-invention, of course, but there's something more important. Tolkien was inspired by an interest in Christian theology and ancient languages, and the dream of creating a language of his own. I was inspired by the raw, sexual power of Robert Plant, and the more cryptic appeal of Jimmy Page, to be the kind of girl I believe they might have wanted.

His mother had him peel off his shirt and then she scrubbed the dirt from his back. As for his hair, there was so much more of it than either he or his mother had ever experienced. It dripped in his face and fell over his mouth and his mother threatened to cut it, to which Samuel declared, "Never!" He was so overrun with grass and burrs that the water seemed to turn to mud for an instant; the twins had to resume their rounds with the buckets and warm water. When at last his mother was satisfied that he no longer appeared so bewitched and abused, she left him to strip the last of his clothes alone. His mother planned to burn them, which Samuel pleaded against, although he did so out of principle. If they had not been from the Queen's issue, he would have gladly assented to his mother's request.

Samuel was instructed to summon the girls, if he so desired, for more water. A fresh shirt and trousers were laid out for him on his parents' bed, and a drink and plate of bread and fruit were set on the nightstand.

There were so many questions to ask, about how the twins had grown, how business had fared in his absence, which horses were due to be shod in the coming weeks, which had been put out to pasture; and then there was Jenny's book to be savored. He had secured it into his sack before he had been ordered into tub, and as he now removed it to open its cover, he handled it as if it were parched skin under siege from a bandage. The pages were embossed at the beginning, with pictures: ink and pencil sketches of a meadow, a sunrise or a sunset; it was not possible, in the tones provided, to know which event was being depicted. The layout of the stables was also set down in those pages, and then portraits of various horses, left anonymous. Some special attention was paid to the hooves and shoes of mounts; from what Samuel could read of the drawings without proper shading and proportion, there was something wrong with these mounts. Founder had set in, or shoes were not changed soon enough.

He skipped over some pages, and some more, and then he found floating between a raft of blank pages, a message, without a title:

In the consequences of echoes I was conceived
and my voice effaced; a process not as simple

as violence, but for that I would have been so
much more gracious. For that I would curtsy and
bend and even celebrate: if the air as we know it
would chisel my skin with an understanding of
slate: the metamorphoses of the soil's discards
switched with grains; the water that we dream of
would split my bones so the blood would run
white. Instead I must balance, I must burn, I dodge
the songs and calls that in the glossy fields chafe;
the somatic differences between plants and animals,
the necks that flare and pump in mating sessions
versus the stems of weeds and daisies. They wait
for the descent of wings, the trespass of hands
and adhesive legs, just as I do, crowned in my
dignity, patience, and shame.

Samuel blinked. The penmanship was not the most polite, but these
were most definitely words, a form, and imaginings; it was language that had
never before been spoken, a voice that surged through his limbs and organs.
He swallowed, as if to preserve the sensation, stuff it back into his body before
it could escape. He swallowed again and shut his eyes, and turned the page,
to find this:

I too often think of salt
as my only way of speaking,
speaking through the eyes
of others who must register
my message, on the trail
of my cheeks and nose
as if they were the pollens
of dandelions; deposits
for an unseen, unpromising
spring: Should I slip this parcel
into your palms, knowing sweat
devours everything.

Samuel set the book down gently, as if realizing only now how frail were these pages, how he might destroy them should he become careless. He was afraid of the book, and yet he was **thrilled** ❀ by it. His forehead, his ears, his nose: all of him went numb with a peculiar recognition: that no part of him was necessary, except for the part that spoke. In his chest, his throat, his mouth, the blood felt as if it had been alighted: these were the facets that had bore him that illness when he was younger, and these were the facets that Jenny had worked to heal and preserve. His hands and arms, his eyes, his legs and feet—any part of him that enabled him to forge, to shovel, to work, to march, set an arrow to a bow—were, in comparison, worthless.

❀ When I started working at the Faire, I was alternately scared and **thrilled** by everything: the job I had at a dunking booth, the acting I was to do in an Elizabethan accent, spending the night on the wild and woolly fairgrounds, and most of all, the people I would be doing all this with. They weren't just teenagers like myself, but older adults, who had taken a few detours I never before imagined, before growing up.

A good share of these folks were real burned-out cases from the 1960s: former and active addicts and activists, along with a sprinkling of stereotypically disturbed Vietnam veterans—or at least men who paraded their life story as one following that narrative. There were also some serious carneys on what was then a kind of Faire circuit, selling their wares, their talents, their skills and their brawn to set up and take down the festivals as the year wound down to Christmas. In 1979 this circuit consisted of the spring Faire in Agoura; the Rainbow Gathering, in a spot always determined at the last minute; the summer Faire in Northern California; the Pumpkin Festival in the fall; and the grand finale, the Dickens Christmas Fair, in the Cow Palace in San Francisco.

It seemed to me, so well equipped for life with my straightened teeth, straightened nose and my college preparatory curriculum, that some of these people must have never had parents. I'm talking about the kind of parents who would take them to a dentist, or a dermatologist, for that matter. Their bodies were host to grotesque combinations of oral diseases and tattoo ink poisonings, or other consequences of hard living. At the stable we had a phrase: "ridden hard and put away wet." It was meant to apply to that old-fashioned notion of a working girl who worked a little too hard, if you take my meaning. At the Faire, it could also apply to men. And why didn't they have careers—not just jobs, but meaningful 9-to-5 obligations? Some of them might have, as welders and carpenters, but they did not show it, and their occupations were all those with a status not immediately apparent. They lived free of life agendas or generational obligations beyond fulfilling their sensual needs, like looking for the next buzz.

If you think that I, the casual user of a gateway drug, was judging them, I was. They didn't seem to judge me, though, and they offered whatever I wanted. And despite all the mores and ambition my parents had drilled into me, all of the good grammar and mainstream culture, I could just as easily see my way to living as they did, on a long, slow path to deformity and delirium. Some of them had kids, too, stringy-hair waifs and urchins well into joining what my parents and grandparents derided as the great army of the unwashed. I tried to accept everyone as my equals as Americans in education and refinement, but in order to do so, I realized, I just had to keep my mouth shut.

When he re-opened the book, he did so gingerly, as if equipped with only his fingertips, and not the tendons, muscle, and major appendage attached to them. With each touch of his fingers, his skin seemed to burn at the page:

> In all my futures I am faceless
> yet not silent, my voice an
> unguent of honey-white; between

your ribs it balms before it rises
and ignites; my hands pressed
clean of soldering metal and branding
iron; my skin like the flesh supporting
pear coverlets, with green spring
inextricably woven into the bark;
my eyes, should I ever find them,
poured into yours, the source of
all my air, and all my might.

He wanted to speak, acknowledge what was racing through his body, what pushed up inside his chest and goaded the heart to squeeze and the lungs to pump faster, and faster, but there was more silence around him than he had ever experienced. He wanted to be heard. He wanted to call her name and have her answer back with his: it was possible. It was possible now. If not the next time they met, then surely in the dreams they would send to each other.

"I must see her," he said as his father woke him.

"I know," Thomas said. "But not yet."

✿ ✿ ✿ ✿ ✿

The dining room table was outfitted in all his favorite indulgences: pheasant and pork, and balls of fish that had been rolled in flour; and tiny red tomatoes that fell on his tongue sweetly and with a spark. The apples were tangy and the cheeses were smooth and soft, and for dessert the twins—as they had rushed to inform him—had made a shapeless tart of lemon that slapped up against the sides of his teeth with its sugar.

As he chewed and gulped, his mother watched in some amazement, and remarked that she had never seen her son so hungry before; Thomas congratulated Samuel on a job well done. When he thought he was sated, Samuel finally noticed that the twins' hands no longer needed his guidance with the eating utensils, and they seemed to drink their buttermilk faster than their mother could pour it. Samuel was handed his customary cup of

Jenny's recipe, but he could not bring himself to drink it. Instead he gripped the warmed mug tightly, as though someone might try to extract it; and he watched its steam rise gracefully, if not mournfully, long without an obvious source or inspiration.

The house smelled of bread, lilies and cattails that the twins had arranged as a centerpiece in a vase: they hung on him with their embraces and kisses, once the meal was finished, and they sang him songs in both his ears and made him promise never to leave again. He was surprised by how natural it all seemed, to be back with his family, in a cool, clean house where the fire chased away the dampness. His time in the Queen's Service had been overrun with moisture: his clothes soggy, his food furrowed through with mold, his joints stiff with a weight he could never rid himself of, but only learn to balance. The fires of his father's shop, his mother's hearth, of all the homes in the village, slaked away whatever moisture threatened in the air; scents were sharper, more vibrant, and Samuel was hungry all over again. His mother fried dough and pears in butter and cinnamon, and his father brought out wine that had ripened into pomegranate brilliance.

After they had plied him with drink and delicacies, the stories of the twins' growing up, the Bible passages they had mastered, the songs and letters they had learned, Samuel felt his lips and eyes growing heavy and awkward with the wine. He could not speak, and there was so much he wanted to ply from his parents. But there were ghosts in Thomas' face, and his mother scurried the girls off to their beds. Before Samuel could regain his wits, Thomas announced, "You have business outside."

"Do I?" Samuel asked.

"Indeed," Thomas said, and he lifted his son out of the chair at the head of the table and guided him out the door. The night was immediately darker than he had known in the past year, bereft as it was of lanterns, night fires, and steeping tobacco and pipes. Home had turned dangerous in his absence, as if he had fulfilled one responsibility only to shirk another. His unmet obligations taunted him now, in the form of grass, weeds and branches, and unfamiliar dips in the ground.

"Work? Now?" Samuel asked, because despite the blankness pressing against him, he had the distinct feeling they were headed in the direction of the shop. "But Father, " he tried, as Thomas' hands pulled his shoulders this way and that. It was as if Thomas' hands were backed up against Samuel's mouth and throat.

He heard the sound of gravel beneath his boots, and he felt the heat that still pumped forth from the shop's equipment, even when it was at rest. The irons, the anvil, the cauldron: the presence of these objects that he had missed so dearly slowly made itself known to him, but still he could not see it. Only by his other senses was the workshop comprehensible.

"Good evening, Samuel Bright," Samuel heard, and out from under a hooded cloak came a lantern, and a face. Sir Robert Drake stood against the shop's back wall, beneath where the hammers and tongs were hung. The lantern left him in a red haze.

"I keep my promises," Sir Robert said as the lantern gave shape to the body beneath his cloak. "Now you must give me your word on this." He raised a finger to his lips, then lifted his arm so that his cloak turned into a kind of curtain. When a figure stepped out from behind, **Samuel fell to his knees**. ❀

❀ **Sam was short**. Real short. As in possibly a hairline shorter than I was, and I would not spring up to my pinnacle—5 foot 3 1/2 inches—until I graduated from college, four years in the future. I did not have an inventory of physical characteristics for my potential boyfriends to possess, but everyone—men, women, sometimes even the children I baby sat—was taller than I was. When I met Sam, it was abundantly clear that I might quite possibly have something over him, and I had never had anything over anybody. Not that I yearned to lord my height or any other of my qualities over anyone. But at least now I would have the chance of taking on an equal.

I met Sam at a pre-Faire party at Sa's house; actually, it was in her sister's small cottage, which was attached to the main house but still afforded an adult sense of privacy. We started the evening with Sa's best friend at the time practicing her skill of hypnotizing boys—literally—so they might fall in love with the proper girl and swear an everlasting obsession with and to her.

None of us was into alcohol all that much and we didn't have any drugs.

Sam's celebrity had long preceded him, in the form of stories I heard through a growing cadre of mutual acquaintances beyond Sa. He was a Faire veteran, having started out at the archery booth four years earlier and then graduating to an actor, which upped his prestige in Faire society to no end. His persona, or Faire character, was a member of Clan Colin, the Scotch-Irish contingent, the Hell's Angels of the shire.

According to the lore of the age, the Celts had made a cold peace with Elizabeth I, but continued on with their raucous and war-like ways. Their stage shows included a good deal of boasting as to their riotous powers and battle calls. Their headquarters, which really was nothing more than a gathering a hay bales and a burlap covering, displayed their weapons: buck knives, shields, swords and pikes. Whatever the Celts did during their time off from the Faire was mostly likely decent, their hobbies including nothing less than the rehabilitation of moribund languages (Gaelic and Elvish).

I don't believe I was not planning to meet the boy who would change my life that evening, but I certainly prepared for it. I had already re-jiggered my interests—my musical and movie tastes. I also ripped off my sister's groovy wardrobe; she was skirting around the edges of the punk rock scene engulfing the Sunset Strip at that time, and no longer needed her Indian-made peasant blouses and painter's pants.

Sam, by way of introducing himself, said the loops on the painter's pants, meant for holding hammers and other equipment, were devices for capturing "cute girls." He grabbed onto one and mock-dragged me across the carpet.

Ooh la la.

She ran her fingers across his forehead, as she had done when he had recovered from his illness, as she always did, greeting him by remembering

to herself his face in fever, and how she had rescued him from it. Her hands must have found the beard he had started, and possibly how he had aged without her. But how she had interpreted him now, he could not say. He could not see her, not the way he wanted, from her brow to her smile. But he could feel, through his breathing and her own, how much smaller she had become. She was also kneeling.

"Jenny," he breathed upon her lips, but she raised a finger there to quiet him. He put his forehead to hers as if he might read her thoughts in the dark, just as how she must have written those words. She smelled of hay, of leather and white, sweet roots. She was made from all the things he loved, and his heart begged his chest to be released, where she could see it plain, aching as it was, but joyful. He hugged her as deeply as he could, to dive into her scent, but his arms and hands found bones where he should have felt flesh. He could only hug her even more tightly, as if to shield her from the hardships that had made her so thin.

"Jenny, Jenny," he whispered. "I must say it." He was aware of Sir Robert, off to the side, of his own father, standing somewhere behind him. They swayed like animals in a barn, and paced ever closer. "You have spoken to me, and I must answer. I must marry you, Jenny, I must."

She answered by clasping his hands in hers, and kissing them. His knuckles were led up to her eyes, and from there to trace the graceful curve of her cheeks, down to her chin. When she returned his hands to him, they smelled tart, of salt and her strength. His knuckles, his hands, were wet.

"I will come for you," Samuel promised, and as he rose, he lifted her to her feet.

"Samuel." Thomas had clasped a hand around Samuel's shoulder. Jenny had turned her head as well, presumably toward where Sir Robert had been standing. Sir Robert spoke: "We must be off, lest we be discovered."

"But here?" Samuel heard himself pleading.

"Our absence," Sir Robert said, "would be all too telling." Jenny slipped behind the curtain Sir Robert's cloak made, before Samuel could bow to her as he wished. Before he could thank Sir Robert properly, the pair disappeared.

❀ ❀ ❀ ❀ ❀

Sir Robert, Jenny, the promises exchanged, the feel of tears and skin: it was over as soon as it had begun. Samuel wondered if it had been real. The ghosts still in Thomas' face told him it had been. He tried not to see them through the dark as they walked back to the house, but they glowered at Samuel's happiness. Still Samuel said nothing, as if the sound of his own voice would shatter the dream of what had just transpired.

Inside the house, Thomas sat down at the table where they had celebrated. The light that had so animated his father's face upon Samuel's homecoming had been that quickly smothered. "Samuel Bright," Thomas intoned, as he had when Samuel was a young boy, and had committed some offense requiring a dour punishment. Now he was waiting for his father's blessing on his engagement, and yet he did not want to ask for it.

"Your father is so proud of you, " Thomas said, "and yet, he is so frightened."

"But I have come back well enough," Samuel said lightly. "In one piece, more or less," Samuel added, to encourage a laugh out of Thomas. He found no success. Thomas' eyes were set on his hands, knotted up as if in prayer—as if in despair, and begging for succor.

"Father—"

"Samuel," Thomas would not even let him begin. "There is too much you don't know, about what has passed in your absence. And it is best if I do not tell you."

"But if it concerns Jenny—"

"It is best, Samuel, if you can plead ignorance." Thomas' face held onto its dire cast, but he rose from the table. And in his height, he seemed to have recovered a portion of the courage Samuel had for so long counted on.

"Now in a few days' time, you will go to the Queen, and formally ask for Jenny's hand," Thomas declared.

"But why is that necessary, if she is—"

"An orphan," Thomas corrected him, before he could voice it. "As such she is a property of Her Majesty. But in a few days' time, Samuel, so as not to raise suspicions."

His father's voice had returned to him, enforcing the last word on the issue. But its re-emergence told Samuel—he dreaded what it meant—that in the time they had walked to and from the shop, his father had aged. Samuel considered what he had always considered impossible, that the courage and forbearance Samuel had always loved and admired in his father had left Thomas. Or perhaps, Samuel dared to think, his father had surrendered those qualities long before these past moments, in the year Samuel was away at war. It was only now, back in their home, in the silence that seemed to be struggling between them, that Samuel recognized this fact.

chapter eight

A daughter **learning** ❀ the Lord's
transferred words is merely
censoring the throat's shadows.
The tarn of her thoughts is
bottomless yet mirrored,
a tunnel to what is material
in bone, her ancestors.
Yet if the girl is summarily
orphaned, as if in the stage
of an insect, those shadows
will distend into a cloak
of independence, and the winding
of rhymes and psalms will be
foreclosed, the nests of blankets
and inheritance will be unsowed;
and no one will share the diligent
practice of secrets. This is how
sound and meaning fail to breach
the soul of a chrysalis.

❀ Before each run of the Faire opened to the public, the Faire
managers held **a month of workshops** for participants so they

could brush up on their street theater, costuming, folk dancing and use of BFA—Basic Faire Dialect. Everyone except for the noblest of the nobles, I suppose, was to use this BFA, and it was taught by a rather robust and demonstrative woman who also portrayed Queen Elizabeth I that particular Faire season. This was the one workshop I attended, and I was intimidated by the differences between "you," "thee" and "thou;" the requirement that all public utterances should trip so perfectly off the tongue; that everyone around me could quite spontaneously quote Shakespeare and Marlowe—the ladder being someone I had never heard of.

So I resolved to never, ever, leave the booth where I'd be working. I would not be engaging in street theater or folk dancing or any type of conversation. The busking I would have to do from the top of the booth—singing "Dueling Buckets" at the top of my lungs, or reciting our advertising slogan, "I take a bath once a year, whether I need it or not"—was quite enough of a challenge, thank you very much. Though I was as far from shy as a person could be, and the overhaul of my personality did not include affecting a case of timidity, I was going to have to be demure and deferential. I was in way, way over my head, and it must have been obvious.

Once the Faire began, and I took my place on the balcony of the Dueling Buckets dunking game, I had to learn to use my upper body: my job consisted of lowering a bucket into a burlap-covered vat of water, filling it up, and then throwing that water into a gutter, or directly onto the customers playing the game. When Slayer tried to teach me how to use a stick shift (an exercise in futility), he had said, "You can do this, you're a dancer, you can use your arms and legs at the same time." But of course I wasn't that kind of dancer, an accomplished one, and while my legs were in pretty good shape, my arms were a little short of atrophied and useless. The only way I could lift those buckets was to plant my legs into the floor of the booth as if they were pegs, and then hoist. It worked well enough, so I didn't worry about any consequences to the rest of my body.

In the days that followed, Samuel began his mornings with one of the writings Jenny had left him. He did not entirely understand them, just as he could not quite fall into the routines of his father's workshop: loading the fire, pounding, and molding. In the afternoons he sat with the twins, and made excuses to go to the Market. He found reason whether there were errands to run, or not; whether flour or sugar or a bail of string was needed; whether there was a chance of encountering Sir Robert there, or Jenny herself. But those last two possibilities had long since been foreclosed, and Samuel knew this; that Thomas and Sir Robert, and perhaps Jenny herself, had arranged it this way, so that when he asked the Queen for permission to marry, there could be no possibility of an incident that would upset Her Majesty.

> The world should have silenced
> my eyes, rather than the equipment
> it has; if I should not see, if I should
> not feel, the nape of daisies as if they
> were the birth of new alphabets, or
> the curtain of nightfall, a massage
> of darkness; or the calluses that grow
> in tandem on my palms and soles,
> crenalated like mint but not soothing,
> as if containing a message from
> somewhere deeper than my knowledge.
> Had I been denied these attributes, rather
> than the grace of vibration, like awakening
> to the withdrawal of winter's caul,
> then I would have nothing to speak of,
> I promise, rather than this well: its
> breach and rise and slop of intentions,
> a fool's conceit that prods at my dumbness,
> for I am a fool: to believe that a swell

could compete with any true sound.
A bell or ice setting a fractured branch,
glass hobbling in its frame and cell:
through stretch and polish the wind
crafts these vowels. The consonants
come later, with the cruelty of whispers
and spring thaws.

Samuel wondered how Jenny came to such ideas; or how such ideas were born and so deeply felt. Reading Jenny's words, he was not gladdened by her silence, but he was willing to consider the possibility silence had birthed these pictures, their arrangements; if this was what was said within the mind that could not speak for itself. He continued to search for Jenny, in a crowd at the Market, during a glance at the stable courtyard, in the corners of the shop in the morning, when darkness made its last gathering before the true dawn. Every swatch of black hair held the possibility of Jenny attached to it; and in the conversations he heard, in stalls and on the streets, he hoped to catch if not words about her, then one of those silences. He tried not to ask the twins if they had any of the same observations, for they had taken to a particular form of commentary whenever he spoke to them. Giggling. Samuel, meanwhile, was too mucked up in his daydreams for their laughter to register.

Within the political mimicry
of fingers and wings,
in the pleats and ruffles
where earth is drawn to air:
birds dwell as if buttons,
suiting the equation together.
The waist of the world hovers
through us, and when we speak
our words are delivered through
feathers. And if one bird should
fail in its stitching, its bonds
and threads refuse to adhere,

must it also lose its song and
ranking, its neck now agile for
no purpose, and its silence a
punishment, a solidified dare?
I am not unaware of decisions,
declarations, scolds and a
sublimated sense of anger;
In mute conversation I have
indulged in all of them; they
have nested and fed and flown
through the whole of my
symmetry, just as a tuneless
bird breathes without notes
to share. Yet the calculations
of nature prove immeasurably
cruel; what is not cultivated
rips as if overused fabric,
knots and basting unravels
as if fastened without much
care. Still in the proportions
meant to call or signal, this bird
and I regret our separation;
our sentences not so much to be
served as to be borne in the
rise of moments: in all of the
spring or on holy days, when
the difference between song
and language is much too clear.

Samuel was waiting. For his throat to swell, his chest to squeeze down
upon itself; for his legs to turn heavy as with filled with dust. When he relived
his last meeting with Jenny, when he read and re-read her words, those were
the sensations that came upon him. He was paralyzed, as he was when he fell
ill. But when he was ill, she was always with him. As she would be, when they

were married. Samuel was waiting for his life to begin, and it felt as though he were dying.

> From whence does the sound return
> once it exits the teeth and tongue:
> into the blazes, the furnace of cudgels,
> or into the divine finality the ocean cools,
> which we race in the ships of adventure
> stories? Does it store itself where the first
> die were thrown? Do I lose my intentions,
> my breath, my origins in stilled minutes,
> by denying them names and expressions
> In public? Words in the air, not in correspondence
> stretched across the bands of the planet,
> but in speeches, dialogues, the betterment
> for contracts and disagreements. They dissolve
> as if minerals when the rain comes down
> in gimlets, tenderizing the mountain top,
> and winter reveals its lesions. Meaning
> slipstreaming, it deposits not in roots or
> in any celestial rotation. When my father died,
> I was not silent, and yet the sound carried
> off beyond all records, and comprehension.

❀ ❀ ❀ ❀ ❀

The Queen was beautiful, although not in the way he now understood Jenny to be, of course. Jenny was beautiful—in thought, in language, in appearance— all beyond his experience. The Queen, dressed in the spoils of her Service's conquests, was a catalogue of magnificence. Her breasts, neck, and face were powdered, her cheeks inflamed with what had to have been the debris of roses. Each one of her features was clear, individual, and distinguished, as if an artist had painted on her delicate nose, her sharp mouth, and knowing eyes, and her hair was severely reddened.

Samuel had seen the Queen before, but only from a distance. Naturally, there was no comparing the splendor of the Queen to any of her subjects. But compared to Jenny, Samuel could not help but think, the Queen was a slightly coarser specimen. It was this thought he held onto as the commander of his regiment, in his court regalia, introduced Samuel to her.

"Samuel Bright," the commander said as Queen Marion entered the great room where Her Majesty held her audiences. Samuel could see himself in the wax and polish of the floor as he lowered himself to one knee and drew his eyes away from Her Majesty's face. The ceiling was high, as if in a church, mimicking the rise and arch of the Heavens. He had registered in his vision the single piece of furniture in the room, Her Majesty's throne of gold and red velvet. The distance between himself and that throne was so thick, Samuel thought he could not simply walk through it. It would require an exercise that called on all the limbs and digits, a maneuver more like swimming.

The Queen's ring appeared before his eyes, and Samuel kissed it. The length of her hand appeared next, and he kissed that also. "I know your father, " she said. Queen Marion spoke as though addressing a council, not a lone, meek soldier seeking to begin his life after war: "Your Service has done such honor to him," the Queen went on. "And to me, and your country as well."

"Thank you, Your Grace," Samuel said, looking up for the moment. Then again, he averted his eyes.

The Queen directed the commander to leave them alone for the moment. "Rise, Samuel Bright," he heard the Queen direct him, and he climbed to his full height. The scent of her hand, a strange flowery coverlet, remained on his mouth and nostrils. "I believe you are seeking **permission** ❧ to marry," Queen Marion said to him, directly.

❧ **Permission** to work at the Faire was easy to get, and it was not. My parents quite surprisingly said yes. Their marriage, unbeknownst to all of us at the time, was in its death spiral, and my mother's pleas to my father to allow me to attend probably wound up being one more hinge in the coffin of that relationship. I had to get one other signature, however, that was not so easily got.

Of all the many reasons why the Living History Centre undertook production of the Faire each year—educational, artistic, self-enrichment—granting teenagers access to the most bodacious orgy of their young lifetimes was not one of them. Yet that was one of the primary attractions of working there. Some actors received stipends or passed the hat; others were sometimes compensated only with free admission and meals. Booth workers, like myself, worked for nothing but the thrill of it, and the chance to "sleep" overnight on the Faire site. No doubt Faire administrators were mindful of the possibilities a lewd crew of hippies and hangers-on offered to adolescents at the peak of their soul-searching. So said administrators demanded each participant under the age of consent have an on-site sponsor, a grown-up to watch over them.

If you were a grown-up and were asked to be responsible for a seventeen-year-old girl feverishly starved for food, shelter, and acceptance, what would you do? I fretted and I was rejected by a few grown-ups who had already taken on more teenagers than they could handle. I eventually persuaded a magician, who was happily sponsoring several other girls my age, to take me on. Once he had signed my documents and I got my night pass, I rarely saw him.

Yet Friday nights or early Saturday mornings, when I would depart from my home for the Faire, remained a nail-biter of an experience. There were no televisions, telephones, newspapers, or modern plumbing on the fairgrounds, and I had no intention of introducing my father to the magician, who favored silk purple shirts, moustache wax, and pantaloons even for his day job. During the week my father stewed in his rage over these circumstances, his anger stoked by my renewed interest in dance. Thanks to Sa, I was back at the ballet studio two days a week, and added a class in modern dance that she was taking. So much jumping and flipping at a time when my focus should be on academics. But that wasn't the half of it.

My father had barely kept his sanity during my first experiment in dating (my grandfather referred to Slayer and his family as *Tobacco Road*, owing to their depressed economic circumstances; it was an assessment my father heartily agreed with, and what did I know about *Tobacco Road*, other than Will Geer, formerly of the Old Left and then currently of *The Waltons*?). With my leap into the Faire, my father faced a new blight, living with a budding Anglophile.

You must understand that for my father, it is always the eleventh hour of November 29, 1947, and Clem Atlee's government is spewing and scheming to hold onto its precious mandate and prevent the United Nations' partition of Palestine. For thirty-some years my father had been boycotting all things British (except for the British writers he revered since he had bought all that stuff years ago. His complete collection of the works of George Bernard Shaw also was particular dear, but Shaw was Irish; and when Wendy Hiller or Alistair Sim or Alec Guiness showed up on television in some old movie, they were most graciously welcomed, since their appearance was free and no currency on his part need be exchanged). To have the likes of Monty Python and hobbits and elves quoted within his fortress of Ben Shahn and Chagall was more than he could take.

My Faire friends—two Jewish boys, by the way: Sam and his best friend, Adam—would telephone and he'd scowl, "Some guy with a biblical name called," and then he'd pad back to the bedroom, to conjure the ghost of Edward R. Murrow on his black and white television. By the time the weekend rolled around, he was a cauldron of diminished expectations, and I never quite knew if he was going to release me into the bosom of the Golden Age of England. Under no condition was he going to drive me there himself, and I practically swallowed my fingers until a friend, usually the owner of the dunking booth, strapped me into the passenger's seat of her car and we took off.

The Faire ran for six weekends between April and June,

and during one of first weekends I was there, a letter of acceptance from a college arrived. It was not from UCLA. My father panicked. He called the admissions office and lo and behold, there on its roster of the anointed, was my name, and the letter of confirmation, which could be photocopied and framed without violation of the UCLA trademark, would be sent out shortly. I had distinguished myself as a citizen and a scholar in my community (or so the actual letter of acceptance said, when it finally arrived and my father helped me thumb-tack it to my bedroom wall), and for the first time that I could remember, my father was actually proud of me. I pretty much had no problem doing anything, or going anywhere, after that achievement—for the time being.

"Yes, Your Grace," Samuel said, and he wished, then, he was still on one knee to address her. Despite his summation of her appearance just seconds earlier, he now felt it was the only appropriate position from which to engage such a woman.

"I am flattered that you would do so," the Queen said. "But you know that it is not wholly necessary."

"Yes, Your Grace," Samuel responded quickly, and he nodded as if the gesture could replace another supplication. "But my intended, she is—" He hesitated, then switched his glance to his feet. It was a conscious action. He did not want to gloss over anything so plainly in front of her. "She is an orphan," Samuel pronounced.

"I see," the Queen said, but she maintained the neutrality of her posture, and position. "Is this orphan known to me?"

"Yes, Your Grace," Samuel said, but he could go no further with his answer.

"Is she known by a Christian name?" the Queen prodded.

"Yes, Your Grace." Samuel swallowed; he blinked to see his feet in his boots; his boots mere seconds away from slipping out from under him.

"Just tell me her name, dear," the Queen urged him on, gently, and yet she seemed so merry.

"She lives in the stable." Samuel spoke as slowly as he could manage, as if the gaps between his words would give him time to gauge the level of risk, as it built. "Her Christian name," he said, "is Jenny."

The Queen turned abruptly toward her throne, but she moved no closer to it. She was as rooted in her position as Samuel was in his own. "Samuel Bright," the Queen said with her back still to his face. "You know that is impossible."

"It is impossible for me to live without her," Samuel tried.

"I am sure you believe that," the Queen said, and she began to walk, to march away from Samuel. Her voice rose with more force as the separation she created grew firmer and firmer. "But it is belief, merely, and can be overturned."

"She saved my life, when I was very ill," Samuel said. He tried to make his voice follow her. "She saves my life everyday, now, with her kindnesses, and her words."

The Queen neither spoke nor acknowledged Samuel with a glance until she reached her throne, and when she did, her appearance was that of a haunted being: her face was ablaze in fury and offense, but she was petrified into a stillness.

"That girl has no words. No voice. She is as dumb as any animal."

"No, Your Grace," Samuel said, and he thought of producing the book of Jenny's words, as proof of her spirit and intelligence. "Though she does have her own way of speaking."

"Impossible," the Queen declared from her perch.

"No, Your Grace," Samuel said as slowly as he could. "She knows her letters; we learned them together, and she—"

"If I had known that your father, an honorable subject of Her Majesty's if there ever was one, deigned to teach that creature, I would never have allowed—"

"He did not teach her, Your Grace," Samuel said. "She taught herself. She copied me."

The Queen appeared puzzled, her face a rash of pinks. She shook her head as if to clear it, and declared from her perch: "That girl is an outcast."

"Yes, Your Grace," Samuel acknowledged. His hand was at his heart, where the book lay, inside his shirt. "I shall be one as well."

"Do you not have parents to consider, your sisters?" the Queen asked. She was quickly regaining her agility, the dexterity in her face and argument.

"I could not have come here without my father's blessing." Samuel said.

"Still, it is not up to you, or your father, to make that determination."

"Then allow me to speak with those who do," Samuel was begging. He could not help the desperation in his voice, how it pushed him forward toward the throne, where he wanted to throw himself, upon its steps.

"Your persistence is verging on impertinence, young man," the Queen said.

Samuel considered everything he could pour into that moment, for disrespect was never his intention. But his priorities had changed—while he was away, or perhaps earlier, when he was rescued from death. It was only being away that had made him realize how close he had been, then, to the end. He explained it all in the only way he could:

"I am in love, Your Majesty."

"I will allow that you believe that, too," the Queen said, with an edge of generosity in her voice. It was welcoming, and familiar.

"But only because of what I know you believe love is," she said, and with that caveat, all of that generosity dissipated. "It is not for me to instruct you on such topics. Yet it is for me to protect my subjects, my society, my nation. You are not to see this girl again."

"Your Majesty—" Samuel said, for suddenly there was no other response possible: his mouth was dry, his heart enlarged, now pressing on the borders of his throat, his eyes stinging from the whiteness of the Queen's face, her pearls, and her hands.

"Your Grace, " he again attempted, all his facilities under siege. "I—"

"You have privileges, having served me as well as you have, and you may seek **introductions** ❀ to any number of young women."

❀ Despite Sam's absences, or perhaps because of them, I still saw **plenty of action** at the Faire in a way I had never experienced before. I think I must have hit puberty with the beginning of the Faire season, because suddenly my face and body were engendering an interest heretofore dead in the opposite sex, or at least in serious hibernation.

To the boys my age who worked with me at the dunking booth and elsewhere, I was not particularly attractive; most came armed with their steady girls and were none too interested in anything but them. But to others, mostly older and perhaps more experienced with the vast variety that is acceptably feminine, I wasn't anything to sneeze at. One man, a partner in the archery booth and father of one of my newfound friends, referred to me as the "Jewess with the lovely breasts," and I didn't even know at that point that I possessed breasts. Indeed, my flat chest was particularly pronounced at the Faire, given that I had to wear a bodice. Bodices were meant, at the Faire, at least, to produce some enticing cleavage, but you had to have something to contribute to the process. Yet this man noticed whatever it was I had, and although it was wildly inappropriate, and perhaps unwise for him from a statutory standpoint, I was ecstatic.

I don't wish to give the impression of the Faire as a gathering place for pedophiles, but the atmosphere supported a good number of mashers and letches—not quite as old as my father, but certainly old enough to be my father. A letch, by definition, is overly keen to notice the wiles of a seventeen-year-old girl, but I was overly keen to be noticed. I became an object, possibly blunter than most, and as the weeks went by I felt I no longer had to feign a personality to attract attention. It was enough just to be my age, and particularly my height and weight, and I loved it. I loved every second of it. Once, behind the Main Stage on a particularly hot day, I tried to steal a glass of lemonade from the dispenser that was reserved for actors. An older guy told me I could only have some if I gave him a kiss. And boy, did I give him a kiss. There was one night when I was either out of my mind or determined to prove something to myself, and I did some things in the back of a pickup that to this day are quite unspeakable. But the person I did them with doesn't remember me (I asked him many years later). So let's pretend they didn't happen. Sa also introduced me to another man, whose nose was as prodigious as my own, and he kissed me gently on the nose. I was back every morning at his booth to collect another kiss. In fact, each morning just as the Faire was opening, I made my rounds, to the various booths and encampments where I was sure to be noticed, to collect my kiss on the hand, a hug, or a more passionate reminder of my biological destiny, finally after all these years fulfilled.

"Yes, Your Grace, but I do not wish—"

"If you wish for your family to continue living under my rule; if you wish to continue in my Service, as a soldier, or as a civilian; if you wish a future for your dear sisters; if, young man, you can put aside your petty selfishness," the Queen said, and Samuel knew she was only just beginning. "You will forget this girl, and you will do whatever is necessary to forget her. If I am to hear of any contact between you and this outcast, I will have to punish you, and her—further. Now," the Queen demanded, "you may take your leave of me, young man. " She was forced to summon the commander seconds later, because breathing was the only action Samuel could command of his own.

❀ ❀ ❀ ❀ ❀

In his face and chest, Samuel felt strangely cold and frightened, as if the anticipation and promises that had been circulating there had been **wrenched out** of him. ❀

❀ Swelling was one of Sam's first **symptoms**. He was incredibly strong in my eyes, particularly at the Faire, where he sometimes wore chain mail or other odd pieces of armor in addition to his kilt and boots; he could dance and hoot and feign disobedience and raise a pleasant ruckus with the best of the Celts. But he was beset by the onset of random illnesses—first a swollen tongue, ulcers in his mouth and throat, a fever without its attending irritations. As quickly as the fever abated, he was beset by a sore throat and runny nose: a cold that was akin to a cardiac emergency. His skin blistered and peeled, he confessed, in difficult, private places, which prevented him from indulging in certain activities. His aches and pains were obviously far more serious than my own hypochondria, but their cause was not unspecified. I at least had dancing to blame. Sam's illnesses kept him out of workshops, or had him arriving late on a Faire day, or missing a weekend altogether.

His knees and feet, meanwhile, were invigorated, with a new kind of anger. His first impulse was to find Jenny, and the lower half of his body felt determined to carry him to her, at any cost. He was walking toward the stable, but his breathing stopped him; surely it would be roiling with the Queen's spies—her guards, nobles who perceived themselves as her exclusive champions, the stable rats and scullery girls who would suddenly be inspired to a new loyalty. Samuel next thought of the Market, any random corner, at which he might come across Jenny on an errand, but he just as quickly knew the Market would be teeming with fools and merrymakers and all sorts of similar characters. At his home, the shop, on the land and in the kitchen and bedrooms which he had helped his father to erect, soldiers and members of the Queen's guard who had never thought of visiting a country blacksmith would be lined up, to have their horses attended. Samuel surveyed the world he knew and realized it had collapsed at his feet; every treasured location, now an obstacle.

He resolved immediately to **say nothing** to his family, ❀ to protect them, if nothing else. He also decided against contacting Sir Robert, for any contact or correspondence could be easily traced back to either one of them, and they lacked a code, a clandestine language, by which Samuel could explain this new situation. Samuel was also unsure as to how much trust he could place in Sir Robert. Sir Robert had done nothing to raise his suspicions, but Samuel could not understand how he had allowed Jenny to waste away while Samuel was away, at war; Samuel thought Sir Robert had promised him more.

❄ Sam had yet to sit me down and **confess** the source of his problems, although he came close, once, in a tale he told to impress a bunch of us. We—an assortment of actors, Dueling Bucketeers and other stragglers—were comparing adventures in narcotics abuse one morning after a night of Faire partying. More than experimenting with marijuana and parents' medicine cabinets, children's dentistry provides the gateway to any number of incidents involving anesthesia and harder substances. I of course had nothing to contribute, since I never even suffered a cavity. Sam, however, proved himself the veteran again in terms of pain, suffering, and graphic detail.

I may not do this justice, but here it goes: Sam awoke one morning with a headache. A splitting headache that did, in fact, lead up to the severing of some connections in his body, to ease the excruciation. This headache continued for an untold number of days, so he was taken to the hospital, where he was given a spinal tap, which did the trick up nicely. The puncturing of his lumbar, he said, felt like a swift kick to the solar plexus, although it took place in his ass. He never told us what the spinal tap revealed about his condition and how the headache was specifically relieved, but by the time he was released, he was feeling quite dandy. His story took the day.

Samuel saw that he and Jenny were alone as well as apart. He could live this way, hounded and ostracized, he convinced himself; he would not be giving up his family, but protecting them from a capricious royal edict. He could live this way, but not without the love that had brought him to this point; not without the love that had restored him when his next breath was in doubt. He could live but not with this dissonance of feeling, an imbalance between what now bit and chilled at his chest, and blazed in his gut.

Samuel told himself he was not about to relapse, but he did not want to return home in this condition, so clearly in need of Jenny's comforts. His mother's first reaction might be to immediately send for her, and Thomas would also be alarmed, and together they might draw upon Samuel too much interest. He could not garner such attention. He would have to live differently, now, that he had committed himself to Jenny, against the Queen's wishes. He could not order out from his thoughts just when he had made this pledge, to keep to stealth no matter the consequences; but he knew, without having to explain it to himself, that he was committed to such an existence the moment he left the Queen's presence. What he needed now, then, was Jenny herself; and if he could not have her, he would at least have her knowledge: the roads she took, the passages where she hid, the fields and flowerbeds where she collected her herbs and crafted her medicines. Samuel led his mount in that direction.

He slackened his hold on the reins of the horse once he settled into the saddle; the horse was likely to know more of the way than Samuel did himself. Jenny had taken all of the horses out there, at one time or another, to sooth their hooves with licorice or mint, to graze while she picked flowers, to gallop without the smell of the shop in their nostrils. As a child, and as a younger man, before he left for the Queen's Service, he always thought Jenny smelled strange after her outings: unclean and rustled. But as he considered it now, as he willed those scents to come back to him, to fill his own nose, his face, the coldness that was overtaking his lungs, Samuel thought of how Jenny must have smelled of grass: young and on the verge of something wonderful. There was a cave, as he remembered it, where she hung her plants to dry them out, before they could be crushed and assembled into powders; a cave made from the exposed roots and fallen branches of the oldest of trees, as if it were the skeleton of some beast, the skin long since wasted. It was that corridor in the forest that he sought out now as much as it was his memories of Jenny, what he had before now had always taken for granted.

When he was ill, she did not leave his side, he realized; she slept on the floor, beside his bed, when his mother tended to him, and his father held the scented cloth Jenny had prepared against his forehead. But this could only have been for seconds, shreds of the hours Jenny stood on her feet, either administering a cool draught to his sweating neck, or rubbing an ointment on his chest or below his nose, to guide his breathing. She was everywhere in that room, in his body, if not chasing the illness away from his organs, then battling it with her hands, her touch, her fingers. During the long nights, she kept a candle at his bedside, her hand on his, her other hand on his wrist, her eyes fixed on the rhythm his chest struggled to sort out. When he awoke for moments he thought he had stolen from the sickness, he would see her there, reading from a book, or weeping over his forehead; and still she was always bright in her face, expert in her touch, and once, he was now certain, her lips, her neck, and her tongue were moving.

"Did you speak to God then, Jenny?" he asked out loud, as he and the horse pressed into the woods that were soon knitting themselves about hooves, knees, flanks, and ankles. "Did you speak to Him on my behalf?" He coughed as if he could push out the dread that had been rising in his chest, and knew that he would never find any answers like this, panicked and potentially lost in the trees. But he had to know: he had to know all of it: from the moment of Jenny's birth to those nights in his sick room; from the day she arrived to live with his family to that night in his father's shop, when he pledged his life to her.

Samuel might have let his eyes fallen shut; he might have let the reins slacken, his posture drop. He couldn't say, because he was somewhere between the voluntary twilight of gentle sleep, and the blackness that comes when consciousness is drafted into illness. But then he registered something: a touch, foreign, tugging on his boot, blocking the horse's next steps. It removed his feet from their stirrups, his legs from around the horse's girth, his seat from the saddle.

Samuel was on the ground, his shirt open, but his throat still struggling for air. A familiar pair of hands were upon him, at his lips with a sprig of bitterness, for him to consume; at his chest, their massage begging him to breathe; then at his nose, with a fervent scent that cleared through his head, behind his eyes, and through to his neck.

"Jenny," he said as he awoke, gasping. In her eyes he saw the reflection of whitened branches that embraced them, just as a pair of wings might gather up flightless offspring. "Jenny," he now whispered, as he recognized that he had arrived in her sanctuary. "You knew, didn't you? You knew Her Majesty would reject us."

She did not nod so much as she bent her head in a kind of apology, and embarrassment.

"How, how did you know as much?"

Her eyes, which had fretted away from his, now could find no place to rest, as though they feared finding the answer. Samuel sat up, wanting to take her in his embrace, to shelter her from what she must have known, but could not have told him. The branches immediately above them were most certainly dead, and yet everything around them, around her, felt stunningly promising, alive, as when the air is first kissed by a storm. No one knew where they were; no one could hear or reach them. They were astonishingly alone, and yet anything they did or said had the power to echo beyond the dead branches, the trees and the grasses, into the rest of the universe.

"It does not matter," Samuel said. "There are other Queens, other sources of law, other realms. Without wars, and sickness; without outcasts."

No, Jenny shook her head. She tightened her eyes into a furious, closed grip. No, she shook her head again. She refused to hear it.

"We will find them, Jenny. Please."

No. She insisted. She was standing now, as if to distance herself from Samuel's suggestion, but she had to balance herself between the roots that had forced their way up from the ground. Samuel rose to match her, to explain how his fate too was consigned to the Queen's whims. The branches overhead and the roots, like shoulders of an emerging beast, formed a tunnel around the two of them, as though they existed only within the confines of a heart. The Queen's heart, Samuel imagined it to be: to leave it would be to die, even for Jenny, the outcast, consigned to its darkest, coldest places, far from its core.

She put her hand into his shirt, as though she was about to examine him a second time, but instead she pulled out the book she had given to him only days ago, and turned its pages. When she handed the volume back to him, it was at this poem, the only one with a title.

For my husband

Had I ever met him, I know my soul
would be too heavy for his sparrow
shoulders. I would have to shut
my eyes with an immediacy that
would prevent him from entering
any such gate, pass through their
imperfect motives. I wish to God my
eyes were not so clear, like gasps from
sun as it ditches its children and turns
its back on others' creations. God gave
me these eyes for a reason, I must believe,
and yesterday, in the courtyard, the shadows
of the twins playing at partners and dance
came not from the sun but from the sound
of my own wishing. I wish I could lock
those girls into coats of straw, distribute
them about my hems like protectors, love's
sentinels, against perils deeper than
knowledge. I tried to breathe in the trees
and bushes of my walk, but everything smelled
of the wings your touch travels on. Not my
husband, but the oil and scales upon which
your travels must float; the ginger stretches
of your flesh and stature, warm from the embers,
alive and glorious.

"Sometimes, when I read these," Samuel said, "I feel as though I am looking into your soul."

Jenny nodded, and set her eyes on him; proudly, it seemed to Samuel. Her pupils widened and breathed deeply in their motion, like the heart of a flower exposing itself to the sun. Her eyes did not take pride in herself, he knew, but in him, the man she had saved, the man she was creating. While he watched her eyes, he felt her attempts to put the book back in his shirt. He stopped her, and took a hold of her hands.

"Would you, Jenny, consent to a different kind of ceremony?" Samuel asked. "I will marry you here, in our own way. And we will remain married in this manner, for as long as necessary. Until the Queen relents, or—"

Samuel stopped; Jenny had shut her eyes again. She did not want to consider the possibilities. And yet, with her eyes closed, she nodded once, gravely. She kept her eyes closed until she could smile again, and those eyes were brilliant in that moment, as though they had somehow taken light from an unknown source.

"Now stand then, my Jenny," Samuel commanded, although he was quite sure Jenny understood, as he did, that he had not the slightest idea what he should say or do next. Samuel faced her anew, and realized she was looking up to him; she had suddenly turned small in his arms.

"Since no one has gathered with us," Samuel improvised, "there should be no objections to this union, unless the crickets dare say anything about it."

Jenny nodded in confirmation.

"Jenny has already fulfilled one of the promises of a true marriage," Samuel said, "nursing me back from death, even when my own parents thought I was lost. So I make the same promise to you, to protect you, to never desert you, to never surrender you to the worst circumstances, to accompany you, always.

"And I promise, Jenny, to let no man tear this bond asunder, no God, no religion, no monarch—"

Jenny lifted a finger to Samuel's mouth, and shook her head, forcefully.

"No being, " Samuel corrected himself, "shall tear this bond asunder. I am yours, forever. Now Jenny, what might you promise, that you have not already given me?"

Jenny released his hands, and looked down at the ground. She ran down a quick length of the tunnel and found a stick. With great ceremony, holding it aloft, marching down the imagined aisle as she walked, she presented it to Samuel, and then put it on the ground before him.

And with her hand recommitted in his, she jumped over it, guiding him over with her.

Samuel knew he was too full of joy; he could not contain his laughter.

Jenny tried closing his mouth with her hands, shushing him with her fingers, but he simply lifted her up; she was so small, so light; so generous in all her thoughts, in all her expressions. She only succeeded in making him laugh more. If she could have laughed, she would have, he was certain, for he had never seen such color in her cheeks. Brave it was, and sweetly pink toward her eyes, and on her forehead.

When he could hold her up no longer, she spilled out of his arms, gently, and pulled him down where they had been sitting moments earlier, in a different world. On his forehead, then on his nose, she dispensed neat, almost sisterly kisses. On his mouth, her kisses lost their discreet nature.

She remained as quiet as ever. Even her breathing was muted. It did not thicken, or roughen, or take on any kind of tension. Samuel didn't know what he had expected from her. But his own breathing had always been so tender, so changeable. Now it was coarse, almost vulgar.

He could not stand to look at her face, or perhaps it was he could not stand to have her look at his own. So her hands, her knuckles, tight and drained by the grip they perfected, became the whole of his focus. As he pushed and pulled at her, as they rocked back and forth, her knuckles in his whitened, a white like a long, hot scream. Samuel's hands were going numb. He thought this numbness would travel up his wrists, his elbows, up to his shoulders and he would lose her: he'd let go, she would fall, he would damage—break her.

When he thought he might have to let go, she pulled his hand up to her throat. Her neck, her throat—it was what she showed to him now, as she kept her grasp on his other hand. She was arching her neck, exposing it to him, and she laid his hand there, held it there, and there he could feel the muscles of it. He could never have imagined what an intricate instrument it was, in someone who could not use it. But it seemed to skip beneath his palm, to pulse and bend, and before he could discern its pattern in the push and pull of their hips and hands; before he could get a glimpse of her face as it pitched upwards, away from him; before he could get his next breath, all that was her neck and skin and bone rushed up and out of her mouth. Jenny was moaning. The sound of it was sudden in Samuel's ears. It shot through his head, down his spine, and into **his loins**. ❀

❀ There was no such **explicit sex** in my relationship with Sam. That's the shameful and stupid truth about it, so I hope you will indulge me if I am a bit discursive in explaining the whys and wherefores, and most of all, the hows—how I was frightened, ruined my chances, tortured Sam and myself, the regret and guilt I feel about the ridiculousness I created.

On our first official date, Sam and I landed on the sands of Venice Beach, because the movie we were supposed to see was sold out. It was long past curfew and the disgruntled and homeless wandered around us; we were wrapped in a blanket and I was pretty freaked out. This was the first real date I ever had (Slayer and I were more like "friends with benefits," I have come in my old age to realize); and my previous boy-girl relationship, naturally, had exploded into a fiery abyss of drama and recrimination. I didn't want to lose Sam before I had even started, so when he made his move, I came up with a brilliant excuse to stop him. I said, "I'm frigid," which is not exactly what I meant, although the word had been used to describe me and my responses in the sexual arena once before. To which Sam replied, "Well, we'll just have to drag you back to the car with the ice tongs, then," which he didn't, but still he remained a very polite gentleman.

Although we didn't talk about what we would do, when we'd do it (and how often and where and why), I can remember one incident, when we were sitting on a bale of hay during a Faire day, and Sam took out his wallet. It was packed full of food tickets, pictures, identification, the usual paraphernalia, and the perfect shape of a circle had been embossed into the wallet's insides. Sam removed from the billfold a condom as if to explain the offending brand and said, "Sorry. My dad gave it to me, like two or three years ago." Then he replaced his father's little gift from whence it originated, where it went unmentioned for the rest of our time together.

Like me, Sam was no virgin. He had dated two other girls whom he introduced me to without a problem. (One, who was slightly older, was so good to me. The other relationship was serious but did not end well. The girl was sweet, polite and quite pretty, although Sam did not go on and on about her.) So we both knew what we were doing, theoretically, and yet I was so terrified. I worried, I ran away, I ran back, and on the one night during the Faire we had together—he had made it out for the entire weekend—I passed out before he could try anything.

We lay there together beneath a sky that was brilliant without the effects of urban light pollution. For a minute, maybe two. And I was out, like I'd been mugged. Like I hadn't slept in weeks. I slept like a log. I woke up the next morning stunned at what happened. He just sat there, a look of his amusement on his face, tempered by disappointment.

Maybe I just couldn't take all that fresh air. Maybe I couldn't take a day in real sun. I wish drugs or alcohol had been involved, to explain it away. Because it was the last time we would get a chance like that. Ever.

"Jenny," he gasped, and he re-emphasized his grip on her one hand. With the other he reached up to her eyes, glistering at their edges. She did not smile, or let escape what passed for her as a laugh; she was embarrassed, he thought, and she cocked her head, as if to hide her face in his palm.

"Jenny," Samuel found himself repeating. "Your voice. You have promised me your voice."

She nodded into his palm, and her face went from damp to flooding, her tears warm and viscous on his fingertips. "Jenny," he was panting. He pulled her toward him, his chest and torso swallowing her up in his embrace. "You can speak, you can, my darling. Oh Jenny," he said, and felt her trembling against him. "Jenny, you have made me the most wonderful promise."

❀ ❀ ❀ ❀ ❀

Samuel awoke the next morning, on his own pillow, in his own bed, to find a folded piece of parchment directly before his face. It read:

Teach me to speak
to love and hum,
and lead you into
the grass, to complete
my prayer.

chapter nine

To not give away his secret—their secret—Samuel had to pace himself. In his walk, in the gait he allowed his mounts to take, in the questions that he asked, about Jenny, about everything; he had to slow his very heartbeat, for fear that it would overtake his body, his breathing, and leap free from its cage, his chest. There were any number of ways to accomplish this, Samuel was certain, by distraction; he ran any errand that came to his mother's head, and completed any and all tasks in the shop, regardless of whether he was asked to. For the twins there were songs and dances and stories, and at night, when he was certain all were asleep, he took his time, as much as he had, to make the walk from his home to their meeting place in the forest, to soothe his eyes with the sight of his Jenny again.

In the moonlight, when they had moonlight, Jenny's skin took on a kind of frost, it was so white; but an anointed frost, as if it were a mosaic of pearls. On the nights when there was no moon, Samuel imagined the heat from Jenny's chest, her face, and the tender place between her legs; the heat he collected and pressed against himself, as a kind of rose shadow, the kind pearls must give off when they are sequestered in their velvet boxes. She was liquid in his hands; she was sand; she was the raw stuff—the spines of last year's leaves, stems and roots—the tillable riches of the earth. Beneath Jenny's touch, Samuel was steel, and ivory, and the hard cut of minerals. He had never been as strong as when he was in her presence, as if he grew in stature and muscle, under her judgment.

She fulfilled every promise a young wife in her position could make to a young husband, except that she did not speak. She blushed and blanched and rolled about with him in any way he asked, but not once during their encounters did any sound again escape through her throat, not for all of Samuel's efforts. At times when her skin lost all of its cold gloss and turned a flushing red, he would try to teach her a word, a sound; he had Jenny put her hands to his throat, to feel the vibrations her name, or his name, or the names of the twins and Samuel's parents, made there when spoken. She tried, or appeared to try, but something would overcome the mouthing of words or her concentration on her throat. Samuel thought he could almost hear this thing pull back on her breathing, as if there was a catch, a trap in her mouth, or her mind, that kept her from success. The blood would dwindle away from her face and then her eyes filled—not necessarily with tears, for they never fell; but a gauze, a veil, a net for her feelings.

She would fall into his grasp, then, and she was so achingly slight in his arms, so frightened and disappointed—for him, it seemed, for she could not then bear to have him look in her face. Samuel's only solution to this was to quit the speaking lesson, and offer her food, for then he was reminded of how easily damaged she could be, given how exposed she was, down to her frame. On days his mother sent him to Market he took from what he had long been saving to buy Jenny loaves, cherries and cheeses to bring to her in the woods. The meats his family ignored at their own table Samuel stole, even though he was certain his mother might notice eventually. Feeding Jenny was a risk he had to take. Often times Jenny would greet his gifts insisting, through gesture and expression, that she did not require them. But just as often the wan pieces of fruit, meat, and bread were met with a famished excitement that outlasted the life of the gift.

Of all the measures Samuel took in those days, he reserved his all discipline and concentration in not speaking a word about Jenny, not to his sisters, nor his mother; not to his commanding officers and colleagues from the Queen's Service, who came to the shop more regularly than it seemed than there was a need. They brought their horses for shoeing, of course, but they also found fault with their swords, their hammers, the bits and implements that would be more properly molded by the castle's blacksmith. Thomas could not explain the sudden interest in his services. These men boasted to Samuel of their own engagements, the coming of their children; but to such news Samuel tried to do no more than smile. To shake his friends' hands in congratulations, to participate in their amazement or joy, might be taken to mean that he understood all too well his friends' good fortune. Samuel had to deny it.

Working alongside his father during the day, Samuel longed to take his problem to Thomas, to beg for permission to leave the family, should it become necessary. Most of all, he wanted Thomas to tell him more of how Jenny had come to the family; had she ever had the power of speech; what she possibly could have done to have been rejected so: was it her knowledge of medicines, the suspicion of witchcraft, which had excommunicated her from all manner of company? But to pose such questions was certain to invite suspicions Samuel knew he would not be able to deflect, so his skin and soul beat with desire and worry.

Samuel also knew, however, he could not keep his wife in her current circumstances for much longer, given that seasons change. So there was one risk he took: Whenever there was an opportunity to ride to another town or village, to another county, whether to ferry livestock or supplies, to receive a payment, or shoe a horse, Samuel took it. And while he was away, and likely still under the surveillance of prying eyes and tongues, he took notice of the churches in these places, the look of the pastor and the congregants, and guessed at their charity—and none too accurately. He wanted to post to a minister a hypothetical, of course, entailing the marriage of an outcast girl to a soldier, a blacksmith's apprentice, and as he watched the giving of alms at one church, a Mass at another, a wedding at a third, he imagined the answers the men of God would give, without hesitation. They would always agree that an outcast could not be married in church, for although a shepherd must watch over all of his flock, he could not risk running up against the disapproval of the ruling monarch.

❀ ❀ ❀ ❀ ❀

Sir Robert initially did not bother to notice any change in the girl as she tended to his health, and he tried to fend off her starvation. Nowhere had the Queen more spies than in her kitchens, it seemed, and as Sir Robert sent underlings to procure the rinds, crusts and gristle deemed unfit for such noble tastes, he noticed heads cocked and eyebrows arched once too often in his direction. So he instead took to requesting more for himself and his staff when the kitchen made its deliveries, with the intent to carve off a portion for the girl, should she be willing to accept it. She was not. But the couriers of his meals were more than willing to spill whatever gossip they had accumulated about others in their travels throughout the castle, in return for a nip at Sir Robert's rations.

The livestock at Sir William's estate had been poisoned, Sir Robert was to learn; Beechum's crops had been sabotaged; servants and soldiers across the land were disappearing. There were no culprits, no causes that anyone could fathom, although the couriers also brought word of Sir Matthew's entreaties to his fellow nobles of his attempts to reignite the fight against the Gongols. They were responsible, Sir Matthew had charged. Sir Robert, with all his strength and fiber, refused to believe it. What he did believe was that Sir Matthew's desire to return to arms threatened to consume the country once again. But at what cost, Sir Robert wondered; and he especially wondered if there was some way to make Sir Matthew pay it.

Sir Robert was ready to collect that payment. He was ready with his own life, if that was to be required. He was in the midst of making arrangements in case of his demise at the hands of Sir Matthew, when he noticed a change in the girl so devoted to his continued health; the girl who accepted so little in return, it was as if she thought she could live solely on Sir Robert's good intentions. That she may have been aided by others, chiefly the young soldier who thought her to be his intended, did not enter Sir Robert's thoughts. How could it, as Jenny, in appearance, at least, seemed smaller, thinner, a body to be diffusing into nothingness?

And yet, on that morning as Sir Robert sat up in his bed, preparing his last will and testament, the girl moved about the room in a more affirmative manner, as though no longer afraid the ground beneath her feet would break open, with its demons reaching up to grab her. As she mixed the juices and herbs she prepared for him each morning; as she touched his forehead, his throat, the scar **fermenting** ❀ on the back of his head, her hands were no longer so hesitant. Sir Robert did not ask her for an explanation of this change, although he could pretty well surmise the cause of it; and Sir Robert told himself he was not jealous. He was too old to believe in love, or in God, or even in Man. What was left for him to believe was a miracle.

❀ On a weekend when Sam was absent and I was left to torturing only myself, I felt my left knee **corroding** inside my skin. I wasn't struck by a cramp or singular kind of pain, but where there had once been a joint I rarely thought about there was a chronic dullness, a burr and hum that would not let me forget about this facet of my anatomy. Since I was a flat-footed dancer, I was obsessed with my feet: my ankles and that region where I was supposed to have an arch. To now be told by my body that I had another joint to worry about seemed patently rude, and perfectly unfair. But I was in the middle of filling and spewing buckets about, and there wasn't much I could do about it.

I spoke to Sam on the telephone, and he was sympathetic. He also had a bum knee, it was revealed, that had to be drained occasionally, and he suggested I do something about my own. But what I was supposed to do wasn't abundantly clear. I could still walk on the thing, and dance at the same level that my teachers expected of me. But when called on to do the splits during stretches in my modern dance class, my knee would pop out—just a micro-meter—and prevent me from securing my leg to the ground.

I had about as much tolerance for pain as I had patience, and by the end of another Sam-less day at the Faire the following weekend, I was in tears. The knee bulged as if trying to escape my skin, and I hopped around graceless and wounded. My parents, mindful of the family history of orthopedic debacles— my mother's chipped and sprained ankles from tennis; my uncle's foot pain from standing up through hours of surgery; my sister's being born pigeon-toed, and my father's litany of auto-immune cum arthritis disorders—sent me to the family orthopedic surgeon. To summarize his diagnosis would be futile, since years later, I was told that whatever it was I had never really existed.

The doctor took measurements. He took X-rays. They showed indisputably that I had a kneecap, joint, tendons, ligaments, and cartilage. He manipulated both knees in every direction imaginable and asked, "How come you're so flexible?" When I reminded him I'd been taking dance classes for the past eight years, he found the solution. "Quit dancing," he said, impressed by how efficiently he had wrapped up this diagnosis.

"What is it you see, there?" Sir Robert asked as Jenny's fingers inspected the wound in his scalp. Once she was finished, she sat directly opposite him, so that she might track the movement of his eyes; it was one of her methods, to ensure that the injury to his head did not move deeper, as it seemed, into his thoughts.

"What is it you look for?" Sir Robert persisted, to which Jenny smiled—or Sir Robert guessed it was a smile, as she had covered her mouth with her hand, and the lines on her face were his only indication.

"I am looking for something as well," Sir Robert said, to which Jenny nodded, although without much enthusiasm. Gestures such as these had led Sir Robert to believe, during spare moments, that the girl did not speak not out of some impairment; but because she had not much use for other people. She dwelled in a much more considered, cautious realm.

"I am looking to finally end all these quarrels," Sir Robert said. "With the Gongols, and Sir Matthew, this bloody wheel of war. Would you like to help me on this one?" he asked, for Jenny had turned her attention to her bag of medicines, as though whatever communication they might have enjoyed moments earlier had been broken.

"Without you, I was a mere mortal. Vulnerable and obvious. Without you, I would have long since met my mortality," Sir Robert said, rising from his bed to met Jenny at her feet; he bowed to her. "But with you, dear girl, I am alive today. And I can take on anyone, and I shall make my meaning indisputably clear to Sir Matthew."

Jenny backed away from the edge of the bed, away from him. Her face took on no particular expression except for her eyes, which were oddly reminiscent of the last time she was confronted with news of Sir Matthew, and his presence. The green of her irises was suddenly crowded out by a darkness, and whatever color was left strained to make itself felt.

Sir Robert took to his knees. "If he is any threat to you, dear Jenny, it is only through me. And I would be remiss in my duties if I did not make him understand the lives he is sacrificing for his own profit. And I must make him understand that he must stop, for my own good, for the country's, and the Queen's."

At the mention of the Queen, Jenny's eyes shuddered, as if the last stretches of fragile green shoots had been trounced by overcast and shadows. Sir Robert took one of her hands in his, and found it to be excruciatingly cold.

"I cannot fail in this endeavor," he said. "And I cannot succeed without you. It is the only way to stop Sir Matthew and save this nation. Otherwise your Mr. Bright will be sent away again, with so many other young men, until we are depleted of all our health, all our strength, all our hope; not even your medicines will be able to save us."

Jenny wanted to shake her head—no, no, no—Sir Robert could see, but instead she held herself firm and still; so still, Sir Robert thought, that she trembled in a way, as if she planned to repel his ideas solely by wishing them away.

"You need only accompany me on my next ride to Sir Matthew's," Sir Robert tried to assure her. "And to tend to me, if I should need tending, should Sir Matthew challenge me. Then, I will not be defeated. And then—" As Sir Robert rose, she offered him her other hand, and Sir Robert took it, with enthusiasm. "Then we will see what profit you shall derive from this enterprise."

Quickly Jenny released her grip, as if the heat their hands had briefly composed had turned stinging. Her eyes, once so dark, had turned red, rebuking, just as the seasons sometimes turn on one another. Sir Robert was not sure if he could continue looking into them.

"Jenny," Sir Robert said, and he suddenly felt the weight of her name in the air, how it could sink them both; but this could not have been the possibility that frightened her.

"My first aim is to help you, dear Jenny," he continued, as he re-approached her; she was backing away again, with a slow trepidation. "I can get you out of the stable, into a proper home with your Mr. Bright, if that is what you wish. I would not come between that."

She closed her eyes, as if to reorient herself to him, and to the room, which was growing lighter by the minute; their time together, her time with all others, was too limited, and Sir Robert could see how the wound that this fact had engraved in her was deepening.

She could not move, whether out of fright or fascination, Sir Robert did not have time to guess; yet her eyes blazed with a kind of curiosity that told Sir Robert how desperate she was to dream of the possibility he had just described, to possess what all of Her Majesty's subjects enjoyed as a birthright.

"But first, I must know how you came to be in **this position**," ❀ Sir Robert said, and now he placed his hands upon her shoulders: they both needed to be steadied, as though both knew what would be said. "You do know why you were cast out, Jenny," he said, although he only was guessing. He knew he had guessed correctly as he had to grip her ever so tightly, to keep her from collapsing. "Tell me any way you can, and I will restore you."

❀ Medical science being what it was in the 1970s (and even as it is today), Sam was never given an explanation for **his condition**. He came up with his own theory. He blamed the environment. He had moved around a lot as a kid, due to his mother's different relationships and marriages, and for a time the family found itself in Saugus. North of Los Angeles, Saugus was a new but unremarkable housing development near the upstart Magic Mountain amusement park. There also was an asbestos plant there, or perhaps it was gypsum, or something having to do with paint. He wasn't quite sure and he didn't seem very interested in laying blame on most days. If I hadn't asked him, he might never have thought about it in the first place.

She was no longer swaying in anticipation of fainting but shaking, **disintegrating**; ❀ she would turn into twigs, threads and feathers between his hands. He was determined to continue watching her eyes as he pleaded with her to listen, to understand, to allow him the chance of doing for her what she had done for him. But it was too late, he could see through her eyes the drought of his chances; although they were so easily filled with tears at the mention of speech in the past, there were no tears now. Rather, there was something else in their mixture, something beyond horror, beyond shame, beyond any secret a soul could bear for as long as hers had done.

❀ What was **disintegrating** in Sam could have been any number of things. It could have been his immune system, since he was experiencing all sorts of opportunistic infections. It could have been his spleen or his bone marrow, since he also was anemic. I spent the years I worked as a journalist prowling through the Associated Press and other wire services for news of scientific advancements to see if it would ever have been possible to cure him. And I have yet to come up with an answer.

What I have managed to sew together is that something must not have been quite right from the very beginning. Two of his genes fused while he was still in the womb, as it does in one out of every 100 newborn babies. But only one in 100 of these genetically afflicted babies will go on to have a serious illness. Please do not ask me to do the math. Or to explain how the *Journal of Clinical Investigation* was able to come to the conclusion, recently, that a childhood illness is likely to blame. Sam never told me about a childhood illness. He only told me that he passed out in the shower one day, just before he was 14.

To hear the science tell it, though, this childhood illness activated in Sam's body a molecule known as TGF. TGF-beta1 "is a multifunctional regulatory peptide (25 kDa) inducing growth arrest and apoptosis in many normal and neoplastic cells," according to the *European Journal of Cell Biology*. Had this been 2010, at least according to *Nature*, someone might have known how to stop TGF—at least in mice—and then the chain reaction that was to follow might have never taken place. Of course that would require time travel, both to the past to administer this potion and to the future when a human TGF inhibitor medication could be invented; it would require the kind of fantasy I am unable to construct, due to my lack of knowledge in physics, to say nothing of basic arithmetic.

So instead this TGF headed directly to Sam's bone marrow, where it granted permission to all sorts of high jinx: necrosis, and overgrowth, and ineffectual and defective blood cell production. His body was partying with all kinds of nasty. I don't know if Sam's condition was lymphoblastic or myelogenous, granular or of some other measurement; whether it affected his B, T, or NK cells. After thirty years – and the death of my uncle (liver, lung and bowel cancer), Sa's mother (breast cancer), my mother (pancreatic cancer), my sister (breast cancer) and so many others — I'm not going to ask. That would be impertinent.

But I can't help wondering what exactly went wrong in his system, and when, as if there was a date, a particular moment, when the assemblage of his peptides and proteins and enzymes and all those other processes went strangely out of whack. I wouldn't know what I would do with this moment, other than announce it, expose it, as a journalist would a scandal, and hope that sunshine would be the best disinfectant.

I might say this about any number of biological incidents attached to my life (although my father's asthma never prompted such speculation, since there was little to no mystery about it, given it was such a source of nostalgia and dinner table entertainment). But from where and how did my Grandma Stell contract scarlet fever, which lead to her heart condition? Or what launched my mother into the first of her many manic-depressive episodes? How far would I have to go back—to when she lived in Greenwich Village in an apartment with God only knows how many other girls and ate one hot meal a week and spent whatever money she did have going to Broadway matinees? Or when for the Wonderland Avenue School Halloween Festival, she filled up a coffin with candy and asked people to guess how many pieces were inside, so she could give the coffin and candy away as a prize? Did it have something to do with the time one of the neighbor ladies told her she saw my father consorting on Mulholland Drive with a much younger woman? He was talking to his sister, my aunt, and as it turned out, he was handing over some cash so she could get an abortion. My mother freaked out even after my father 'fessed up, the way he remembers it. Or did it have something to do with my beloved grandparents and uncle once said to her, or something they didn't do or say? The life of an Army brat is not only one of travel, but frequent separation, and from the time she was in junior high, she was either missing one parent, or both, or her brother, or all of her immediate family members.

My father used to sit on our patio on the warmer evenings, smoke his Dutch Masters, and contemplate all the things he would do differently. At least that's what he told me he was thinking, when I would ask him. My sister would also engage in such re-running of her life, and she and my father used to watch "Star Trek" together, in its first run on NBC. They never seemed too interested in the merits of the prime directive (Starfleet's dictum that none of its space cadets could ever interfere with the unfolding history of the civilizations they visited). But I sure was, once I was in college and watched the show in syndication. Nowadays, in my approaching dotage, meddling with the prime directive, especially in regard to other cancers I've had the displeasure of encountering, is among my frequent diversions. I do not so much look for a date that diseases started as much as muse on what was happening to a body when it was first stricken but its owner was believed to be unaffected. Did the presence of the cancer cancel out all of the epicurean joys, for instance, that the patient was then experiencing? All of his or her achievements, bliss or even depression? What was the central operating principle of this person's biological being? Does it even matter? And I did indulge in this once Sam worsened, but in a much more practical fashion. I even had a date to draw my speculations around, for all the good that it did for Sam's recovery.

chapter ten

The summer ran strong in Samuel, ❀ his eyes more brilliant and alert with the love being dispensed to him in those months. His arms were thickening too, thanks to his apprenticeship, and the drafts that once threatened his chest had dried up, as though they had been mere puddles left to shrink in the sun. His beard and hair lightened most considerably, as if to rival the gleam of stars now timid in their arrival each evening. The boy's parents fretted that the strength rising in Samuel would attract attention; that its source would be discovered and then destroyed, before they could protect both their son and the lover he had obviously taken.

❀ **Sam was a gas** at the Faire. He did not make it out to the Faire every weekend, but when he did, he was at his best. In the mornings, before the turkeys arrived, he would perform his rendition of Barnes and Barnes' "Fish Heads" ("Took a fish head/to a movie/didn't have to pay/to get him in") as the musicians practiced on their instruments. When he, as a Celt, was insulted on the street, he adeptly replied: "Life's but a walking shadow/That struts and frets his hour upon the stage/ And then is heard no more" from that play no self-respecting theater person was ever to mention. At the end of one day, he brought birthday greetings to a friend in the form of the Mongol Birthday Chant: "Death, destruction and despair/People dying everywhere/Happy Birthday, Ugh! Happy Birthday, Ugh!"

I loved the way he smelled, his calm, salty tartness; I loved the taut confidence he carried about him in his chest; I loved the slow, cool feel of his skin. And he must have really liked me, too, because he continued to stick with me, even though I obviously didn't have the wherewithal to put out for him. If he was ill, gravely and terminally ill as I should have suspected, given that I watched television movies of the week and read Hallmark Hall of Fame books, he had an easy way of portraying a healthy forbearance.

And then, one day, Sam decided to get drunk. A friend of his—I didn't know his name, but he was big, hairy, and older; and tawdry, too, with a heavy metal/armor compulsion he so proudly displayed through his costume—wanted to celebrate his birthday. A little liquid street theater, he suggested, and Sam was game. I could watch if I wanted, Sam said, and I did as the turkeys hesitantly formed a circle around him and his friend. They begged for ale at an ale stand, using a helmet to collect the proceeds, and then drinking straight from it. I saw where this was going; the only thing that scared me more than sex, possibly, was alcohol. So after a single round of begging and drinking, I high-tailed it back to safety—my booth—where we indulged in much more contemporary pleasures. I'd meet up with Sam later.

Dueling Buckets sat at the crest of a hill. From the booth's balcony a few hours later, I saw Sam gingerly tread his way up toward me. He looked fat and fragile, as if his body would burst from all the beer he poured down it. He sat down on a hay bale in front of the booth with an abject look of suffering.

"Are you going to be sick?" I asked, and he said, "Yeah, I think so." There was a terrible gurgle in his voice, as if he was holding back the inevitable. After a pause, he said, "I think I'll just sit here for a while," and so we did. His mother arrived to take him home as if nothing was wrong, and I didn't say a word.

I never found out if he got in trouble, but what would have been the point, all things considered.

Samuel understood this, and he and Jenny enhanced their precautions, if not their passion. Samuel severed all contact with the stable; the twins traveled with Thomas now, should business take him there, and Samuel disappeared himself should any soldier or officer seek assistance from Thomas directly. Every stable rat, every groom, every steward: anyone in the Queen's employ looked at Samuel with new eyes now, he was certain; in the Market they might approach him on false pretenses; at the shop they were too curious about his schedule. Samuel came to wonder if it was not he who had been cast out, for he had studied evasion in the Queen's Service; he moved through his life now as though he were an enemy in his own land, a feeling and practice which only increased his loyalty to Jenny.

They devised new routes to take to their meeting place; and new meeting places, new landmarks, out of the wheat and corn flourishing in the season. In the stalks that extended and thickened with the months, they created codes— the placement of a root on a rock, a line in the dirt, a branch wrested from a tree—to communicate their desires, and their whereabouts. They agreed that there would be no one routine; as still in their absolute beauty as Jenny's face, skin, and touch became to him, she would not settle for any comfort, for any two consecutive nights taking the same path, or resting at the same location. As August trapped them in its heat, and the sweat of their affections, Jenny did not deny Samuel anything, except his attempts to have her speak. One night she emerged from a patch of yellowing reeds as if she had taken on the character of that grass, brittle and tangled, depleted of the strength she had shown the previous evenings. He could not get her to explain what had troubled her so, what kept her fingers worrying over each hand, the skin worn to breaking. So he placed her hands on his throat, and commenced to give her words she might use. But she refused, with a fierceness that startled them both. She scratched at her own neck, as if trying to destroy whatever might speak from within. Samuel soothed her with kisses, her blood on his lips; and a bit of his own tears; but never again would she consent to such entreaties. She had rendered her silence perfect.

Samuel told himself Jenny's re-doubled silence was one more precaution; he told himself Jenny was right in her choice; she was protecting both of them. He devised any number of excuses until a night when the darkness came not too early, but too decidedly in its force; it did not arrive that evening. It quickened. The root on the rock could not beam through its width; the line in the dirt could neither be detected with the toe of his boot, nor guessed at from a closer perspective; and the branch wrested from the tree must have held too fast to its brothers. He returned to each location, and sought her out in all the others, but by the time the moon grew to its full measure that night, there was still no trace of Jenny. It was as if she had evaporated with the summer light.

Come the morning, before his mother would have breakfast at the table, a weary Samuel Bright took his mount into town, and at a distance he believed all involved could tolerate, past the stable. Perhaps from the horses' postures; from their pace, or the idle words of their riders; perhaps something would tell him that Jenny had passed the night there, that she was more than safe, just as she, for some reason, was being more than careful. He had long since instructed Jenny to arrange the hay in her stall into the shape of a sleeping body; he had provided her with blankets for the ruse, and as far as they both knew, until now, it had been working. But the scene at the stable, as far as Samuel could discern, proceeded without any interruption; there was nothing to indicate anything extraordinary had happened, that Jenny was absent from her responsibilities, or that anyone noticed. At home, his sisters, however, did take notice: of the lack of clover in his beard, the one hazard of their meetings both he and Jenny occasionally allowed, to Lucy and Grace's amusement.

"Where have you been sleeping, Samuel Bright?" Lucy asked. "Have you forgotten to bathe, Samuel Bright?" Grace chanted.

"He should be paying better heed to himself, I'll give you that, girls," Thomas interrupted them.

Samuel did not ask his father, in the shop, whether he might forgo lunch to take another ride into town on business; he simply mounted his horse, with a pair of bags for tools, to allay any suspicion. He did not ask his mother whether he could skip dinner, so that he could find yet another new path to the rock, or the patch of dirt, or the tree; he simply took off on foot in that direction. He found nothing at each destination, and he felt his chest numb, his skin tightening, and his eyes and mouth blaze with fear and contrition. Standing at these anonymous landmarks, Samuel watched the night take on an unfamiliar texture, like a chalkiness, impenetrable and choking, as if the air had been drained out of it. He pushed himself through it, toward home, toward the shop, and when he took out a horse from his father's stock, he did not bother to saddle it. He could not rightly remember how he even mounted the animal. It was all he could do, to slip a bit past the horse's teeth and hoist himself as he gripped a handful of mane, in a night that seemed to wrap and bind him. He rode where he knew he must not, to the stable, through the paddock, into the stall where he knew Jenny slept. Her nightclothes swayed from the hayloft although there was no wind, no trace of breath; the blankets he had supplied her with had been neatly folded and stored in a corner. The bed of his beloved had been trampled with the rest of the stable hay, as if it had never existed. This confirmed the worst of all Samuel's fears: that the night, its unknowable elements; that the ways and means that had made Jenny an outcast had now made her vanish.

Samuel's breathing tried to betray him; his chest heaved with tears and panic. But he could not allow tears or panic to overwhelm him, distract from his purpose. He clutched at the packet of herbs that Jenny had prepared for him and that he wore at his heart, and he slowed the pace and fury of what now beat about his insides. He would not so easily surrender. Still on horseback, he urged his mount to carry on with all of his being; the horse reared and protested, vocally, at great risk to their mission. Samuel ordered the horse into a gallop, and the rush and clatter of the command, combined with the horse's hoof beats, might very well have awakened both man and animal from their solid and damp slumbers.

He did not recall commanding the horse in any particular direction, and as the horse gathered and released its legs, Samuel felt his desire to hold onto the animal, the need to guide it toward any destination, slip away from his hands and arms. He could not see where the horse was taking him, as the night re-doubled its darkness so fiercely it seemed that no blade could lance it. Clumps of the horse's mane clung to Samuel's face; Samuel felt their brush and sweat. He felt the horse rein its own gait, the bursts of power from its legs unwinding, lessening, controlling their rage, until the animal was at a trot at the doorstep of the shop.

The horse halted and Samuel could slid off; it walked off, on its own, as though it knew Samuel could not be bothered to remove its bridle, or help it with a pail of water or a brush, to cool down. The horse must have understood how suffocating was the blackness of that night, except for a brief and hesitant light Samuel saw prodding its way out of the shop. Thomas was inside, seemingly praying over the unwilling wax and wick.

"Father," Samuel said, although he felt as though he was speaking through a withheld breath. Thomas, his hands folded together and pressed to his forehead, hushed him.

"Father," Samuel insisted. "I must **speak** with you." ❀

❀ Sam's mother **called me** at home a few days later, saying we had to talk. She had serious business with me. Sam got on the other extension. I had never been to the apartment they shared, but I could picture Sam in his room, tiny and drowning inside a monstrous bed. His voice still had the gurgle it picked up from Sunday's drinking, now augmented by sobs, although he didn't quite sound as if he were crying. It was more as if he was anticipating someone else's tears—my own or his mother's. Both prospects were apparently equally as frightening.

"You know Sam's been sick," his mother said, or something amounting to as much. This was going to be bad, I just knew it. Sam and I were to be hanged from our toes for his drinking. Or maybe Sam was dying. I already knew what was wrong with Sam, because Sa had mentioned it once, in an all-too brief addendum, as she showed me that Polaroid of her first Faire season. I never lacked for information, really, but I had willfully ignored it because of Sam's good looks. Because he was a legend.

Sam was the guy who realized he had forgotten his ticket to the historic Cal Jam concert once he had arrived at the venue after a one-and-a-half-hour-long drive. He was also the guy who marched in the final parade of the Faire one season with a plastic orange Tommy gun as his weapon. He had even been thrown from a convertible during a car accident on Interstate 5 when he and his friends were driving up to the Faire's Northern California location. But he survived none the worse for wear. All of the Faire kids in that accident survived. But something had now gotten to Sam.

Leukemia, his mother said it was, and with everything that was happening to him, he might be coming out of remission. They weren't entirely sure yet; there were tests to do and stopgap therapies to try and they were going to do everything they could to prevent another round of chemotherapy. They were going to keep him out of the hospital, keep him from becoming nauseated, from losing his hair—all of the things everyone has heard about thanks to our pop cancer culture. As she was speaking I felt as though she was enlisting me into something, a great battle against this indiscriminate killer that knew no rules of conduct, no manners and no discretion.

As quickly as she told me all this, and Sam could echo her optimism, Sam and his mother said they had to get off the phone because Sam was so tired. I said something like, "I'll talk to you in a few days," and then the call was over.

I don't remember how I felt, precisely. I probably felt nothing. Not numb, as in shocked and removed, but light, airy, as if my insides had been vacuumed out and now I had no weight to hold me to the earth. I sort of just hovered over where I had been standing, over all the places I had ever been, as if I was no longer an earthling, but an observer, clinical and distant. I must have told my parents, my girlfriends, Sam's friends—I couldn't keep my mouth shut; I had to have told somebody. I must have felt sorry for myself, too, and I shiver to think now of that self-pity and its reverse generosity.

"Samuel," Thomas finally acknowledged. He looked up at his son, all worry on his face dispersed.

"There are matters pertaining to Jenny," Samuel said, as slowly and as carefully as he could muster. "Matters of which I must ask you."

"Don't you think it late for such inquiries?" Thomas said.

"I do not understand," Samuel said, in earnest.

"You cannot now have regrets," Thomas said.

"And I have none," Samuel quickly answered. His father's question had given voice to the worst of Samuel's thoughts, and he felt as though the blood that powered his throat had surged to his scalp, his face, his mouth. "Jenny, however, has—"

"That girl is not capable of regret," Thomas said. "If she was, she would not have survived as she has."

"She is missing, then," Samuel confessed, and what had been a momentary rush in the heat of his thoughts now seemed to be a flood. "I cannot find her, and I have looked. Properly. I have dared looked where I shouldn't, and I—"

Thomas signaled to his son to stop, although there had been no sound that could have warned them of company, welcome or unwanted. Still, Thomas pointed to his own ear, and then drew Samuel close to him, as though he had never grown into a man, and was just a boy who had to be steadied against life and its inevitable disappointments.

"If I tell you," Thomas asked, "might it help you find her?"

"Tell me what," Samuel asked, keeping his voice as small as Thomas kept his; as if the walls of the shop, the walls they had created, repaired, maintained with their own hands, had switched allegiances.

"I have been here every night, praying, begging, that this would not happen," Thomas said mournfully.

"What would happen?" Samuel asked.

"That you would be taken. That she would be taken."

"Taken? By whom?"

"Listen," Thomas instructed. "Listen carefully.

"You were too young to remember; perhaps you had to be, when Jenny came to us. Perhaps you were five, or all of six. Jenny's father took ill, and he sent her to us, we thought, as a temporary arrangement. We were to care for her, but she cared for us; she chatted and hummed as though she were a bird, celebrating a spring thaw. She did whatever was asked of her, and when you were sad, she sang to you. She told you stories when you were restless. You ran and played and danced and cheered together; she was your twin in contentment. When his illness finally sent him to his deathbed, Jenny's father asked that I take her to her mother—"

"Her mother?" Samuel said. And he recalled one of Jenny's poems:

> If my mother should see me, would she be like a fish
> seeing an obstacle? Beveled and reflective, my features
> might appear, because a fish knows not whether
> the planet is curved or flat, aerated or salted, heavy,
> and drenched; a fish does not recognize itself either
> in the clouds, or in a mirror. It would only know, upon
> introduction, that water is no longer infinite. The universe
> is a sudden proposition in childhood, I know, but fish
> have no such divisions, no before or after when knowledge
> is shaped, tactile, and closed to certain existences. Would
> she gasp, flap, and drown in this knowledge, or would she
> run away? Or would she wait, assured anyone so distorted,
> so scale-less, would under her discretion melt? I would
> gladly dissolve not at her feet, but at her tail, to be swept
> up in her wake for a rebirth, perfect in its silence, a pearl.

"She is as alive and well as you or I," Thomas said of Jenny's mother, "and we would not wish otherwise, even if it would be for the benefit of her daughter."

"But—"

"Samuel," Thomas said. "Jenny speaks through this story."

"She speaks now," Samuel said.

"Now?" Thomas asked.

"Jenny can speak. I have heard her," Samuel said. "I have, Father. She spoke when—"

"Do not tell me, Samuel," Thomas said, as if he knew, immediately, the circumstances of Jenny's brief speech. "Now, you listen, so you might understand, how Jenny was silenced, how she was cast out."

Samuel nodded, although only for his father's benefit. For there was nothing to understand, as far as Samuel was concerned. He did not think he would ever understand, but still he nodded a second time so that Thomas might go on.

"Jenny's father asked that I some day take her to her mother, but I did not. The girl needed a home, love she could trust, and we gave that to her. Your mother and I, and even you: we gave her all she desired. She was a beautiful, selfless girl. Yet her mother insisted. For months and months. She sent word, then she sent threats. It was a trying decision your mother and I made, but we kept to it, for Jenny's sake. We knew how it would end. Finally, she was sent for, and we relinquished her for a time. When she returned, she was as you know her. We never again heard another word."

Again Samuel nodded, but the gesture betrayed his frustration. "But who—"

"I can say no more," Thomas said gravely.

"But how can I find her? Who has taken her? Where? Why?"

"Go to Sir Robert," Thomas said, "to your colleagues in the Queen's Service, to the Queen herself, if it comes to that. I will go with you, if you should have me; if you still deem me worthy of your trust."

❈ ❈ ❈ ❈ ❈

The older man, Sir Robert **recognized immediately**: ❈ the blacksmith. The younger man, Sir Robert should have recognized, except that he looked as if he had been stricken, if not by illness or injury, then by a sudden, bracing shock. Surely Sir Robert had been coming to the same realization over the last two days, as Jenny failed to appear with her curatives, her touch, the swiftness and quietness of her methods.

> ❈ Sam was an **astonishing copy** of his father, Don. Don showed up on my doorstep, in the same spiffy kind of Alfa Romeo he had bought for Sam. In the eyes of my parents, Sam's

father should have been awarded some sort of Brownie point for sticking around and meeting his obligations. But he had come to take me to see Sam in the hospital, at the behest of Sam's mother. My parents were not happy about it.

Hospitals represented the sum total of both my parents' fears, and they had no stomach to drive me to any medical metropolis for a visit there with my new boyfriend. Plus the similarity between father and son was just a little too striking. It was as if another teen-aged boy had been conjured specifically to storm the barricades of my father's fortress and make off with one of his daughters. Sa once described Sam as someone who should have been born with hooves rather than feet and hands; so magical was his form and personality. By those rights, Don should have been outfitted the same way, even if it was not the best way to make an impression on my parents.

But they let me go, knowing that Sam was ill, and that Sam's mother was a graduate of UCLA; and possibly because I had no homework that night and my standing as a scholar and citizen in the community would not be jeopardized. And off we went, my hair whipping in the wind thanks to the convertible, and the conversation at levels my father might have appreciated, owing to the volume of the Alfa Romeo's engine.

In the beginning, Sam's father talked a lot; when I said I wanted to go to the University of Missouri to study journalism some day, he said something about attending that school, although it wasn't clear if he had graduated from that campus. The Harvard of the Midwest, he proudly called it. He also said something about losing his medical license. (He was by training a psychiatrist.) He might have worked as a hospital administrator, but it was hard to hear him through the petulance of his Alfa Romeo. I talked a lot too, about my parents, and Slayer when I was asked about my prior experiences; but nothing seemed to impress Don too much. Possibly, after his divorce from Sam's mother; the transfer of his other son, Adam, to other domestic arrangements that included neither his mother or his father, so that he might have a "normal" experience away from Sam's illness; and Sam's illness above all, the man was jaded.

Sam hadn't talked much about his father other than one instance at the Faire one afternoon. We were walking hand in hand when I spotted John Tunney, the former U.S. Senator from California, and son of heavyweight boxing champion Gene Tunney. I said loudly, "Look, Sam, there's John Tunney, the ex-senator." Oh I was so delighted with myself as I emphasized the "ex" in my sentence. My father had crossed party lines to vote for Tunney's opponent, S.I. Hayakawa (my father, former school teacher and long-time disciplinarian, beguiled us at the dinner table with paraphrased excerpts of Hayakawa's *Language In Thought and Action*, and the tale of how Hayakawa had climbed up onto the speakers' podium during a student uprising at San Francisco State College, and unplugged the microphone.) But Sam did me one better and answered back even louder, "Oh, I know that guy. My father once tried to bribe him."

"Sir Robert," the blacksmith said, and he took a sweeping bow before the nobleman. The younger man—the boy, Sir Robert remembered, but now his face pocked through with fear and helplessness—was bereft both of his speech and youthful agility. He bent stiffly while keeping his glance locked on his superior's.

"Thomas Bright. I know you, although not as well as I know your son," Sir Robert confirmed, but the boy was resolute in his silence. Nevertheless, Sir Robert rushed the two inside his room, for whatever the nature their errand, Sir Robert knew it to be precarious at this time of night.

"You come to speak of the girl," Sir Robert said once he had secured the door. He addressed solely the father, because the son seemed unreachable, glowering yet shuffling behind him.

"My wife," Samuel Bright corrected him after a moment, and he spoke with a defiance that seemed to sear the fact of their marriage into Sir Robert's chest.

"You are married." Sir Robert had dared himself to say it, as though only his saying it could confirm it. He realized, then, how much comfort he had taken in the Queen's capricious edicts against the girl. "According to what tradition?" Sir Robert heard himself ask the boy. He could only imagine how cruel his question must have sounded.

"Our own," Samuel Bright answered bravely. "By our hearts, and our own witness." But as soon as that bravado appeared, it dissipated, as the boy explained, "No church would have us."

"Yes, I should have expected as much, " Sir Robert said, more for his own hearing, than for his visitors'. "So now, you seek that sanction from me, perhaps?" Sir Robert asked in earnest, for he could not fathom why the two men had sought him out, in the midst of this night. They were in the steepest depths of the summer, and yet the night was as inexplicably vicious as any in winter.

"We do not require any sanction," Samuel Bright re-asserted himself.

"Samuel," Thomas Bright upbraided his son.

"Then what is it?" Sir Robert asked. But there was no answer—neither in their voices nor their faces. Their intentions remained as though their lives depended upon the silence.

"If it is that grave," Sir Robert guessed lightly, "you'd best get on with it."

"She is missing," Thomas Bright said.

"Missing?" Sir Robert was incredulous.

"I have lost her," Samuel Bright confessed.

"Lost her,' " Sir Robert repeated. "How does one go about 'losing' another person? Did you lose her as though she were a purse, or a family jewel, or a bushel to be packed and taken to Market? Or perhaps you simply mislaid her, forgot where you had disposed her, after you had finished with her one evening?"

"No sir," Samuel Bright answered quickly, and now Sir Robert heard contrition in the boy, but it was too late. Samuel Bright went on to explain how he and the girl had worked out secret passages, mysterious signals, an entire retinue of winks and nods as if they were children playing a game of buried treasure, but Sir Robert did not want to hear it. Sir Robert could only think of his own wife, years before, as he watched her flail and evaporate in her sick bed. All that time, he did not "lose" his woman. He always knew precisely where she was, and what she was suffering. To have "lost" her would have been a blessing; mixed, perhaps, but relatively painless.

"Perhaps she is not 'lost' at all," Sir Robert said. "Perhaps she has found a better arrangement."

"Sir Robert," Thomas Bright responded for his son, whom he now held back with an arm. Sir Robert knew the boy had every right to take offense, but he too was overwhelmed with the possibility the pair had presented to him. "I beg you to remember our girl, this young lady," Thomas Bright struggled to say over his son's seething and jostling. "You know her qualities, her bearing, her loyalty, dedication—"

"Yes," Sir Robert conceded quickly, if only to quiet the pair, because Thomas Bright's words reminded him of the girl, and all too well. Sir Robert raised his hand, as if to block Samuel Bright's response, but he was hailing, beckoning, his own thoughts to return to him, of events just two days before: How the tenor of Jenny's eyes had shifted, descended, it seemed, into dread, first upon discussion of Sir Matthew; and then upon speculation of her future. Sir Robert was confronted with the possibility that it was he who had sent Jenny away; that he, in his zeal to right the world, had frightened her to death— the death of the only life she knew how to live. It was he who had lost her.

"Now," Sir Robert said, his voice gauged to a whisper, "we must hear Samuel Bright's story, clearly and precisely. We must map out all of the places he has already searched; all of the paths and places she might have taken or visited; all of the roads and eddies, clearings and caves he has conceivably neglected. Then we must consider everything that has been said to her of late, and everything she could have possibly heard. We must take inventory of our resources."

"Resources?" Samuel Bright asked indignantly.

"Yes," Sir Robert said, and he hesitated in his calculations. After a pause, he concluded, "We have no allies. Only horses, armor, and weapons."

"What are you proposing?" Samuel Bright asked.

"If she has run away," Sir Robert said most delicately, "she will want us to bring her back, no matter the controversy."

chapter eleven

Through Sir Robert's spies, they managed to ascertain which horse Jenny had chosen for her journey: the same Chestnut that had been provoked to throw Sir Robert. Word of Jenny's choice convinced Sir Robert that his worst suspicions were taking shape, but of this he said nothing to Thomas Bright or Samuel. He simply reported the development to the blacksmith, who was certain to be familiar with the type of shoe with which the Chestnut had been outfitted. Watching for its mark would be paramount, Thomas Bright predicted.

Between the three of Jenny's champions, they divided the areas to be searched, according to where each person would arouse the least interest. Sir Robert was assigned homes and concessions, the roads of a most public nature; Thomas, the stables of other horse keepers, merchants as well as nobles, where Jenny could seek aid, comfort, or shelter; and Samuel Bright, the caves, clearings, and unexplored patches of trees. Should he find her, he might well need more hiding places to maintain his marriage, and if Sir Robert was to keep his own secrets, he acknowledged, he would have to leave some for the boy to also keep.

But by that afternoon, the **sun was steadfast** ❊ in its severe focus on their necks and backs, just as Jenny apparently was determined in her attempt at concealment. No man could find any trace of the Chestnut's hoofprint, although its track would be almost three days old at this point, and possibly unintelligible. Samuel emerged from swamps and the most impenetrable of paths splashed and bruised, but without evidence of his wife. Thomas had neither word nor sign of the girl. Sir Robert met with a similar failure, and as the day drew on, he had reason to believe the Queen would soon enough discover the nature of his investigations.

❊ At the Faire, the weather was **all kinds of hot**, especially the kind of heat you associate with a foreign country or other unfamiliar place, because it would never be this hot where you would bother to live. Granted, it was a dry heat, but it caramelized your insides. You could feel them stoking themselves, particularly in your nose, which bulged with the tangled by-products of dust, blood, and snot. In the morning and evening, a water truck patrolled the Faire grounds, spraying the paths and other unclaimed areas, trying to tamp down the dust. Still this protocol had little effect, since whatever moisture the water truck provided burned up like flash paper taken to a match. The dust that eventually loosened itself and swarmed around us gave me the feeling I was being mummified in some very dirty parchment.

At the workshops before the Faire began, the leaders made it a point to remind participants to keep up their salt and water in-take. Huge pickles were sold at the Faire for this purpose. Whatever the temperature, its effect would be emphasized by the costumes you had to wear. Even we peasants had dressing gowns and several layers of skirts to contend with, long-sleeved shirts and blouses, or tights under trousers. The costumes weren't supposed to come off until 6 p.m., when the Faire shut down and all the tourists departed. People cheated, of course, the men removing their shirts or the women lifting their skirts or wearing their bodices practically *au naturele*, but as I have previously mentioned, I lacked the equipment to do so to any great effect.

The Queen and her nobles were especially torturously adorned. Their sweaty indignities included velvet jackets, woolen tights and trousers, outfits lined with ermine and fox; and underclothes of silk and satin. And once the Faire was finished for the day, they kept those costumes on. For me in my muslin, the heat began with a slow braising. Then I stewed in my own juice for the rest of the day. I looked at those heavily powdered nobles with more awe than respect, but not with any envy. At night I looked at them with a special derision.

I did not have it as bad as most because I worked for that dunking booth. It did a blazingly good business most days, and when the customers got too woolly we had no compunction about cooling them off. How the rest of the shire survived, in their collars and costumes that weighed in on the double-digits, I'll never know. Maybe they didn't, after all.

"It is she who has forced this situation," Samuel Bright declared of the Queen, a bit too convincingly.

"Hush, Samuel," Thomas warned him.

"Your father is right, " Sir Robert said. The three met on horseback, on a clearing off an unfinished path Thomas knew about from his childhood. The day had yet to cool, although a fresh wind had blown up, seemingly conjured from the ground itself. It threw dirt and blades of wild grass about the horse's legs, and the animals protested with snorts and whinnying, as though they sensed, for certain, the enemies the men imagined were listening.

"Who else would wish ill against Jenny?" Samuel Bright demanded.

"You speak of treason, Samuel—" Thomas attempted.

"Then so be it," Samuel said. "It was she who prevented us from marrying properly. It was she who ordered Jenny out of our house. Now it is she—"

"You are assuming far too much," Thomas interrupted.

"I assume nothing. I know my wife," Samuel asserted. "She would not so cruelly abandon those—" Samuel stopped himself, gathered the reins of his horse and directed the animal a few steps away from his colleagues.

Hearing the boy's humiliation must have pained both men, but that pain was particularly acute in Sir Robert. He had not meant his pitiless insult of a few hours earlier to establish such doubts in Samuel Bright, who had no good reason to harbor them independently.

"My son is correct, Sir Robert," Thomas said. "If anything, Jenny would risk her life to protect those she loves. Nor would she flee to save herself. Surely, she could have done that months, or years ago."

"But you do not know those she might be protecting you from," Sir Robert said, and as if to test his misgivings, looked off in the direction of Sir Matthew's estate. They were too far to see any trace of it; it would be deep in the evening by the time they could make it there, their horses, and possibly their own resolve, exhausted beyond reason.

"We are not at an end, not yet," Sir Robert said, as he casually led his horse on that path, and wondered whether Samuel Bright and his father could ever be made to forgive him. The horizon governing the direction of Sir Matthew's lands was merciless, the sky at that far point treacherous in its quake and color. Samuel watched his father follow Sir Robert into that delirious, stony blue; as though some force had scoured it to bring out its gloss and sheen, but had not discovered what it wanted to.

It was Samuel who discovered the imprint of one the Chestnut's horseshoes, beside a creek where they stopped to water their own animals. Samuel had said little as they rode at a strict canter—for speed while preserving the horses' resilience. Should they find what they were looking for; should they have to steal it, as Sir Robert expected, the horses' alacrity would be called upon further; and their search was already beyond a full day's load. Where the road seemed to lift, and the gurgle of the night's insects rose, Samuel finally spoke, directing his father and Sir Robert onto the grass and over a hill, the bottom of which opened onto the water from which the horses could not hold back their thirst.

Where the ground was cool, almost muddy, Thomas took off his boots to sink his feet into the chill. Sir Robert drank and splashed his neck and face. Samuel was to watch the horses but he could not remain in a single spot; he led them to different stretches as he paced, eyes to the ground, a look of enraged hurt overcoming his features. Sir Robert and Thomas did not say they doubted Samuel, when he declaimed a royal M insignia, the mark of a royal horseshoe, in the smooth and dark soil beside the creek. But the sun was giving up on the day, and the heat, and Samuel's discovery could not be easily verified; that mark could easily be attributed to the waterfowl congregating on either side of the creek.

"I would just assume find her myself," Samuel announced, and rushed through the water before he could be dissuaded; he did not find another royal M insignia, but made off for an assemblage of thick yew trees in the immediate distance. Thomas was about to follow his son when Sir Robert held him back, and asked him to wait; the yew trees blockaded from view the rest of the landscape, which Sir Robert guessed was equally as vacant; this was royal land, he suspected, untouched and unpopulated. Together the men waited as the night crawled down from above them.

Samuel emerged, one fist clenched over a bridle; his other arm carried a saddle, with the royal M insignia clearly delineated on the saddle blanket. The Chestnut's tack: Sir Robert immediately identified it, and as Samuel ran toward the pair, they ran toward him. At the creek's center Sir Robert and Thomas were breathless, and Samuel's breathing was strained through with tears. They did not guess what had happened to the horse, or even if it were the right one. Whatever may have happened—the horse stolen, slaughtered, its rider kidnapped, injured, or worse—the only clear message the three could agree to take from this is that someone wanted that Chestnut to appear anonymous.

To their own horses, they did as much as they could to make them appear the same, and tied them to a tangle of brush and trees with ropes they had fashioned around the horses' necks. The saddles and bridles they hid in the branches, before they set off for the yew trees. They could not have imagined the barricade those trees formed, the darkness they completed; it was as if the night first edged its influence between the leaves of the yews, where it twisted and thickened itself so that it was deceitful to their vision.

Sir Robert had the three link themselves to one another with a rope, and took to stripping the twigs and branches with his dagger, as if he could bring more light into the situation. Samuel considered calling on his sword, but knew its blade would be useless against the intricate threads of vegetation. Thomas usually carried a small axe, used in smithing: why did he not use it now? Above their heads, the branches of the yew trees met and mastered their fates together, as if they had agreed on a form of punishment. "Father, the axe, Father," Samuel called out discreetly. But there was no answer other than the sound of Sir Robert's blade buffeting against an idle stem, a green twig. Samuel reached his hand in front of him, where he thought he saw a hole in the vegetation, a tunnel that would lead them through the muck that was becoming the air. But just as soon as his hand left his side, it hit a set of inexplicable thorns, and Samuel felt a prickling wave of pain, a font of moisture running down his palm and arm. He was trapped in a riot of branches, each desperately searching for light, for sustenance.

Samuel felt the rope jerk at his waist, pulling him down; his chin was in the dirt, his chest rammed against an exposed root, his feet and legs seemingly pulled out from under him. He wondered if he was going to have to burrow his way out, like some lower form of life, one that seeks out its nourishment in shards and debris—it would not matter to him if he profited from death by some natural cause, or by some brutally deliberate act. Samuel felt reduced, demeaned, a sensation he had not encountered since the Queen's Service. Husks, bush and twigs rustled in his ears, as if he had been sunk into a moat, and he was struggling to swim. He flailed as if he were a fish groping at the air, or a bird, drowning.

"Oh Lord!" Samuel heard himself cry out in exasperation. "**I will not die by these creatures!**" ✿

✿ Sam was not strapped to his hospital bed, but he might as well have been. A myriad of tubes and their attachments effectively incarcerated him in his spot; tubes and tubes and more tubes by my counting, which were attached to all manner of medical voodoo that delivered onto him **some terrific suffering**.

Despite my grandmother's many stays in the hospital, I had never seen anyone so encumbered. My grandmother, in fact, rarely had anything taped onto or jabbed into her, since for her condition the only remedy, apparently, was rest. Or better yet, complete and utter stillness. This discipline she had to enforce upon herself, for there was nothing to stop her from abandoning the hospital and its insults and walking out the ward door. There were a couple of times, during her last stay in the hospital, that I wished she had done this, considering what a load of pessimists that had been assigned to care for her. They told me at almost every visit that she wasn't long for this world.

Sam, however, was precluded from making such choices. He was enmeshed in a not-so-peaceable jungle of I.V. plastic. But he did not quite look as I might have expected, like a martinet or insect squirming under the domination of some spider. He instead reminded me of one of my uncle's car engines, which he took apart on the weekends to put back together again. My uncle did this while feeding the engines whatever concoctions he thought necessary, through the spare I.V. tubes and bags he collected from the hospital and then adored his garage wherein.

Car engines, of course, cannot leap off their blocks and prance about unsupervised, and neither could Sam, but for his own reasons. His treatment required so much medicine, and therefore so many tubes and hypodermics lodged into his system, that he had to be outfitted with a pair of splints. One was for each arm. They immobilized his arms so that his veins, pocked and resistant from all his prior battles, would not reject the needles and hence the cure that was worse than the sickness. Upon exiting Sam's arms, the tubes ran through beige electronic boxes of some sort and then up to the bags of clear medicines. Each box had two buttons—red for stop, and green for go was the extent of my understanding—and when something went wrong, the red button would flash and an alarm would sound. The alarm was meant to alert the patient, and possibly the nurses, that the medicine had stopped flowing, due to a bent tube or some other technological malady. Said alarm wasn't particularly violent or even loud, but it was a particular kind of irritating interruption. We—Sam and I—could not pretend this entire thing was temporary when that alarm dared contribute to our conversation. When he was conscious; when he was first beginning chemotherapy, and had all his hair and his optimism, he would bang on the buttons whenever a box got out of line.

There also was a story Sam told me as his chemo was beginning, and he had just been outfitted in the splints and he seemed relieved, to a degree, as if he knew now what was going to happen. He told me about an earlier stay in the hospital when he was similarly confined by the arms. He felt worse than dirt, and he thought about ripping out all the tubes and needles and taking a flying leap off the balcony. But he soon thought better of that plan, and decided to stick with the suffering. I don't know why he told me this; perhaps I had made the mistake of asking how he felt, and I got the response that question deserved.

"Samuel Bright," he heard Sir Robert respond harshly. But from whence Sir Robert's rebuke originated was beyond Samuel's comprehension. Samuel yanked on the rope and received no response; he tugged again, to find the rope tightening. It pulled him from behind, but he could not stand.

"Remain where you are. We will come to you," he heard Sir Robert instruct. The splintering of snap of stems and limbs followed. From where the thorns had tracked into his hand, Samuel felt something like pain, as if the whole of his heart beat from his fingers and palm, rather than from his chest. He nursed the hand the only way he could, by drawing it up to his chest, and felt the book, Jenny's book, there, and he pressed the hand against it. If Jenny was on the other side of this thicket; if there was another side to this prison; if this was what Jenny was made to endure, he would endure it as well, as painstakingly as necessary.

"Samuel," Thomas rejoiced. Samuel could see neither his father nor Sir Robert, but he felt the rope relinquish its tautness; he could smell the men, their shared disorientation.

"We will crawl out of here as a column," Sir Robert announced, and his movements momentarily took up the slack their reunion with one another created. Ahead of him Samuel saw a figure move on its elbows and its knees.

"No," Samuel said, and as he slowly lifted himself off the ground, he grabbed the first branch above him in a fist, and wrenched it off its tree. Another threatened his neck; he clutched it with both hands and hung all his weight on it until it splintered. He would pour through those branches as if he were a snake, shedding its skin. "Jenny is my wife; my charge; my life," he declared. "She saved my life, once, without cowering; I fight for hers now on an equal footing."

For a moment, Sir Robert heard nothing from the young man; indeed, the air locked around this impenetrable nest seemed to go rigid, deflecting all evidence of sentience. Thomas might have been holding his breath; Samuel Bright was withholding his. But just as soon as the blood and breath of everything around him seemed to have stopped, Sir Robert's ears picked up on a trail of snapping, crunching, puncturing noises.

"Samuel!" Thomas called out, in his strongest mutter.

The rope tugged upwards on Sir Robert's waist, as if calling to him to move ahead, follow Samuel's clamoring.

❦ ❦ ❦ ❦ ❦

Breaching free from the yews' clutch, Samuel Bright, Sir Robert and Thomas Bright discovered they had been caught in a circular arrangement; the grove and undergrowth had been shielding a building—but from whom? There was no road, no other sign of civilization close. The night had long since sealed its hold on the earth, but this darkness was far more malleable than what had so viciously played with them earlier, in the grove. The darkness seemed to wither out in places, so that the building revealed itself to be a long, low-slung structure, its purpose not immediately decipherable. As they approached it, the building gave up its scents: reedy with an animal strength, leather and grease. Another stable, they seemed to agree without speaking; large enough for five or six horses, and surely a place where Jenny might feel comfortable.

Yet it was unlit, and still, beyond all measure; possibly it had been abandoned, with neither the yew trees' knowledge nor permission. Samuel was wary of showing his back to the trees, should they find some new way to continuing their duties. Walking gingerly toward what appeared in the darkness to be a door, Samuel would not let them slip away from his glance, as he was certain the roots would find some way to travel underfoot, surround them secretly. At the door, a simple sliding mechanism, Sir Robert brandished his dagger, and signaled to Samuel and Thomas to draw their swords. Samuel looked to his father's belt for the axe, but found he could not reach for it; his one good hand fastened to his sword, and the other felled by a consistent ache, and a rigor that came on with swelling.

Sir Robert slid open the door as if he were throwing it aside, and inside there was a figure, caught askance; it screamed, as if to summon others, but its cry was mercifully unheard, at least in the interim. Together the three men dropped upon it, and someone—Sir Robert, or Thomas—gagged it with a cloth. As it lashed and struggled beneath their weight it might have been trying to speak, but it was stifled by both their force and Sir Robert's distinct interrogation.

"You are guarding something here," Sir Robert said, in a voice that did not frighten Samuel, but was uncomfortably familiar in its relish and urgency. "Guarding it for whom?" Sir Robert went on, as he jerked about the figure's waist and produced a pair of knives, a mallet, and other tools that Samuel could not readily identify in the dark. "What is of any worth, in a dark, empty stable? Stolen jewels, silver, sacred keys and sabers? I'm not sure I care," Sir Robert taunted, "when the death of one more of my enemy's men would be so much more interesting to savor."

"No!" Samuel protested. Their quarry tossed and rolled with renewed determination, Samuel having relinquished his grip. "Let him speak, for God's sake."

"He has nothing to tell us," Sir Robert said, and he appeared, through his shadow and sweat, to be throttling the man.

"He is the only one who can tell us anything," Samuel insisted.

"Sir Robert," Samuel heard his father plead. "Our mission here. Our purpose."

Samuel heard a pause, a shuddering of breath. "The girl," Sir Robert sputtered, to which the guard's arm rose, his index finger pointed into one of the stalls as the other hand dabbed at the tools—keys, Samuel could now see—that had been ripped from his belt. Samuel bolted into the stall, swept free of muck and hay, and paced around madly, until his foot caught on something metallic.

Sir Robert threw the keys at Samuel; outside of the stall, Samuel thought, Thomas and Sir Robert made quick work of securing their prisoner. Samuel opened the trap door only to find another blinding darkness, but instead Thomas and Sir Robert came up behind him, with light—torches— and the guard, whose gag had been removed. He was younger than Samuel, too young even for the Queen's Service.

"Take us to her," Thomas commanded, for it was Thomas who held his sword on the boy's neck, and the boy's eyes blazed with a new willingness.

✿ ✿ ✿ ✿ ✿

They could not see her readily, as they entered the cell, but Samuel knew instantly that they had lit upon the correct chamber. He knew it in the breathing he heard, its shallow, wary patter, quickening according to their footsteps. Samuel wanted to leap, yell out that he had found her. But Sir Robert blocked his path, and motioned for silence: there could be other guards, or the girl could have been merely bait, with her captor seeking prey far more substantial.

But Samuel burst through the embrace of Sir Robert and his father; he surged toward the far wall, his good hand in possession of Sir Robert's dagger. From the bottoms of her feet to the back of her neck, Jenny shook with each ding of contact between the instruments and the chains. Samuel felt it. With his arms he squeezed her tighter to himself, as if he could stave off her shaking, until he realized she was responding not to noise, but to something within herself, the grip and tension of pain.

"Faster," Samuel begged.

"The gown I gave her, so she might be presentable to Sir Matthew, when we visited last spring."

Samuel did not want to listen. He clutched at her ever more tightly, but she could not be soothed. There was no conciliation for her limbs, her chest, her throat, her face.

"Likely she was trying to meet with him again," Sir Robert continued.

"Yes, sir," the hostage volunteered, and at that moment, Samuel felt more of Jenny's weight upon him. They had released one of her ankles, and with its release, the rest of Jenny's body seemed to relinquish all interest in that limb. It swayed slightly, and once it swung against Samuel, it felt heavy, deadened, as if its connection, its position in Jenny's life had been abandoned.

"How much longer for the other one?" Samuel asked. Now the guard, Thomas and Sir Robert worked together on the other ankle. "She can't take much more," Samuel said, and now there was no concealing his begging.

"Patience," his father offered back to him.

"Oh God, Jenny, what business would you have with Sir Matthew?" Samuel asked, as if beseeching the girl in a prayer.

"My business," Sir Robert replied for her. "I had asked her. Foolishly. To help me." Jenny's bulk increased at that instant—her other ankle free not of the cuff, but of the chains. The three men took to her arms then, the cuff on one wrist, and Samuel burrowed what strength he had left into her chest, around her back. He steeled his legs.

"Almost, my beauty," Samuel said into her skin.

"To end this war. Sir Matthew's little game," Sir Robert went on. "How could Matthew keep at it with the Gongols, if I continued to challenge him. How could he continue to challenge me if I had Jenny and her powers at my discretion."

"What? As if she were some kind of totem? A charm? A talisman?" Samuel found himself shouting at Sir Robert, so that he could be heard through the chaos: Sir Robert's audacity, the hostage's sobs, his father's grunts and exertion. "She would not go through this for you, you who see her as an object, a piece of enchanted armor or some tool for mesmerizing your opponent. She—"

"Samuel!" His father's voice seemed to spring on him. Jenny's arm dropped as dully and cruelly as that leg had been liberated.

"Her shoulder must have been broken," Sir Robert diagnosed.

"Jenny," Samuel whispered. "Please hold on dear girl. Please. Oh God."

"You know as well as anyone, Samuel," Thomas said, as he, Sir Robert and the hostage moved toward the last of Jenny's imprisoned limbs. They formed a circle around the ruin that was the girl's now static body. Samuel did not know whether she had somehow calmed herself, or whether she was succumbing. He could only keep up his stream of worthless talking. "Jenny must have understood the implications of her talent too," Thomas said.

"I do not understand!" Samuel protested. "I do not want understand! Any of you!"

"Now is not the time for an exposition of the day's politics," Sir Robert said.

"You were using her," Samuel accused Sir Robert.

"Yes," Sir Robert said, and with his admission, Jenny's final wrist was set free from the hackle. Her weight increased one last time against Samuel, and her breath, at least in the form of a scant catch, returned against Samuel's neck.

"But she would not be used, your Jenny," he said, and Samuel was struck immobile for an instant, as he watched Sir Robert smooth away the bangs that adhered to Jenny's forehead, and then the kisses Sir Robert placed there. "She must have come here, seeking Sir Matthew's audience, to beg him to stop his campaign against me; to ask for a reprieve, so that she might not have to repair and revive me, each time Sir Matthew attacked. She wanted only to be Jenny, not some healer or sorceress, or even an outcast, but your Jenny, your wife; helpmate to a safely ensconced blacksmith's apprentice.

"I wanted to end this war," Sir Robert said. "She did this not for me or my cause, but for you. Her husband."

"Come, come," Thomas was saying.

"But she would not answer him. Sir Matthew," the hostage volunteered, unexpectedly. It was the first he had spoken since confirming Jenny's appearance at Sir Matthew's, and his voice was muffled by his shame, his downward glance. He scooped up Jenny's feet to relieve Samuel of some of the weight, and seemed to be addressing them with his subsequent words. "She gave him neither a yes or no when he asked that she perform her miracles for his benefit," the hostage said. "Is she—is she an enchantress?" he asked.

"What was done to her?" Sir Robert asked.

"I cannot say, beyond the usual, sir," the hostage responded, and he looked behind himself, quickly, as if assuring himself there were no spies close by to report this betrayal. "Sir Matthew and the others, they questioned her for hours, it seemed to me. I heard no protest, no remorse on her behalf. They said she gave neither voice nor tears to their measures. She must be—"

"Please, men," Thomas interrupted.

"Yes," Sir Robert agreed.

Jenny's breathing shifted. It was enlarging. The gulps of air were terrible, and rattled and bound through her chest. "I will take her now," Samuel said to the hostage, and with the man's help maneuvered Jenny fully onto his arms, so that he might carry her as a husband carries a new bride across the threshold.

"Is there no other route out of here?" Sir Robert asked, but they had already begun to move toward the chamber door, a slow, bleating mass of exhaustion and panic.

"A tunnel underneath, sir."

"Come on, then, man," Sir Robert said as he made way for the guard to show them. Samuel and his cargo were the last to follow, and though he had rescued Jenny in body, he wondered, whether in her **mind**, she was far, far beyond them. ✿

✿ Sam was either **dazed or comatose** for most of my visits. On one occasion, I was able to learn that he was on morphine; someone had told me he was, and when I asked him, he smiled, although none too enthusiastically. During that visit, he awoke from the dreams swirling around him and asked if we had been fencing at that moment. When I told him no, he closed his eyes and retreated back to wherever he had been.

I don't know what he was thinking and feeling during all of that time. Nowadays we talk about the clouded state some cancer patients enter into upon chemo as "chemo brain," but for Sam, there was no such description of his mental wanderings. He was just out of it, wasted. For weeks and weeks he simply lay there, absorbing and digesting poisons, waiting for them to do their trick. I knew, somehow, that the blood transfusions made him feel like a vampire; this he had told to either his mother or one of his minders, who informed me when I visited. But for the rest of those hours—once or twice a week—he was absent from most contact and all conversation.

chapter twelve

Not until they were able to lay her out in the bed, on the first clean sheets that she must have lain against in over a year, that they were able to see the worst of her suffering. They had not been able to remove the cuffs attached to the chains once they freed her, and now her hands and wrists swelled against them, threatening their confinement. The knuckles and fingers that they could distinguish were a brackish purple. Her feet and ankles, also encased within the iron cuffs, had been spared the same depth of injury that her hands now displayed, but one foot had obviously been abused, possibly beaten on its sole, but Sir Robert could not fathom by what instrument. Her face was clear except for one vividly black eye she could not open; the skin around it seemed to blister and spit, so distended with dead blood it was. Her back and abdomen were plainly marked by lashes that boiled crudely, like oil or tar, dangerously hot to the touch.

Samuel Bright took charge. The young man ordered white sheets for his bride, because she had endured enough of dinge and drab in her life: now she should look most like herself, and everyone should recognize her for the angel that she was. Her bandages were also to be from the same fine white cloth. Her roots, powders and potions had to be obtained—at great cost to their safety, Sir Robert had argued unsuccessfully—from her garret in the stable. Thomas and their hostage were dispatched for that task, and when they returned, a broth was prepared according to a recipe of Samuel Bright's recollection. At first she waved away the liquid, just as she shook her head when first introduced to the clean, bright linens. But she could not resist, ultimately, and she succumbed to these luxuries as well as sleep, as though her soul had been broken.

Possibly because she could not speak, she trembled as if to demonstrate her wretchedness, but Samuel Bright insisted on speaking to her. Not for a moment did he stop, keeping his mouth to her ear. He, too, refused attention to his wounded hand, so that he might bathe and bandage her injuries, even as that hand became fairly useless. With the other hand he stroked the girl's hair and forehead, and tried to pacify her skin's natural processes of bleeding and scarring. Sir Robert tried not to listen as Samuel pleaded with his wife, offered her balms and prayers, a stream of pleasantries and desperation. It was an all too familiar combination for Sir Robert, who had once resorted to the same measures with his own wife, years before. He would have liked to have pulled Samuel Bright away, demanded he get his rest, but knew his efforts would be just as ineffectual as Samuel's. Instead he scooped up Samuel's neglected hand, washed the blood from his forearm, applied ointment to the fingers and palms, and wrapped the scratches as best he could.

Once both husband and wife were bandaged, Thomas sat at the foot of the bed. His expression—the gray eyes alternately searching for and neglecting sleep, his mouth girded so tightly Sir Robert could see the working order of his jaw—was one of bitter shock. They had spent a day and a night retrieving the young woman, and now the first light in Sir Robert's chambers was rough and anemic. Clouds swallowed what rose from the sun. The sky spoke at this hour, of winds and rains that would scrape away the heat soon enough. To Sir Robert it seemed the elements were demanding relief from their condition. Rather than seek it through a thunderstorm, they wanted it from the girl, who once could offer anything, but now had nothing to spare.

Sir Robert wondered how long it would take Sir Matthew and his men to establish what had happened the night before; to calculate the meaning of their missing guard (he sat with them now, petrified, watching for signs of the young lady's recovery); the trap door left open in the stable, and their prison robbed of its prized tenant. How long might it take Sir Matthew to frame some type of specious complaint to the Queen, and to have that complaint delivered in person; how the uninformed Queen might act in response: Sir Robert examined the possibilities as evenly as he could. Jenny was at the axis of this maelstrom. Should they be discovered—when they were discovered, Sir Robert understood—exile might be one appropriate punishment for consorting with the outcast girl. The Queen could likely demand far more agonizing penalties, given her particular distaste for this one, ruined quintessence of a girl. Or perhaps it was the girl's suffering that the Queen had such disgust for. That Jenny was now suffering for the sins of Sir Matthew struck Sir Robert as a scandal. Perhaps if they were discovered, for they would be discovered, eventually, he now hoped, the Queen would finally be confronted with the sins of Sir Matthew and his ridiculous war.

"Where are you going?" Thomas asked as Sir Robert lifted himself out of the hard stool where he had been sitting. Samuel stole his eyes away from his wife, and toward the nobleman.

"On an errand," Sir Robert said. His eyes met Samuel Bright's, and Sir Robert could see in them the grief that was drowning the young man's being. Sir Robert could not risk disappointing him. "An errand I neglected yesterday," Sir Robert explained, as graciously as he was able, for now he had finally located the true source of his anger over this affair, ablaze in his gut and in the person of Sir Matthew.

❀ ❀ ❀ ❀ ❀

It was not his pity that made Jenny so beautiful, Samuel told himself. It was the milky calm of her skin, about one cheek, her forehead, her chin; it was her hair, lush even in its tangles. He longed to see the green of her eyes, their resilience and delicacy; for so many years, he had been entranced by those eyes, and since their marriage, their green had grown as shoots mature into blossoms. To see those eyes now, Samuel prayed, would be a kind of forgiveness, for he had failed her in all the ways he had pledged to keep her: safe and honored.

She was so beautiful, Samuel thought he could not bear it, and he wrested his sight from her and lodged it toward the ceiling, where he could let his eyes seethe unnoticed. Sir Robert had left, and Thomas was snoring. Tears clamored up Samuel's throat, begging for release; his eyes stung from balancing what he would not spill. He shook his head as Jenny would: not so much saying "no" as refusing the alternative. He would not cry, so long as Jenny did not; Jenny only cried, it seemed to Samuel, when her silence was threatened. And yet the Queen, who insisted that she be cast out because of that silence, had turned that silence against her; just as Sir Matthew had done, because he failed to understand that silence. Samuel thought by marrying Jenny, he could free her from whatever kept her mute; give her stature and the security that comes with it. But by trying to do so, he feared, he only exposed his own cowardice. He could not live without her.

His tears temporarily stayed, Samuel returned his glance back to Jenny. With his one good hand he arranged her hair over the blackened eye so he might see Jenny as he best remembered her: a little playful but a little inscrutable as well. He lowered his head to rest on the pillow beside hers, to smell her hair, her lips, the jasmine she was fond of collecting; he closed his eyes and brushed his knuckles against her cheek, her eyelids, and still saw every slope and current of her, the serene design of her smile and forehead. He promised himself he would rest there for only an instant; and he remembered how she had done just as much for him, if not more, when he was similarly trapped, in his illness.

Samuel knew Jenny must have left his side during that time, if only for practical purposes: to fetch water, towels, blankets, new medicines. She had to have eaten, to have washed her brilliant face, how she appeared to him at every moment of his sparse consciousness. She was never worried, always astounding in her hopefulness, even when he awoke to find her hands over his as if she were engaged in prayer, or some other remote meditation. She had never been permitted to go to the church because of her speechlessness. If God could not hear her pray, the pastor said, there was no point to her attendance.

But Samuel heard her prayers, her voice, her humble beseeching. He thought he heard it when his limbs ached and she bathed him in salted water to draw out the fever. He thought he heard it when she rubbed almond oil and arnica into his skin afterwards. There was no explanation as to why he was so ill, why his chest suddenly denied him the pleasure of breathing; although his lungs had always been brittle. If he ran too hard, or the weather turned too quickly, his lungs might seize up, as if to protest the change in circumstances.

Jenny had always been able to call his lungs back from their inflexibility, and as Samuel grew older, he believed she had healed him completely. But one afternoon, while pounding out horseshoes under his father's tutelage, Samuel drew in a raft of heat as if to **scorch his breathing**. ❦ As if in reply, his throat embarked on a string of coughing. Once finished, he was to return to the house to cool off, possibly drink a medicine of Jenny's making; but the short walk left him winded. Sitting up proved too taxing. He was laid out in his parents' bed for a brief rest, but by nightfall he was bedridden.

❦ **The hottest days** of the year also sickened my father, according to the tales he and my grandmother would gleefully recall together. The High Holy Days, as if to match the dread which surrounded the arrival of Rosh Hashanah and Yom Kippur in a quickly- secularizing family, tended to be the worst in terms of weather. There are no dog days in a desert climate, but there is a dry heat that scorches and consumes the air as if it were accelerant. Being that this weather coincided with the start of football season, my father and his friends decided to play football, and as a concession to the heat, they moved their playing field from the park to the sprinklers on someone's front lawn. My father has claimed he could play football all day when he was a kid, and perhaps on this occasion, before there were smog warnings and heat alerts and other officially kinds of common sense that were broadcast, he did. All that my grandmother knew, though, once he arrived home was that he could cough and wheeze, but no longer breathe. Perhaps at great offense to our Lord who deemed automobile driving a sin on holy days, my father was rushed off to the hospital (once again).

Aside from this being the time period when the Great Book of Life is open for Jews to inscribe their good will and intentions in; and the Days of Awe and Atonement; this was also the start of the school year, which my father, who had apparently missed one too many school years, was going to have to sit out through as well. He had pneumonia, the worst case of it he endured. My father and grandmother like to make my father's childhood bouts seem like fun and games, but for this one illness they do not provide such details. No one seems to have been told exactly what happened afterward, although we do know my father eventually recovered. And that his father—my grandfather—dubbed the illness, in his Eastern European accent—"No Money-Ya," as if recording the cost of this malady.

The fever had the walls of his chest bearing down on whatever air he could capture for a moment. His exhalations came back agonizingly hot, as if from a furnace. The next morning, his parents sent for a surgeon. Amidst the commotion of parents, visitors, the surgeon and the twins, Thomas was to tell Samuel later, Jenny came in, with her equipment: a bowl of cool water, a simple cloth bag; odd pieces of fruit with herbs and other material stuffed within. When Samuel's breathing had calmed and afforded him some rest, Jenny slept, too, on the ground, beside the bed.

His recovery was not one of steady progress, however. On what might have been the third night, or the fifth, or the seventh, his breathing was particularly coarse. He felt as though he was calling on every ounce of his strength, from what kept his ankles in his feet to his eyes in his face, to draw on the air; and cuttingly cold it was, not as if it were a knife, but a blade, injuriously blunt, in need of sharpening. Samuel believed he saw his parents: Thomas strangely distant, his mother frightfully arrayed in sobs and mourning clothing. He saw Jenny too, although not at the same moment. He saw her later, when the room was empty—of light, of his parents, of air itself—he was choking.

He did not actually see Jenny, he remembered, but felt her presence; beside his ear, as if she were breathing air into it, because his mouth, his throat, his lungs had become useless. On his chest she had piled her hands atop his; she pinched and she pressed at his hands, as though they could squeeze out whatever in that chamber was ailing him. Samuel could see that Jenny was on her knees, begging, beside him, and he heard a sound in his ear, words—*Live, Samuel Bright, live*—she used to revive him. Spoken words.

In your affliction you collected
apparitions of sound; visions of
prohibited meaning; the firmament
that germinates during broken
respiration, before it is restored
to innocence and pride. I wiped
your mouth and cooled your brow.
But I suffered onto you no influence.
It is impossible to suffer when you are
mere visage, a perennial, a fact of light
and size and occasionally the movement
of the sun: The working results of the humble,
illustrative organ, I am, although I would
rather nest farther, into that syndrome
that dared to deliver you to these aural
revelations; fabulous as you believe
them to be, they are so profound, dangerously.

Samuel remembered reading this poem in Jenny's hand, and he remembered then, too: "You spoke to me then, didn't you Jenny?" he wept into her ear. "You spoke to save me. But what if I cannot save you now?"

✿ ✿ ✿ ✿ ✿

Samuel awoke to more words: greetings, apologies and arguments. A blur of voices he sorted through as he played as though he was still sleeping: his father's, contrite and humble; Sir Robert's, hard and spiteful; and a third, female voice, which he thought he must have known all his life, yet it was too tight, too distant for him to place readily. Samuel inhaled a raft of Jenny's skin, the slender wilt of her hair, and knew she was asleep, beside him. Yet her scent seemed stronger now, as if refreshed by fresh cuttings, and the woman's voice he could only call familiar suddenly was known to him, in all its detail.

"You brought me here at your own peril, Sir Robert." It was the Queen speaking. "To say nothing of your colleagues in this endeavor—Thomas Bright. I expected better. And your son. He was specifically instructed—"

"I apologize for my son," interrupted Thomas, "and my daughter-in-law."

"They are married?" the Queen asked, as if all the authority in her speech had somehow been taken from her.

"They consider themselves as such," Thomas explained. "Your Majesty, you know this was inevitable."

"I know no such thing," the Queen answered. "I do know that you, Sir Robert, and your son have placed my rule in jeopardy, and I cannot allow—"

"Yet you prefer to allow Sir Matthew to continue his handiwork. Here!" Sir Robert declared, and Samuel heard a swell, then a kind of belting of the air. Sir Robert had removed the blanket on the bed, to reveal the bruises and lacerations on Jenny's legs, the swelling of that one foot, as if it were turning putrid. "This is what Her Majesty would rather allow! See his actions! And whom do they place in jeopardy? Whose life and limb?"

Samuel heard nothing, save for a dread silence, and the precise footsteps of the Queen circling the bed. She came to rest on the other side, and delicately she placed herself beside his broken wife on the mattress.

"What would you have done, had this been your beloved?" Sir Robert asked quietly. "What will you do now, seeing how your esteemed Sir Matthew conducts himself?"

"Enough!" the Queen declared in a strained manner. She might have feared arousing Jenny, Samuel thought. All he could hear now were the elaborate layers of the Queen's nightdress settling against the linens. Samuel lifted his head, as though only now he was awakening, and saw the Queen's face inspecting Jenny's. There was a terrible similarity between the two, in how they registered pain, as though they perceived it not in themselves, but in each other.

"I am sorry, your Grace," Samuel Bright could not help himself from speaking. He neither rose to bow, nor averted his eyes under the Queen's gaze to show his respect. "I confess the guilt of my actions, but I do not regret them."

"Yes," the Queen murmured, and the lock of hair Samuel had so lightly placed over the black eye was brushed aside by Her Majesty, who suddenly gasped, although she must have known what awaited her beneath it.

"Your Grace knows she saved my life, once; that I owe her nothing less," Samuel continued. "It is the same maxim that bound us in Her Majesty's Service, that binds us as a nation—"

"Yes, yes, yes," the Queen assented.

"Please, your Highness. Let my Jenny live what little she may have left, in peace. Then you might—"

"And then I might what?" the Queen responded, her fury fully restored. "Your selfishness is sublime, if not dangerous, Samuel Bright. Your little romance has interfered with my ability to not only lead this nation, but any attempt I might make to defend it. Can you even conceive of what is at stake here?"

"I can only conceive, your Grace, that we would not have found ourselves in such circumstances," Samuel said slowly, "**had you** permitted Jenny and I to marry in the first place." ❀

❀ **If only, if only…** This is the most salient thought I can recover from that time, as side effect upon side effect were heaped upon Sam. In the hospital, his knee swelled; his tongue swelled; and those are just the effects I remember most vividly. I remember the knee for the obvious empathy I was able to apply to it; and I remember his tongue swelling because even when he was conscious, he could not speak. Each time it seemed that he was making progress, getting closer to getting out, something would befuddle his blood count, his spleen, or his immune system and more time, more chemo, more cocktails of blood transfusions and pain killers would be added to his schedule. And I could only think, if only. If only. If only Sam hadn't started whittling that day before he was taken to the hospital.

He was feeling great, he said, as he sat down on his bed to whittle at some wood. I don't know if he was planning on making something or was just trying to get the day to go by faster, so the Faire or the summer would get there sooner. Both of us—me with my high school graduation coming, him with his entire life ahead—were impatient. He sat down and whittled but he had to bend a bit to apply some of his weight to the knife and get some traction on the wood. He remained bent over for a couple of hours, or perhaps only a few minutes, before he discovered that he could not sit up again. His back was frozen in the whittling position. He had to call me from the hospital to explain what had happened, and his voice popped and bubbled in a way I could not understand; as if he had to apologize for taking this foolish risk, and if only he hadn't.....

"Samuel Bright," Thomas despaired from where he had also been made to bow.

"But your son is correct, Thomas," said Sir Robert, who had lost all manner and posture of deference. "Her Majesty is as responsible as Sir Matthew for this girl's suffering, and only for her own enigmatic purposes."

The Queen did not answer, deliberately. She fixed such a stare at Sir Robert that Samuel thought the man would break to look into her eyes, green like a kind of steel Samuel had once seen pulled too soon from the fire.

"Maggers," Sir Robert said with **a softness and new sympathy**. ❀ "How could she ever be a threat to you and your magnificence?"

❀ I wouldn't say that my relationship with my father necessarily improved during that summer. I was still dreadfully afraid of him in many respects, and although **he had to lighten up** considerably once I was accepted into UCLA, he remained distrustful of my "extra murals." The Faire was over and I was no longer dancing, which might have reduced a fair portion of the strain between us—he always said, with I don't know how much of a degree of joking, that he'd break my legs if I became a dancer. But I was also making a movie, of sorts, with Sa and some other girls from the Faire. We'd been recruited by Rick Sloane, then a fellow Hollywood High student and aspiring filmmaker. He is now the B-movie impresario behind

Hobgoblins and a part of the *Vice Academy* franchise, but back then the most original project he could come up with was a kind of *Dawn of the Dead* and *Rocky Horror* mash-up that we filmed in the same cemetery where my Grandma Stell had been installed in a wall. We were also working on a conference of *Rocky Horror* devotees that Rick was trying to stage that summer at the Hotel Roosevelt. Yes, without the Faire, most of us were terribly, deeply adrift.

Worst of all for my dad, he had to drive me each morning to my job as a typist at Petersen Publishing (proprietors of such fine titles as *Guns And Ammo* and *Motor Trend*). He hated chauffeuring me and my sister around. And my sister was in a punk rock band by this time, with rehearsals and even club dates far and wide in the great Los Angeles basin. My father was particularly taxed in ferrying my sister to all-ages nightclubs. But to allow either one of us to drive would have required more tolerance and patience than he could not part with. So he stuck with a responsibility he hated, and relished the disgust he engendered while doing it.

When my Faire friends and I finally ran out of projects, we spent our days in rapt anticipation for the coming Monty Python movie, *Life of Brian*. It was garnering all kinds of controversy as it made its way across the Atlantic, and my father was also intrigued, especially given its subject matter. Once it was released he declared he had to see it, for any movie the goyim objected to so strenuously was something he had to see, even if it did mean breaking his inviolate boycott of British cultural products. So we went, before my friends and I could organize our own trip to the theater. There was much in the movie he either did not understand, due to his deafness, and much he didn't like, owing to his own cultural prejudices.

But what he liked left him in hysterics, particularly the joke about the warring factions of Israelites—the People's Front of Judea and the Judean People's Front. This also is known as the "Two Jews, Three Arguments" aphorism among us chosen people. The scene in which Israelites are selling stones for an upcoming stoning of some unnamed offender had him laughing so much, I thought he'd have an asthma attack. He and my mother had finally made their big trip to Israel just the year before, and after the movie, he explained that for a country that had next to no natural resources, if it had any item in abundant supply, it was rocks to throw at other people. There would never be a need to ever buy them.

Samuel was breathless as the Queen released Sir Robert from her vision and returned it to Jenny, still unconscious. Her Highness' expression might have been unreadable beneath her powders and rouges, but her gestures were tender. She smoothed Jenny's brow and took her hand to Jenny's cheek. A string of tears arose from Jenny's closed eyes, as if to reply, and they made the bruise and swelling slick and brilliant. Samuel raised his good hand to his chest as the Queen continued to study Jenny's face, and a new kind of quivering began in Jenny's throat. Her bandaged hands, with the iron cuffs still fastened upon her wrists, pawed imprecisely at her neck as during those times she was afraid some sound might escape from there.

"My mother has come," Jenny said distinctly upon waking. Her stare was unquestionably directed at Her Majesty. "To witness my death, she has come. Finally."

"No!" Samuel cried, and the Queen instinctively withdrew from her position. "God, no! Not now, Jenny, when you have spoken."

"It is a fitting end," Jenny continued, "to an unsuitable princess."

"Yes," Samuel said quietly, to match the diminishment in her voice. "You are a princess."

"Yes," Jenny answered. Her voice, free of the tremors that besieged her body, was small in the space it dared to occupy. And yet it had stilled all the other sounds and voices that could have competed with it; voices with more aptitude, more to dominate with. "You have made me your princess, although I know not for how long."

"As long as I have breath in my lungs, a spirit in my heart, you shall live,"

Samuel said, although neither he nor his audience could rightly distinguish his sobbing from his statements. "You cannot die, Jenny. I do not know how but I will make it so, I swear it."

"Yet in this condition, I cannot live," Jenny murmured. She gathered Samuel's bandaged hand up to her face, her lips, and tried to kiss it through the cloth, as if a final act of healing.

"You are right, my darling," Samuel said, and just as quickly he turned away from her, to face the Queen, colorless now in all her astonishment. "Your Grace," Samuel said firmly, "you must marry us, at once. Before there is nothing left of my princess; before she is cast out a second time, alone into that after-life."

chapter thirteen

"How is she?" the Queen inquired, as she stood in the doorway, seemingly afraid to enter a room where she had earlier presided as both Sovereign and Mother of the Bride. The sky showed not a hint of morning light, yet the bells had long since proclaimed their call of midnight in a heavy, pitiless rhythm. It was as if they foretold the remaining length of the princess's life.

"She is resting," Samuel answered quietly, but formally. He was sitting up in bed, beside his Jenny. One leg stretched out beside her, while the other dangled so that its foot could be firmly placed upon the floor: He was not to sleep until she was fully recovered, the Queen could see. She wondered how many of such nights Samuel Bright could endure.

Jenny had fully tired herself, ❀ smiling and nodding and holding the hands of the Bright twins, Lucy and Grace, during the wedding. Before the ceremony, she had permitted them to douse her hair with flowers and to kiss her more than Samuel might ever have an opportunity to do, once the Queen rightly pronounced them joined forever. Now she was stone still in the candlelight Samuel maintained by her bedside, and her skin was as white as the petals of a camellia. It wounded the Queen at the crux of her being, to witness her daughter's wedding night in this manner.

❀ **We wore Sam out** once he was released from the hospital. His mother finagled his release a few days early, so we could celebrate his birthday in late July outside the hospital. Sam's mother took me, Sam, and a few of his friends to see *The Muppet Movie*. I knew nothing about the Muppets and was thrown a little off balance when I discovered Sam was practically an aficionado. Despite his delicate condition, he nearly rocketed out of his seat when Kermit's nephew, Robin, hopped onto the screen.

We went to see *Moonraker*, which turned out to be my introduction to the James Bond movie franchise. My uncle had stockpiled all of Ian Fleming's books, but the movies were apparently too base for us to attend. Sam was more than eager to acquit me with all forms of Bond information: his women, his controls, and especially his archenemies, whom Sam had committed to memory. I was far more taken by *Dracula*, in which Frank Langella re-created his Broadway performance, and Sam noticed. He began referring to Langella as "that Italian actor," with a sardonic edge in his voice. It gave me a thrill to hear him speak that way, our first in-joke that we had created so spontaneously.

I had decided for myself, sometime during the run of the Faire, or perhaps earlier, that I would make my mark in the world as a walking encyclopedia of cultural debris. But Sam had beat me to the punch years before, glomming onto movies apparently too outré for even the Z Channel. He could act out significant selections of dialogue and direction, such as Bud Cort's hara-kiri sequence in *Harold and Maude*, or Kevin McCarthy's final warning, atop a car's windshield, against the pod people in *Invasion of the Body Snatchers*. There wasn't anything he didn't know, and very little that he hadn't done. Once he even ate a communion wafer—it had been given to him by the mother of one of his mother's boyfriends—and although it didn't burn his tongue, it tasted nasty. Very nasty. The only activity that evaded him was skydiving. The powers that ran the skydiving school wouldn't let him jump, for fear that he had ulterior motives due to his illness.

We spent a lot of time in his apartment, his mother always somewhere in the background, and even more time on the telephone, because I was working during the week, and didn't know how to drive to get to him on my off-hours. Sam's own Alfa Romeo had also been suffering lately, from some congenital defects far less yielding to treatment than his own cancer; and he really was also too weak to drive, as I remember the one and only time I most definitely saw him cry.

I was visiting him on a Friday or Saturday night; my mother or father must have dropped me off to have dinner with him and his mother. When it was time to leave, his mother gave him the keys to her Lincoln Continental and said he could drive me home: this would have been a real turning point for Sam, who was still bald, terrifically pale, and remotely shaky in his walk and voice, as though afraid he would relapse without warning. Off we went to the garage with a feeling of triumph, to navigate through all of life's obstacles.

The parking garage at Sam's apartment building was actually the vacant space beneath the stilts that held the apartments slightly above street level, and it required a certain adeptness with the steering wheel to maneuver through it. We were also supposed to get gas, for this was the summer of the 1979 oil crisis and there was never enough gas to buy to keep that Lincoln's tank from starving. The first move required was to back out of his mother's space before wriggling our way around the other parked cars. But each time Sam touched the steering wheel, the horn would go off.

The horn went off and then it went on and on, and each time it stopped, Sam would try another tact out of the garage, and the horn would go off again. We were burning rubber, fumes, and probably a few pounds of our own as we became more frightened and frustrated with the car's shenanigans. With the horn blowing and the indicator on the gas tank bobbing downward, Sam began having trouble turning in the driver's seat; his entire body seemed to be stiffening, and he could not see where he was going. Finally he gave up on getting out of this fix and told me to get his mother upstairs. It was as close to crying as I would ever see him, the former gurgle in his voice returning and threatening to spill out of his throat in a catharsis I was in no shape to handle. I was more than happy to leave him in the car while I dashed back up to the apartment for help.

His mother either chauffeured us to the rest of our adventures or came with us, such as the time we went to the Fox Hills mall to loiter about. Sam's mother was a social worker, arranging adoptions in Los Angeles County, and some type of adoption event was being held at the mall. Sam and I dressed in matching white overalls; I wish I could remember why. Sam's mother sat at her booth answering questions about adoption and we roamed the stores and food courts as I wondered why people were looking at us as if we were aliens. We were also the only white people besides Sam's mother in that location but that didn't seem reason enough to me. When I remarked on it, Sam told me to keep my feelings to myself, because, he said, "it's their neighborhood."

We had a day alone, though, at the Venice boardwalk, near where our relationship started. Sam's mother dropped us off with some lunches and a couple of sodas; she had dressed Sam in the floppiest hat, long sleeves, long pants, socks and heavy shoes. I was a little grateful for this, since it meant I didn't have to wear a bathing suit myself. We moseyed and sat on benches and drank our sodas until we were confronted by a hippie selling fresh, organic, holy cosmic fruit juices. Sam raised his toxic soft drink in a toast and said, "No thank you, we'll just stick with our cancer juice here."

"May I?" the Queen finished her request with a nod and a gesture toward the bed.

"Please," Samuel said, and he granted entry with a similar nod: the

Queen took notice as to how regal it had become over the space of the day's events. Samuel Bright had yet to cloak his gestures with a stature of imperiousness, the Queen thought, yet he had easily become convinced of his new power and influence.

"Please, " Samuel repeated. "Do not upset her."

The Queen took her place on the hard stool where Sir Robert had sat, and found herself, at least in thought, bowing to Samuel Bright, who by all rights now was a prince. He took from her the candlestick she had been using to roam the castle and placed it beside his own. Together they dispelled that fraction of the night pressing against Jenny, even as the princess' husband and mother despaired that any combination of light, wax, and wick could stay the darkness gathering around the sickbed.

"Has she spoken since—"

"No," Samuel said. "That would be your only concern?"

"**I have been wrong**, Samuel Bright, in so many ways," ❀ the Queen offered, "but now I wish to do right. You must believe that."

❀ **If only** I could have acted differently, at what turned out to be the end of Sam's life; if only I had known; if only I had known better. I don't know exactly what I would have differently, to affect a better outcome, but I would have done something so that I was not altogether so ashamed of my behavior, so that this confession—any confession—could appease that shame, or at least lessen its grip on my persona. Some day I will have to tell my daughter about it, I suppose, so she can understand the limitations of her mother. For such is the culmination of every coming-of-age novel or memoir: the realization that adults, particularly parents, are merely human. Or in my case, as applied to my knowledge of myself, sub-human.

Sam had organized mass expeditions of Faire folk to the movies missing from my education, but as for his actual attendance, he had to beg off. So I went solo, happily enough, although sometimes he had his friend, Adam, accompany me as a "surrogate Sam." When a print of *Monty Python and the Holy*

Grail sailed into town, Sam was bound and determined. Maybe he insisted on going because the summer was plummeting toward its end; I would be moving across town soon, to go to college. Or maybe he was so motivated because the film was playing on a triple bill with *Beyond the Fringe* and *And Now For Something Completely Different*. It was to be an afternoon of class-fueled humor interrupted only by psychedelic animation.

Sam rustled up whatever stores he could find within, and ventured with us. And wow, it was fun. We were in a hopped-up Chevy Vega that belonged to someone's new boyfriend, and went to the Nu-Art theater, an art house so hip it sold milk and ginger ale instead of regular Coca-Cola and 7UP. Sometime during the climax of the afternoon, the showing of *Holy Grail*, however, Sam became terribly uncomfortable. He shifted, fiddled with his elbows, and rubbed his head as though he might rake free whatever feeling radiated throughout his naked scalp. But he couldn't find any relief. He said he was going to go out to the car to lie down for a while, and that he'd be back in no time.

I stayed in the theater. I did not check on my boyfriend. I kept laughing, and the only misgivings I had were about the end of the film. It was a little disappointing. I was expecting them to actually find the Holy Grail, whatever it was. I had yet to fail at a career or in a marriage or even at motherhood, so I did not know anything about defense mechanisms, or denial. Yet I doubt it was instinct taking over as I cackled and guffawed while my boyfriend lay in the back seat of a Chevrolet in a fetal coil. I know I was simply too much in the thrall of everything—the movie, my friends, how unique and un-bourgeois we were. So I laughed as though I could blast the marrow out of my bones as the marrow perilously curdled within my boyfriend.

After the film, my friends and I returned to the car to find Sam rattled by the pain surging back and forth through his organs and skeleton. He might have put his head in my lap once

I climbed in the back; I might have stroked his back, though not his head, as that seemed to be where a great deal of the pain started. The Vega's verisimilitude to the Grand Prix experience was a real point of pride for its owner. But its lack of reasonable shock absorbers and efficient muffler were punishing for Sam. It was imperative that we return him home as quickly as possible, as if something could be done for him there. That he had already been suffering a good while before our wild ride was not entirely lost on me. I had no idea how I would explain all this to his mother.

We tossed Sam into his mother's arms and drove away, with me in the back seat. From there the car's exhaust system echoed the smell and sound of Sam's condition. I know I was freaked out by my own guilt. I had killed my boyfriend, I was certain. The best way to avoid this problem, I decided sometime during the days that followed, was to ignore it, since otherwise it wasn't likely to go away. Although it did go away, it seemed for the others involved: they have never mentioned it, and they certainly have never held me accountable for what followed about a week later.

Samuel nodded silently, as if restraining his thoughts. But his discipline was wanting. "I wish to take her home," he volunteered suddenly.

"Yes, of course," the Queen consented, if only to be diplomatic. "For now, I shall have more private quarters prepared for you."

"I wish to take her home, once day light makes it possible," he asserted.

"But she should not be moved just yet," the Queen began, although she suspected her effort would be useless. Nevertheless, she had to continue: "Especially in light of the coming events. Sir Matthew may soon deliver us with a redress, if not a war to restore his status."

"I do not wish for her to die here," Samuel said.

The Queen possessed no sufficient rejoinder to change his focus.

"She should be with her family, my parents and sisters," Samuel went on.

"She is her mother's daughter, first," the Queen attempted. "Allow her to recover in the home she should have had, had her mother not been so … distracted."

The Queen was not accustomed to the silence that followed; her pronouncements would usually receive some sort of assent, congratulation, or compliment, and if there had to be silence, it would be one of respectful awe. This silence, however, was the same kind that had threatened the wedding earlier, as the Queen conducted the ceremony; or when the twins' singing would stop, or the toasts were dutifully recited; when the twins commented on how beautiful the bride appeared. Never had such silences had been delivered to the Queen so deliberately, from what she could remember; usually it was the Queen who would dole out such silences, as a form of derision or penalty.

"Perhaps 'distracted' is the wrong word in this instance," the Queen said.

"No," Samuel answered, and somewhat haughtily to the Queen's hearing. "It is perfect, except in one regard. Distracted by what, I might ask? For what would distract one so much that she would abandon her daughter? No—not abandon her—renounce her, making her less than human, less than an animal—a horse has at least shelter, a measure of dignity and respect—Jenny was denied her birthright not as a princess, but as a person. I dare you to explain that!"

"And if my explanation cannot justify—"

"And if she can no longer ride her beloved horses, nor walk with her husband or her sisters-in-law, nor stand on her own power; if she cannot hold her own babes in her arms, what then?" Samuel said bitterly. "And should she not live, where for that should I seek justification?"

They held each other in a cold stare—-Samuel in his burning determination, the Queen in her now curious position. But the longer Samuel kept up his stance, the better the Queen could see how unnerved he was: he was trying to hold back his tears as they ripened harshly in his eyes. It was not clear whether he was crying for the damage he was doing at that moment, or the damage the Queen had already done to herself.

"You are a prince now," the Queen said, and she left the hard stool and stood at the foot of the bed, where she could face Samuel Bright at a distance he might mistake for deference. But Maggers was still the Queen and she would act and be treated as one, no matter the circumstance. "And I suppose you are therefore owed an attempt at explanation."

"There is none," Samuel declared as he tried to stifle his crying.

"Yet your father knows it," the Queen continued. "That is why he would not send Jenny to her mother when she was called for, when I requested it."

"How do you know that story?"

"It is not a story, Samuel," the Queen said. "It is the truth of this catastrophe."

"Why was I never told earlier?"

"Out of concern for your safety, Samuel," the Queen said knowingly. "For your family's too; for all of us. Even Jenny's."

"That I refuse to believe," Samuel said. "Jenny has never been considered, in all of this."

If Samuel Bright chose to believe as much, the Queen doubted she could convince him otherwise. Still, she had to try, just as she had to be near to her daughter at this moment: to touch her upon her forehead, smooth her hair away from her face, linger about her brow and check the pace of her breathing. The Queen advanced toward the other side of the bed, and sat herself beside the fitful, sweating princess. Not a trace of blood had strayed into her face, and yet she struggled at every instance to hold onto her life.

"Your father's friend—Jenny's father—he was the royal blacksmith, when I was but younger than you are now, I believe," the Queen said. "He was as fine a man as your father, and far more admirable than all of the men available to me—if ever I had been interested. I had, like your Jenny, an affinity with horses. I thought I could enchant them, although I was only applying the lessons the blacksmith taught me, and what knowledge my father had of them. Certainly they were far more amusing than any human company I would otherwise be confronted with.

"Of course Edward—my father—was beside himself with frustration, that I should be so resistant to a more traditional form of companionship, to not even think of a marriage; but I was young enough that he thought it might not yet matter, and I thought myself a horse princess, content to be the Equine Queen, someone out of a fairy book, really. I lived in fantasy and Hal, the royal blacksmith, would be my royal consort. I would need no other assistance.

"But this was before the war, before Good King Edward sought to extend his influence, and his resources. My father came back from his conquests physically weakened but royally assured; and Hal returned a wasted man, one-half of him useless, and the other half needy, and perhaps a little resentful. I was resentful too. We shared that, I suppose. We shared too much, I am certain."

The Queen paused so she might pull back from her daughter, as though she had a need to not just tell this story, but to re-enact it, in physicality and emotion.

"She was taken from my arms within seconds of her birth," the Queen said, and she began to pace about the edge of the bed. One hand, with neither jewels at the wrist or the fingers, skirted the blanket, as though it offered one last touch of Jenny, yet a touch that did not risk waking her. "And given to her father; that was Edward's decision. My father gave him servants, and money, but it was not enough for his condition. He really could not care for her.

"I think you know the rest," the Queen said.

"No," Samuel complained. "You have explained nothing. Nothing of her talents, her silence."

"Yes," the Queen conceded, and she sat down on the small, hard stool again, as if completing a penance. "Once my father died, and I ascended, I had Jenny come to me so that I could explain—who she was, what it meant, and—" Here the Queen found her own voice wanting for an instance, as if it snagged on a notch or a nail left carelessly somewhere. She looked away from Samuel, as if his audience threatened her composure. "I explained to her that she must say no word of this, to anybody," she carried on as best she could. "The rest of her silence—that was her decision."

"The decision of a scared little girl."

"Yes," the Queen acknowledged. "And she had reason to be. For like me, she was born with a terrible responsibility. And like your bride, Samuel Bright, I have kept silent as well."

"I do not understand," Samuel replied, and it appeared to the Queen that it was now Samuel who was frightened of what may follow; she was not.

"It is not a talent that we possess," the Queen said. "It is more like an instinct, knowledge that we need not communicate to our daughters, and yet they also inevitably display it. It must be what made us royal, once, although our mothers have always warned against practicing it. It could be used for such hatred and wickedness.

"You must understand, now, why Jenny had to be removed from your home after your recovery," the Queen concluded.

"But Jenny would never—"

"But she could be used for such purposes, which is why she had to be made an outcast. You see what Sir Matthew wanted, even what our Sir Robert had attempted. I see now that Jenny made the only choice that she could have made. If she could not enjoy her birthright, she could at least live and be loved for who she truly was. She sacrificed her voice in order to do so."

The Queen had expected Samuel to react in some way—an apology for his own hasty judgment of the situation, or perhaps some sort of acknowledgment of the dilemma the Queen and her daughter faced. But he maintained his resolve. He would keep his distance and distrust of his mother-in-law, Her Majesty, Most Fallible.

Queen Marion rose and smoothed out her gown and jacket as though she were presenting herself to the young prince for the first time, and said, "If you are offended by the injustice of this affair now, please try to imagine what would have been, had I not been able to succeed my father with this secret intact. Imagine yourself and your family under the love and protection of any one of my councilors: imagine what the fight for succession would have been. Any one of them, possibly even Sir Robert, I fear, would have been far less judicious in the number of dead men they might have collected, to say nothing of what they would have done with their living prisoners."

"Still, that cannot—" Samuel tried.

"It justified everything," the Queen said. "Do you not think I would have liked to run away with my young man restored in purpose, in strength and vigor, and raise my child? Or to save my own father, on his deathbed, to have him live on a few more years, days, moments? But I had a nation to think of, a mortal being, made up of sweet and fallible creatures, my subjects. A nation that was not ready for me: a witch of a Queen with her bastard princess."

Her Highness turned her back on the prince, and moved to leave her daughter once again. She continued to head toward the door even as she heard Samuel gather himself together out of her sight; even as she imagined his lifting himself away from the bed to walk after, and kneel before her.

"Your Majesty," Samuel said from his knees, his despair having drenched the disgust he must have held for her. "Please, for the love you once held for Jenny's father, you must save her now. If not for forever, just so long as I might live and love her."

"Hush, Prince Samuel," the Queen said, and she put a palm to his cheek, and swept the tears away with her thumb. "Hush, for I already have."

chapter fourteen ❀

❀ **Jenny, meanwhile, recovered** quite nicely once she was healed by her mother, Queen Marion. Jenny and her mother never quite overcame the breach in their relationship, but Queen Marion found peace and happiness as a grandmother, for Jenny and Samuel gave her many grandchildren. Queen Marion adored each and every one of them and spoiled them terribly. She died at a ripe old age, of natural causes, for she would not allow Jenny to use her healing powers, just as her father had done with her. Such was the tradition, especially since this is not a Huxley fantasy, even if some of its conceits owe something to that author, a favorite of this author's father and the subject of many subsequent father-daughter conversations.

Once Queen Marion died, Jenny ascended to the throne, and promptly moved to make herself into a purely ceremonial monarch. Of course she outlawed war, pestilence, and all forms of elitism before a bicameral legislature and free and independent judiciary could be established. Sir Robert served as the interim Prime Minister. Once a formal system of elections was established, however, Sir Robert did not seek office, although he did oversee a truth and reconciliation commission to sort through any war profiteering or war crimes against the Gongols. Sir Matthew Payne and his minions were neither jailed nor fined, but embarrassed before a huge audience on national television.

Sir Robert subsequently retired as a revered statesman much like Jimmy Carter has become in our own age, even though the author's father still accuses Carter of being too pro-Arab.

Samuel continued on in his father's shop, becoming a skilled blacksmith in his own right, and taking over the operation when Thomas retired. He and Jenny lived much like the peasants did in the May Day sequence in the movie version of "Camelot," in a cabin stocked with dried garlands and clean sheets and much singing and rejoicing. Lucy and Grace grew to be Jenny's ladies in waiting until they were married and had families of their own; they sent their children to Jenny for horseback riding lessons and to Samuel to find honest work in smithing. They might have gone to University, as the author's father would have demanded, but please remember what kind of story this is meant to be. Everyone is supposed to live happily ever after.

And they did, especially Samuel's parents. They were able to retire to Florida on the pension Samuel and Jenny provided for them, and they were frequently visited by their passel of lovely grandchildren.

Sam died on Saturday, September 8, as I was getting ready to go to my first UCLA football game to sit in the student section. The admissions office had mailed me a yellow pass explaining my status as an incoming freshman and I was eager to use it. So eager, in fact, that I had called some people I had previously attached myself to, in pursuit of Slayer, my first boyfriend. One was already a sophomore at UCLA and the others were part of that solid gold sound that was the UCLA marching band. Pretty spiffy company for a barely-burnished co-ed, if you ask me. No one else was asking.

I was excited to be going to college. I wasn't going to be taking any dance classes in college, as I had initially planned, but I was going to live in my own apartment. I was overwhelmed with trying to find a place close to campus (I still didn't drive) and packing my things. Sam's mother had been calling during the week before the game to say he was feeling terrible, and could use some cheering up. I called and told him about apartment-hunting and some other college nonsense. He answered a few yes and no questions, but his voice teetered on torment. It was obvious that he was nearing the end of his slow, painful descent. I don't remember what I felt about all this, but I can recall how the kitchen looked whenever I spoke to him: dark, but not from a lack of light. It was more as if the ceiling was lowering itself, to meet the floor, and although I did not think I would be crushed, I thought I might go blind when the two surfaces met.

I always promised to call back in a few days, but on that Saturday, his mother beat me to it. Sam had died in his bed with his brother, among others, at his side. My UCLA friends showed up within minutes of this phone call, and I had to tell them to turn around and go without me. I distinctly remember not being hysterical—such was my reputation that I did not wish to further it—but I should have been. For during those days that Sam was dying—and I was given a description of them only recently, by Sam's brother, with a few details I wished I had been spared—Sam must have been woefully disappointed in me. It is also possible, I must concede, that he did not think of me at all, for he was so exhausted and had so many other things to think over seriously. "I just want to sleep," he would tell his mother, although I don't know how. His tongue, so long the focus of his disease's side effects, was disintegrating in his mouth.

Two memorial services were held for Sam, in Los Angeles and Northern California. At the Los Angeles service, held in someone's backyard, Clan Colin came out in full regalia, and my friends and I also wore our Faire costumes. The bagpipes played "Amazing Grace," another Christian staple I had never heard of. I was not crying, but heaving great gobs of air, as though my breath was unduly large, selfish, an offense to the rib cage it shook and rattled. During the singing and remembrances, a friend's mother latched her arms around me and would not let go, possibly because she knew that I was about to dissolve, or explode. I don't know which one for certain. I'm sure it was the alternative that was most damning, or embarrassing.

I felt pretty sorry for myself for a long time after, and shed many a tear at inopportune moments, such as the tail end of a German class that fall semester. I was exhausted with homework, hungry because I could not cook for myself, and more lonely than I had never been, living in a one-bedroom apartment with a girl who listened only to disco music. So it all came out in one 8 a.m. session of practicing salutations and singing Beatles songs. When the German instructor tried following me out of the classroom, I made it a point to furiously outrun him. I lacked the vocabulary, in any language, to describe what I was feeling. I understand now that I was crying out of shame, for what I had not done, and for not crying earlier.

That New Year's Eve, I met a man who said that only he had a year worse than my own: he had lost his lover (they broke up), his job (he was fired), and his cat (it died). Together we wallowed in our ridiculousness and felt much better about things, probably because we could laugh at how pathetic we had become. I eventually began dating one of the employees he had formerly supervised. That boy made me feel famous in a way, with his persistence and affections. That relationship was doomed for many reasons, and it ended none too well, as did many others. But I came to some sort of settlement with myself over Sam— or so I thought—the summer before my junior year of college, when I visited the Northern California Faire site, where the second service for Sam was held.

Sam's ashes had been placed along the edge of a forest that unfortunately overlooked the privies, i.e., the port-a-toilets for both participants and visitors. I sat there for a while as my boyfriend-of-the-moment roamed through the Faire's pleasanter sights and smells. I wished that the wind had lifted the branches of the forest trees in some particular way, or that I sensed a particular stirring in those minutes, but I didn't. Later that afternoon, though, I spoke to one of Sam's friends, an older man who was also Jewish, and he told me of saying Kaddish (the Jewish prayer for mourning) for Sam in the synagogue. I could not say Kaddish because my father, in his infinite and liberal wisdom, did not believe in sending girls to Hebrew school. The culmination of that study, the Bat Mitzvah, was a feminist innovation in the religion, he had said, and he would have no part in it. Still, I felt what the pop psychologists nowadays refer to as closure, knowing that this last prayer had been said for Sam. He had been properly put to bed; waking him, after a fashion, would only cause more suffering.

It was also around this time that my parents divorced, which helped immeasurably in my relationships with both of them. My mother was finally free to be herself: a world traveler, book and toy collector, and generally curious person about anything that fell within her line of vision. Age, and specifically menopause, helped too, she said; it smoothed out her moods and kept her from brutalizing her friends when she was angry with them. As she aged she became both entertaining and eccentric, and I fell in love with picking her brain and its vast inventory of experiences and ideas. The divorce was not as kind to my father, who became something of a hermit afterwards, but it stripped him of all that sanctimony he had armed himself with. My father was the one who told me of the divorce, initially, during a dinner at a cheap coffee shop; he started not by using the big D word but by sheepishly apologizing for all his boorish parenting techniques. Years later, he tried to retract that apology, and even in this present day, he backpedals it, explaining that the only crime he ever committed was raising two girls while their mother was figuratively out to breakfast, lunch, and dinner. But I remember that first act of contrition and in fact refuse to forget it. It makes listening to my father's pre-Brown vs. Board of Education views on life in the 21st century much easier to stomach.

Through a much-protracted process, I eventually grew up from that girl I was. I could tell you exactly how, but that might take volumes. And they may not be all that interesting. Suffice it to say that I now teach writing and occasionally African American literature, which I developed an interest in while working as a journalist covering racial issues. Today I have a friend, a citizen of the United States as well as a British subject of Jamaican ancestry, with two passports to prove her tangled ethnicity. She says white liberal guilt is the pond scum of human emotions. But I am a guilty white liberal, which perhaps illustrates how little I have evolved from my beginnings. So be it.

I do have one great accomplishment, however, and that is the daughter my husband and I have produced, although the miracle that she is, is pretty much her own doing. She wishes to become a killer whale scientist and she is, according to the school transcripts—hers and mine—much smarter than I was. Photographs confirm her superior beauty; the records of her pediatrician, as well as those in the store where she buys her shoes, detail her superior health, feet, and strength. Her father, meanwhile, is a man without the frustrations my father wrestled with. At the very least, he does not yell nearly as much as my father did, and his beliefs and parenting strategy are not nearly so obtuse. That he is also successful in his career, as well as the material and philosophical aspirations he has had for his life, also may help. And his wife, for one, has not been carted away by the men in the white coats. We also have the products of a far more advanced psycho-pharmaceutical industry than was available to my mother to thank for that blessing. Overall, my daughter's immediate environment is much healthier than the one I navigated, free of the scourge of celebrity, mental illness, and mid-century Puritanism.

She is teased occasionally and disappointed often, but among the many reasons why I love my daughter is that she has found such setbacks to be surmountable and temporary. I have it on pretty good authority that her reality is at least as good as her fantasies, whatever they might be. At least when we exchange our nighttime dreams over breakfast, or confess our desires and ambitions at dinner, she speaks of rescuing cats and sea mammals, or celebrating some occasion with members of her family. My own ambitions at her age were woefully based on—well, just read the memoir. It accompanies this naked analysis of my personality for a reason.

Still, I am compelled to tell her much of my childhood, if only because she finds it so entertaining. "Tell me the story of your life," she often encourages me at the dinner table, and I realize that her interest, and even dependence on me makes me somewhat of a celebrity in her eyes; finally I am famous, for I have lived through all sorts of natural disasters and witnessed all sorts of tragedies as a former journalist working on small town newspapers. She is most entertained by these stories at dinner, tales of floods and mudslides, fires and car accidents— along with other accounts of silliness occurring on the schoolyard among children and teenagers. I am also famous for being her mother: the other parents, particularly the moms, at her school immediately recognize me and my responsibility. Finally I have stories to tell and a rapt audience to hear them—especially the stories I tell the other parents about her.

I did not include Sam in my dinnertime stories for my daughter for reasons that have more to do with my age, than hers. But popular culture, in part, eased Sam back into my thinking. Most of the cult, avant-garde, and cutting edge products Sam was so comfortable and familiar with, that I sought to associate myself with as part of my constant psychological tinkering, have become part of the mainstream. The Frank Zappa Sam once danced to in his convertible when we were stuck in traffic is known to my daughter. He is the father of Ahmet Zappa, author of one of her favorite monster fantasies. Monty Python and Mel Brooks have been inspiration for Broadway shows she sees advertised all over our New York City Theater District neighborhood. The Ian Drury and the Blockheads Sam sang to me are responsible for a common phrase— sex, drugs and rock 'n' roll—that is shorthand for all the things I warn her we will have to discuss some day, since she doesn't want to hear about them now. In short, Sam bequeathed to me a time and a place, and a way of looking at a certain time of my life that for so long I have avoided.

Or perhaps my need to re-think, re-live, or again atone for my time with Sam is just simple nostalgia, the by-product of my own aging and the growing, gaping distance between myself and my youth. Maybe it's because of the release of Peter Jackson's *The Lord of the Rings* films when my daughter was a toddler. A nickname pinned on Sam at the Renaissance Faire echoes one of the character's in the film: "Samwise." "Samwise," of course, was the simple gardener who accompanies Frodo on his quest in Tolkien's relatively simple universe, and when I heard that name, it upended whatever delicate balance I had affected in the very real world. In those films I heard and saw places and people I had previously only witnessed in my waking fantasies, and one of those fantasies became too real not to share.

The setting for those fantasies is different in place, appearance and administration now. The Southern California Faire has moved three times by my last count and the Northern California Faire has also moved, and is run by a separate organization. New generations of actors and concession owners have given it an entirely different vibe, from what I've been told. Family-friendly is the motto of this re-invented tradition, so that much of the sex, drugs and rock 'n' roll that motivated our attendance has been put into exile. Yet for my friends whom I made through Sam; for the friends I still make through his memory, for he is far from forgotten; for all of us, the Faire is still the place where we gather, either figuratively or literally, to remember the people we were, and the people we once aspired to be. The fact that I fell so short of my goal, and did so quickly, is nothing that I can change. But perhaps I, too, can be rehabilitated, as this one last circuitous explanation should demonstrate:

In sixth grade, we were taken to the home of Edward Kienholz, an artist who is mentioned in the very first pages. Kienholz was famous for his satiric pop art installations, which were, for the most part, recreations of reality. We children knew him as the creator of "The Beanery," an elaborate tableaux of the notable Hollywood bar and restaurant. Our parents knew him as the creator of "Back Seat Dodge '38," a sculpture demonstrating what those Dodges were really best for, in those days. Los Angeles politicians tried to remove the piece from the Los Angeles County Museum of Art in 1966, because it was "pornographic." Kienholz's older daughter, Jenny, was a proud graduate of our campus and his younger son was in our class. For this field trip, our parents had to sign all of the standard permission slips, which included a promise from the school that the trip would teach us how a real artist lives.

So we poured through Kienholz's kitchen, his bedroom, the bedrooms of his children, but nothing like an artist's studio or garret, from what I can piece together. There were televisions in every room, even the bathrooms; we philistines all got a good laugh out of that. But what I remember most of all was how I confronted Mr. Kienholz, asking him, "Why isn't there any art in this house?" He answered by escorting me to a wall in one of the hallways, where a wood-framed mirror was hanging by itself. "This was a toilet seat," he explained. "It has been removed, polished, and the mirror inserted. What do you think of that?"

About the Author

Jane Rosenberg LaForge was born in Los Angeles and raised in the suburb of Laurel Canyon, where she attempted to rub shoulders with the hip and famous. Though she was not successful in that endeavor, she rode horses, took ballet lessons, participated in the Renaissance Pleasure Faire, and graduated from Hollywood High School. After finishing her bachelor's at UCLA, she worked as a journalist in California, Maryland, and upstate New York. She studied writing in the Kate Braverman workshops of the early 1990s in Los Angeles before attending the University of Massachusetts, Amherst. At UMass, she was a Delaney Fellow and a researcher for two of Jay Neugeboren's books on the public health system, *Transforming Madness* and *Open Heart*. Since earning her MFA, she has taught college reading, composition, and literature part-time in the New York metropolitan area; published critical articles on African-American literature; and four volumes of poetry: *After Voices* (Burning River 2009); *Half-Life* (Big Table Publishing Co. 2010); *With Apologies to Mick Jagger, Other Gods, and All Women* (The Aldrich Press 2012); and *The Navigation of Loss* (Red Ochre Press 2012), one of three winners of the Red Ochre Press' annual chapbook competition. She has been nominated twice for a Pushcart Prize (once for poetry, and once for fiction) and once for a StorySouth Million Writers Award. She lives in Manhattan, New York, with her husband, Patrick, and their daughter, Eva.

Acknowledgments

Sheila Ashdown, founder of *The Ne'er-Do-Well* literary magazine, edited and published the essay that became this book's foundation. Dan McLaughlin was this book's first fan. Then Jess Winfield, who did right by me. Linda Lenhoff tried too. Adam Tauber for reading and Debra Di Blasi for accepting and Sharon Bially for the enthusiasm. Jim Meirose in general. Sa Winfield for introducing, creating, exploring, and discovering; any and all Dueling Buckets-associated characters: founders, workers, social climbers, happy campers, lawyers and judges, crooners, activists, outside agitators, nurses, doctors, unattended minors, artists and thieves, actors, significant others, barkers, minstrels, innocents, criminals, slummers, bankers, swindlers, hangers-on, fellow travelers, wannabes, and poseurs. I hope that covers everyone. Michelle Hoover and Kate Southwood for their work and expertise; Michelle Valois for encouraging the poetry; Elisabeth Fairfield Stokes and Patti Horvath. And of course and most of all my husband Patrick LaForge, who has had to endure the most; and our daughter Eva LaForge, my chief inspiration.

Discover more great books at Jaded Ibis Press

jadedibisproductions.com

Jaded Ibis Press
sustainable literature by digital means™
an imprint of Jaded Ibis Productions

be smart. get smarter. read better books.™

CPSIA information can be obtained
at www.ICGtesting.com
Printed in the USA
LVHW03s2300200618
581477LV00001B/191/P